Cambridge Studies in Social and Emotional Development

General editor: Martin L. Hoffman

Advisory Board: Nicholas Blurton Jones, Robert N. Emde, Willard W. Hartup, Carroll E. Izard, Robert A. Hinde, Lois W. Hoffman, Jerome Kagan, Franz J. Mönks, Paul Mussen, Ross D. Parke, and Michael Rutter

The development of social knowledge

The development of social knowledge

Morality and convention

ELLIOT TURIEL

University of California, Berkeley

CAMBRIDGE UNIVERSITY PRESS

Cambridge
London   New York   New Rochelle
Melbourne   Sydney

Published by the Press Syndicate of the University of Cambridge
The Pitt Building, Trumpington Street, Cambridge CB2 1RP
32 East 57th Street, New York, NY 10022, USA
296 Beaconsfield Parade, Middle Park, Melbourne 3206, Australia

First published 1983

Printed in the United States of America

Library of Congress Cataloging in Publication Data
Turiel, Elliot.
The development of social knowledge.
(Cambridge studies in social and emotional
development)
Includes index.
1. Socialization.   2. Social ethics.   3. Convention
(Philosophy)   4. Social interaction.   5. Cognition and
culture.   I. Title.   II. Series.
HQ783.T9   1983   303.3'2   82–14762
ISBN 0 521 25309 8 hard covers
ISBN 0 521 27305 6 paperback

Contents

Preface

The development of social knowledge in children and adolescents is a broad topic requiring some choices regarding the focus of analysis. Those choices are naturally guided by one's theoretical orientation to social reasoning and its formation and transformations in the process of growth. My orientation, which is structural and developmental, has led me to a focus on categories of social reasoning. Much of the research for the theory presented in this book had its origins, about ten years ago, in close analyses of delimited domains of social knowledge. The research was aimed at discerning the differences and similarities in moral judgments and concepts of the conventions of social systems. It quickly became apparent that moral reasoning and concepts of social organization constituted two fundamental and separable aspects of children's understanding of the social world.

In the intervening time my research on morality and convention has gone beyond the original focus to include other important aspects of social development. Moreover, the analyses of categories of social knowledge have provided the framework for an understanding of children's social interactions with peers, their relations with adults, their processes of development, and the relationship between social judgments and actions. A central thesis of this book is that social life is guided by rational processes and that the construction of fundamental and distinct categories of social knowledge begins in early childhood. The idea of distinct categories of reasoning does not imply a dualism of thought and action or of individual reasoning and cultural content. Rather, it is proposed that the separation of domains of knowledge provides a basis for understanding the interrelations among thought, action, and cultural content. The theory of social development is interactive. It proposes that social development evolves through children's reciprocal interactions with the social environment.

In part, this book is aimed at bringing together the various components of the research programs undertaken during the past ten years. Some of the research findings are being presented for the first time. There is also extensive discussion of relevant findings from a set of previously published studies. Much of that research was conducted by colleagues (in collaborative and in independent efforts) who have shared an interest in issues related to the development of domains of social knowledge. They include Allen Black, Philip Davidson, Larry Nucci, and Judith Smetana.

The book has two main goals. One is to further understanding of how people reason about morality and convention and how those domains of reasoning develop from early childhood through adolescence and early adulthood. The second goal is to provide – through extensive and detailed analyses of morality and convention – documentation for the proposition that individuals form stable systems of social knowledge that are organized around domains. In this sense, the present volume is meant to build an empirical foundation for some other theoretical propositions to be presented in a subsequent volume. To achieve these goals, the book is organized in the following way. I have begun with definitions, hypotheses, and theoretical assumptions regarding social knowledge and development. This is followed by discussion of research findings bearing on the hypotheses and propositions. Last, there is a consideration of the implications of this research for a general view of social development.

I would like to acknowledge my gratitude to those who have assisted me in the writing of this book. The early stages of the research were facilitated by a fellowship from the John Simon Guggenheim Memorial Foundation. The actual writing of the book was aided by a fellowship period at the Van Leer Jerusalem Foundation in Israel. The Foundation provided time and a very stimulating setting for thought and writing. Thanks are due to Raphaella Bilski and Yehuda Elkana at Van Leer. Throughout the past few years I have been given research support by the Institute of Human Development at the University of California, Berkeley; I thank the past director of the Institute, Paul Mussen, and the present director, Ed Swanson.

Paul Mussen also provided helpful comments on an earlier version of the manuscript. I also thank Carolyn Hildebrandt, Melanie Killen, and Larry Nucci for their comments. Finally, thanks to Helen Clifton for her excellent work in typing and retyping the manuscript.

Berkeley, California   Elliot Turiel
October 1982

1 Introduction: Approaches to the study of social knowledge

This book is about the ways individuals develop social knowledge through their interactions with the social environment. Knowledge about the social world is, in large measure, socially derived knowledge. The proposition that social knowledge is socially derived, however, can be interpreted in two very different ways. It can be taken to mean that it is knowledge transmitted to the individual by other persons, so that the knowledge acquired is dependent on what is transmitted, or it can be taken to mean that it is knowledge constructed by individuals specifically about social phenomena. The analyses presented in this book are based on the latter interpretation of the social derivation of social knowledge. The analyses document that, starting in early childhood, individuals form conceptual systems for interpreting the varied elements of their social experiences. Social development is a process by which individuals generate understandings of the social world, by making inferences and forming theories about experienced social events.

The study of social development requires two interrelated analyses: the nature of realms of social interaction and the explanation of processes of acquisition or development. Social scientists have extensively considered development and categories of social interaction, culture, and society. However, each of the concerns has been dealt with by separate social scientific disciplines. The most extensive and explicit investigations of individual social development, as would be expected, come from the discipline of psychology. The major psychological approaches (e.g., Baldwin, 1897; Freud, 1923/1960, 1930/1961; Miller & Dollard, 1941; Piaget, 1932, 1951/1962; Skinner, 1971; Watson, 1924) have attended to the explanation of the means by which children acquire social behaviors and social knowledge. Among social scientists, it is mainly anthropologists and sociologists who have studied systems of social interaction through analyses of culture and society. For their part, students of culture and society have generally disregarded systematic study and the formulation of explanatory principles of psychological functioning and development. Instead, the tacit – and sometimes not so tacit – assumption is made that individuals are molded by and come to fit

[handwritten marginal note: seems there are other possib...]

1

their social contexts. The assumption is that individuals accommodate to the patterns or elements of the culture or social system, thereby coming to mirror the culture in their personalities, thinking, and behavior (Benedict, 1934, 1946; Geertz, 1973; Shweder, 1981; Whiting & Child, 1953).

A concern with acquisition, however, must go beyond assumptions to direct investigations and explication of the process of development. The nature of the individual's relation to the broader social system, the ways in which behavior is influenced by social experiences, and the genesis of the individual's social makeup are all issues requiring explanation. Are individuals shaped by the social world, or do they develop conceptual systems for understanding and transforming the social world? Analyses of culture and social systems require corresponding analyses of psychological-developmental processes if one is concerned with the integration of individuals into such systems. In turn, psychological investigations of development need to be informed by analyses of categories of social interaction. The study of the individual's social development, thinking, and behavior requires identification of the types of social elements typically made by students of culture and society, including categories like economic, political, religious, moral, and social organizational systems.

The research described in this volume documents that individuals develop theories about categories of social interaction. Those theories, however, are not simply about each specific or isolated social interactional element experienced. The elements are organized into more general categories of thinking. But social interactions are not conceptually organized to encompass all of social thinking into one system. A main proposition of this volume is that social judgments are organized within domains of knowledge. A related proposition is, therefore, that the study of social development requires classification and identification of domains of social judgment. One of the tasks, then, is to study the organizations and reorganizations of thinking within domains of social judgment. The meaning and boundaries of domains of thinking are considered throughout this volume, and especially in Chapter 2, where the general theoretical framework for the study of development is considered. The theoretical perspective is a structural one that is most closely associated with the work of Piaget. Many other researchers have also taken a structural approach to development, including a recently burgeoning interest in the development of social judgments.

Domains of social judgment

The domain of social interaction has a significant bearing on the individual's thinking, action, and development. The theoretical and empirical analyses presented in this volume address the question of the relations between social interaction categories and the development of social judgments and actions. The focus *define Social judgement*

of this volume is on two social domains: convention and morality. Social conventions are behavioral uniformities that serve to coordinate social interactions and are tied to the contexts of specific social systems. Conventions are based on arbitrary actions that are relative to social contexts. Through their participation in social groups, such as the family, school, or with their peers, children form conceptions about social systems and the conventions, the shared expectations, that coordinate interactions.

Whereas conventions are determined by the social system in which they exist and constitute part of the definition of the social system, the moral domain refers to prescriptive judgments of justice, rights, and welfare pertaining to how people ought to relate to each other. Moral prescriptions are not relative to the social context, nor are they defined by it. Correspondingly, children's moral judgments are not derived directly from social institutional systems but from features inherent to social relationships – including experiences involving harm to persons, violations of rights, and conflicts of competing claims.

They're not? No way how about fam1y or media?

This volume presents detailed analyses of morality and social convention and a theoretical point of view on the development of social judgments and, in particular, on a domain-specific interpretation of social reasoning. After considering the general principles of structure and development (Chapter 2), definitional criteria for the two domains are presented in Chapter 3. As discussed in Chapter 2, a structural approach proposes that thought and action are closely linked with each other. The links are twofold. The development of thought stems from the child's actions upon, and interactions with, the environment. Whereas action is the source of conceptual development, social judgments – once they are formed – are not distinct from actions manifested in behavioral situations. Relations between thought and action are considered first in Chapter 3 and later in Chapter 9. Chapter 3 includes analyses of the experiential sources of social judgments and describes a series of observational studies of children's social interactions in naturalistic settings.

Before dealing in Chapter 9 with the relation of social judgments to behavior, several chapters present analyses of the organizations of moral and conventional thinking. The conceptual features of each domain and the characteristics that serve to distinguish them are considered in Chapters 4 and 5. The data presented in those two chapters offer evidence that morality and convention constitute distinct and non–age-related domains. Developmental changes are apparent within each domain; Chapter 6 deals with the development of concepts of social convention and Chapter 7 with the development of moral judgments.

The analyses and documentation presented in this volume provide the foundation for extending, in a subsequent volume, the domain-specific interpretation of structure and development to a more general theoretical framework regarding social development. The broader framework, which encompasses morality and convention, is based on the identification (Turiel, 1979, in press) of three general and fundamental categories of social-conceptual knowledge, as well as the differentiation of social-conceptual knowledge from social-informational knowledge. On the basis of the assumption that the individual's social world includes other persons, relations between persons, and institutionalized systems of social interaction, it is proposed that the child's structuring of the social world revolves around three general categories. These are (1) concepts of persons or psychological systems (the psychological domain), (2) concepts of systems of social relations and organizations (the societal domain) – of which convention is but one component, and (3) prescriptive judgments of justice, rights, and welfare (the moral domain).

Social understandings or social control

This book is also about the individual's relation to and interaction with the social environment, how to characterize those interactions and, especially, how those interactions influence development. The starting point for the analyses of morality and social convention is the premise that through their social experiences children develop ways of thinking, or theories, about the social world. One type of theory central to social development pertains to moral issues. Children also form theories of social organization, through which they understand the meaning and function of conventions. In coming to understand social systems, people act like social scientists, attempting to observe regularities and explain their existence. Correspondingly, individuals attempt to understand and critically or positively evaluate the sources, functions, and justifications for the rules they are expected to obey. In other words, social life is not detached from thought processes. Indeed, in a long tradition of research, judgment or cognition has been regarded as central to social development and behavior (Asch, 1952; Heider, 1958; Kohlberg, 1969; Köhler, 1938; Lewin, 1935; Mead, 1934; Piaget, 1932; Vygotsky, 1934/1962; Werner, 1957; Wertheimer, 1935). A tradition of research on the development of moral judgments was originally pioneered by Piaget (1932) and extended by Kohlberg (1963, 1969) some years later.

However, the cognitive perspective of social domains is not shared by all students of development or of social systems. A contrasting view of morality and convention is that they represent variants of externally determined standards, which serve to shape and guide people's behaviors, as well as delimit or control their choices. From the societal viewpoint, morality and convention, which are not always distinguishable, serve a controlling function, forcing individuals to accommodate to the group.

As mentioned earlier, some anthropological perspectives posit the primacy of culture and assert that culture serves to exert control over individual behavior.

The concept of culture is still less than clear or precise, still evolving, and, as with most central concepts, unanimity does not exist within the discipline regarding its meaning or functions. Differences of interpretation exist at general levels of analysis. Some anthropologists view cultures as homogeneous, integrated wholes (e.g., Benedict, 1934, 1946; Whiting & Child, 1953). For others (e.g., Geertz, 1973; Schwartz, 1978; Shweder, 1979a,b, 1980), all cultures, including small communities, are characterized by diversity and elements that are not necessarily integrated with each other: "Even the most minimal community would reveal a . . . distinctiveness of personal and cultural variation which, when viewed against the scale of the culture and by the concerns of its members cannot be considered trivial" (Schwartz, 1978, p. 420). Within either the integrated or the diverse view, culture has been regarded as performing controlling functions.

As an example, the thesis that cultures are homogeneous, integrated wholes was posited by Benedict (1934) in her analysis of *Patterns of Culture*. For Benedict, the coherence of culture produces consistency across domains. The type of integration found in one culture, however, is likely to differ from that of another. Moreover, because a cultural pattern is posited to be internally consistent, the practices of one culture cannot be compared with those of another. Benedict's type of relativism stems from the idea that the practices of each culture make sense with regard to its form of integration. Benedict maintained that all social regulations are culturally determined customs, whose meaning and importance could be understood only in relation to their role in a cultural pattern. The unity of culture is replicated in the individual. It guides the ways children are brought up, so that they come to manifest in their personalities and behavior the patterns of culture or what is sometimes referred to as national character. In *The Chrysanthemum and the Sword*, for instance, Benedict describes child training in Japan as successfully geared to the formation of a Japanese adult whose personality mirrors the culture. This was consistent with her earlier premise that the individual's social behavior reflects a nonrational incorporation of the standards of the culture: "The life history of the individual is first and foremost an accommodation to the patterns of standards traditionally handed down in his community" (1934, pp. 2–3).

The proposition that individuals are controlled by the social environment is not always associated with a holistic or integrated view of culture. The idea that the individual is shaped by the social environment has been combined with the view that culture is a series of mechanisms of behavioral control. As Geertz (1973, p. 44) put it, "Culture is . . . a set of control mechanisms – plans, recipes, rules, instructions (what computer engineers call 'programs') – for the governing of behavior . . . Man is precisely the animal most desperately dependent upon such extragenetic, outside-the-skin-control mechanisms, such cultural programs, for ordering his behavior." Conceived in less holistic terms than by Benedict, culture is, nevertheless, the means by which the behavior of individuals is controlled. The individual requires a narrowing of behavioral possibilities, a channeling of capacities into a social order: "Undirected by cultural patterns – organized systems of significant symbols – man's behavior would be virtually ungovernable, a mere chaos of pointless acts and exploding emotions, his experience virtually shapeless" (Geertz, 1973, p. 46). A governing thesis of these approaches is that culture is primary and dominates the individual. It is assumed that a correspondence exists between individual behavior and what exists in the culture.

The presumed correspondence between efforts at social control and individual behavior should not go unquestioned; the extent of correspondence is neither self-evident nor empirically verified. Whether one assumes a greater or lesser extent of correspondence, however, it does not follow that social control is the causal mechanism for the formation of social behavior. In addressing the question of social psychological development, a series of issues must be posed and answered with specificity and detail. First is consideration of the nature of the person's inherent capacities and orientations. Are they such that living in a social world results in narrowing and channeling, so that "the breadth and indeterminateness of his inherent capacities are reduced to the narrowness and specificity of his actual accomplishments" (Geertz, 1973, p. 45)? Or are they such that social life results in a broadening of social interactions and expansion of knowledge? Although the concept of control is applicable in the former case, it is inappropriate in the latter. The nature of the individual's inherent capacities is not unrelated to a second issue: the nature of the individual's interaction with the social environment. Is the emphasis to be placed upon the control exerted by society, or upon the individual's attempts to understand and manipulate his or her environment, or upon the point of intersection between the two processes? In turn, we must inquire into the nature and courses of change that individuals undergo. Is social development best represented, as Benedict put it, as an accommodation to the community, or is it the construction of modes of reasoning about social categories? Does it involve an increasing accumulation of environmental content or a progression of qualitative changes in mental-psychological organization?

These questions are central to developmental analyses. Answers to some of these questions are implicit in theorizing about social and cultural systems that assumes causally imposed environmental control over the individual's behavior. Such implicit theories are, in a general sense, consistent with some explicit theories of social development – most notably, those of behavioristic and psychoanalytic theorists (comparisons of these noncognitive orientations with the cognitive ones are made in Chapter 8). It may be said that for behaviorists social development is under environmental control, whereas for Freudians it is under cultural (or societal) control. Behavioristic theories have explained the development of morality through the psychological mechanisms of conditioning and the learning of values and rules. Morality is thus seen as a combination of fixed habits and direct mental representations of values and rules. Freudian theory has explained moral development as the formation of a conscience (superego), an internalized mental agency whose function is to control, regulate, and transform instinctual impulses that conflict with societal functions.

Although there are important differences between behavioristic and Freudian theories, they share the assumption, along with the theories of culture discussed earlier, that the social environment serves to regulate and control human conduct. From this assumption three tenets follow: (1) a dichotomy exists between the individual and the group; (2) a dichotomy exists between self-interest and other-interest; and (3) nonrational or irrational processes predominate in determining behavior in the social domains. In these conceptions the individual is regarded as entering the world with impulses, needs, drives, or, according to Freud, with complex patterns of instincts. Whichever way it is put, in analyses of social development this translates into a view of a child whose initial state of *No. This* selfishness and impulsiveness must be curbed and made social. The developmen- *is too* tal process is one in which originally external content residing in the group (in the *simplistic,* form of standards, regulations, prohibitions, etc.), becomes incorporated by the child. That is, with increasing age the child's behavior is modified or socialized so as to render it more consistent with group interests and standards. Socialization is aimed at modifying the child's natural self-interested tendencies into group attachment and altruistic tendencies.

The proposed dualities between the individual and the group and self-interest and altruism are rooted in the view that the social domains are primarily nonrational. Social behavior is, in the main, guided by emotions; reason is, at best, secondary. It is needs, drives, and passions that motivate the child's initial interactions with the social world. It is rewards, punishments, and threats, along with their resultant fears, anxieties, and ambivalences, that cause the shift from self-centeredness to greater sociability.

Indeed, if the social environment only serves to regulate and control, it does follow that the social domains are nonrational. However, the social environment does not merely exert control upon individuals but is understood by them. Paralleling the diversity of culture is the diversity of the individual's understanding of the social world. Development entails an expanding social knowledge and an increasing complexity of social interactions. The child is not motivated solely by needs and drives that conflict with social obligations and that make for a dichotomized relation of the individual to the group. Rather, the child is in a reciprocal interaction with his or her environment, through which descriptive and prescriptive concepts are constructed.

Unfair. The Geertz/Benedict argument has been lumped in w/ the Freudian one.

2   Structure and development

The analyses presented in this volume are based on the assumption that individuals define, interpret, and judge social relations. The individual's interactions with the environment are characterized by efforts to understand other persons and relations among persons. Hence, the individual is in a reciprocal interaction with the social environment. The research discussed here was designed to examine the social judgments of children and adolescents, the developmental course of those judgments, the relations of social experience and development, and the relations of social judgment and social behavior.

The developmental approach to social judgment currently represents one of two main trends in psychological research emphasizing the role of cognition in the social domains. Within the subdiscipline of social psychology, attribution theorists (e.g., Jones & Davis, 1965; Kelley, 1967, 1973; Nisbett & Ross, 1980; Ross, 1977) have been primarily concerned with causal inferences in the individual's predictions and conceptualizations of the behavior of other persons. Developmental psychologists have paid relatively little attention to children's understandings of the psychological attributes of persons, concentrating to a greater extent on the study of children's concepts of social relations (potential relations between the two approaches are discussed by Ross, 1981, and the place of the psychological domain in developmental formulations is discussed by Turiel, in press). The developmental approach to social cognition has its origins in a related, but somewhat different, tradition of structural psychology from the origins of attribution theorists. Whereas attribution theorists were influenced by Gestaltists (e.g., Asch, 1952; Lewin, 1935) concerned with social psychological problems, the recent work in developmental social cognition draws heavily on theories concerned with the relations between structure and development, such as those of Baldwin (1906, 1915), Vygotsky (1934/1962), Werner (1937, 1957), and especially Piaget (1929, 1932, 1936/1963, 1947/1950, 1970a,b).

Piaget conducted some extensive research on children's social reasoning during what may be considered an early, exploratory phase of his work. Included among those early studies were investigations of perspective-taking, communica-

8

tion (1923), and moral judgment (1932). Undoubtedly, the early research has had a substantial influence upon recent concerns with social cognitive development. However, more important influences – particularly for the point of view and the research findings presented in this volume – have stemmed from Piaget's later theoretical formulations regarding thought, structure, and development. A distinct shift was evident in Piaget's approach starting with his work on sensorimotor development (Piaget, 1936/1963, 1952). In addition to an exclusive concentration on nonsocial cognition in his later work (e.g., logic, mathematics, physical relations, causality, probability), Piaget formalized his structural and developmental conceptions. Whereas the earlier formulations characterized the child's thought as progressing through general and global phases, his later formulations included a series of distinctions serving to differentiate types of knowledge. For instance, distinctions are drawn between logical-mathematical concepts and physical concepts, as well as between operative and figurative forms of knowledge (Turiel, in press). Moreover, several researchers (e.g., Inhelder & Sinclair, 1969; Inhelder, Sinclair, & Bovet, 1974; Kohlberg, 1969; Langer, 1969, 1974, 1980; Strauss, 1972, 1981; Sugarman, 1979), along with Piaget, have provided systematic formulations of structural development.

Those principles of development are outlined in this chapter, without an extensive or comprehensive explication. The purpose of this discussion is to provide an overview of the basic concepts and to serve as a general guide to the presentation of research procedures, findings, and interpretations in the subsequent chapters. Of course, the remainder of the volume includes further extensions of the theoretical framework.

Interaction, construction, and structure

An overriding premise of the structural approach is that thought is *organized* and that it is *constructed* out of the child's *interactions* with the environment. The meanings of construction and interaction and their interrelations in a developmental context have been summarized by Piaget (1970a, p. 704):

In order to know objects, the subject must act upon them, and therefore transform them: he must displace, connect, combine, take apart and reassemble them. From the most elementary sensory-motor actions to the most sophisticated intellectual operations, which are interiorized actions, carried out mentally,...knowledge is constantly linked with actions or operations, that is, with transformations....Knowledge, then, at its origin neither arises from objects nor from the subject, but from interactions...between the subject and those objects.

The initial sources of the construction of thought and knowledge are the child's sensorimotor and interiorized actions upon, and interactions with, objects, events, and persons. The thesis is that thought and knowledge are neither givens in the biological makeup of the individual (the subject), nor do they stem directly from the environment (objects). The thesis, therefore, is interactional and not maturational. However, over the years the proposition that thought is constructed through individual–environment interactions has often been misinterpreted to be a nativistic or maturational one. As early as 1930 Isaacs (p. 58) critically stated her view that Piaget's

> views on the development of the child's language and thought, judgment and reasoning, and conception of the world, constitute the most arresting modern statement of the theory of maturation.... But Piaget's conclusions are, I think, lessened in their final value because he does not use the concept of maturation (which he expresses as the structure of the child's mind at different ages) sparingly enough nor critically enough.

More recently, Wilson (1978, pp. 68–69) praisingly observed that Piaget

> spent a lifetime charting the often surprising stages children pass through in their more purely intellectual growth.... It is no coincidence that he calls this conception 'genetic epistemology', in effect the study of the hereditary unfolding of understanding.

In all likelihood, this assimilation of the hypothesis of interaction and construction to a maturational one stems from the often-made assumption that children's development, and behavior in general, are causally determined by two factors, heredity and environment. If development is not explained as a direct function of experience, it is assumed that one must be positing a nativistic or maturational explanation. Among those who take innateness and experience as the sole factors, the disagreements are over the relative emphasis placed on each factor. Most have regarded innateness and experience as representing dual causes of behavior. However, some place the greatest emphasis on innate factors (e.g., instincts, predetermined structures of behavior or ideas, maturationally determined capacities), others regard the acquisition of environmental content as primary, and still others attribute more or less equal weight to the two factors.

A paradigmatic example is provided by the long-standing debate over the determinants of human intelligence waged by those using psychometric measurement (the familiar IQ tests). Within that tradition, intelligence is defined as a trait or capacity possessed by individuals to a greater or lesser degree. Psychometric measures of intelligence are presumed to provide a reliable estimate of the amount of intelligence possessed by an individual (relative to others). Competing explanations of the sources of intelligence vary usually with regard to the degree to which it is determined by innate capacities or by experience. Some have maintained that intelligence is primarily a genetically determined capacity only minimally affected by experience. Others have argued that, in spite of some contribution of genetic traits, intelligence is primarily determined by experience. Experience is said to account for most of the individual differences in the amount and content of acquired knowledge. (Some have also urged for a more balanced contribution of the two factors.)

The psychometric view of intelligence will be considered in the context of a discussion of methods of study. For now, the point to be made is that from a structural perspective intelligence is viewed not as a capacity or a trait but as a process of cognitive activity. Accordingly, the concept of intelligence is not characterized as a quantitative attribute of persons, but as systems (or forms of organization) of thought, which in ontogenesis undergo transformations, that is, constructions. It is indeed true, as Wilson wrote, that Piaget referred to the structural theory of intellectual growth as genetic epistemology. However, the use of the term "genetic" is meant to connote development and not a hereditary unfolding. In its developmental sense the term has been used in two contexts, genetic *epistemology* and genetic *psychology*. Genetic epistemology is not restricted to individual development, but refers to the wider sense of the growth of all knowledge including, for example, branches of scientific disciplines. In any case, the developmental connotation of the term "genetic" has been explicitly stressed by Piaget and Inhelder (1969, p. viii):

To dispel any ambiguity about terminology, let us note first that the word 'genetic', as used in the expression 'genetic psychology', was introduced by psychologists in the second half of the nineteenth century to refer to the developmental aspects of psychology. Later, biologists began to use the term 'genetics' in a more restricted sense. In the current language of biologists, 'genetics' refers only to the mechanisms of heredity and does not include the study of embryogenetic or developmental processes. The term 'genetic psychology', however, continues to refer to individual development (ontogenesis).

This is not to say that there is no biological basis to development. It is to say that organizations of knowledge are not proposed to be preformed in the nativistic sense. The biological or inherited factors contributing to the development of thought are, in addition to *general* capacities for cognitive activities, the dual functions of assimilation and accommodation (Piaget, 1936/1963, 1970a, 1980a). Assimilation and accommodation are inherent to interactions between biological systems and the environment; through assimilation the individual modifies events to fit his or her structures and through accommodation the individual's structures are modified to fit events. Moreover, assimilation and accommodation are functions that operate in individual–environment interactions at every level of development, including the activities of infants and adults. The process of assimilating environmental events can be seen, for example, in the infant's attempts to suck objects like rattles or blocks, thus fitting the objects to a sucking schema. In addition to assimilation, experienced events produce accommodation of existing schema to the structure of the object. Infants accommodate their sucking schema to the type of object; they suck the nipple and thumb in different ways, and blocks become nonsuckable objects.

The concepts of assimilation and accommodation imply a reciprocal relation between the subject's structuring activities and experienced events. That is, it is necessary to analyze responses to stimuli in their reciprocal form. Responses are not determined entirely by external events, such as the characteristics of stimuli or associated positive and negative reinforcements. As an illustrative example of how a response entails a structuring of the stimuli eliciting it, consider the classic experiment conducted by Watson and Rayner (1920). The experiment, which presumably demonstrated the conditionability of emotional reactions in infants, was based on the hypothesis of a unilateral connection of stimulus and response ($S \longrightarrow R$). Watson and Rayner claim to have conditioned a fear of rats in the infant by pairing the appearance of the rat with the onset of a loud noise (the durability and generalization of the response to other white, furry animals is open to some question; see Harris, 1979).

Watson and Rayner maintained that pairing an aversive stimulus with an originally neutral stimulus was sufficient to produce the fear response. Presumably, the source of the fear response (the rat) was initially arbitrary and was made nonarbitrary by the conditioning process. However, the results of experiments (Bregman, 1934) using the same conditioning techniques with different stimuli have shown that the relation of the subject to the object contributes to the learning that occurs. Using methods similar to those of Watson and Rayner, Bregman attempted to condition infants to fear wooden objects and cloth curtains of various shapes and colors. Bregman's experimental efforts were unsuccessful: She was unable to condition fear responses to the inanimate objects.

The Bregman and Watson and Rayner findings demonstrate that even at the level of experimental efforts at conditioning fear responses in infants a reciprocal relation exists between responses and stimuli. The findings can be interpreted to mean that the nature of the stimulus, in concert with the child's schema, are significant determinants of responding and learning (Nisbett & Ross, 1980). From the point of view of an infant, animate objects are more likely to have fear-evoking qualities than a block of wood or piece of cloth. Development during infancy, however, goes well beyond the learning of discriminative emotional responses. During infancy, or the sensorimotor period of development (Piaget, 1936/1963, 1952, 1954), the initial cognitive organizations are constructed that lead to the formation of representational thought and symbolization. Piaget has traced the development of infants' means–ends activities, through which their actions are coordinated with desired objectives. The focus of that research was on the early constructions of physical knowledge, that is, knowledge of objects (e.g., the onset of object permanence), spatial relations, temporal order, and causality.

Recently, some important discoveries were made by Langer (1980) regarding the origins of logic. In extensive, detailed, and precise research on infants' (6 to 18 months of age) manipulations of different types and shapes of objects, evidence has been obtained of the early formation of elementary logical structures.

The research focused on part–whole transformations: the transformation of objects from one form to another, and the formation and deformation of objects into parts and sets. The infants were presented with a small series of different objects (e.g., rings, columns, and spoons) made out of nonmalleable and malleable materials. The analyses were based on detailed recording of the spontaneous activities of infants, as well as their reactions to specific manipulations of the objects by the experimenter. The logical operations found to be part of that early period of cognitive development consist of combinativity (e.g., composing and decomposing), relational operations (e.g., addition and subtraction), and conditional operations (e.g., negation and correlation). The cognitions of this period represent only the beginnings of later constructions. Indeed, they have been termed (Langer, 1980, 1981a) "proto-operations" and characterized as "protologic" to signify that they are precursors to the later logical operations and inference structures of childhood (Inhelder & Piaget, 1964) and adolescence (Inhelder & Piaget, 1958).

This is not the place for an extensive discussion of the sensorimotor origins of physical cognitions and logical operations. The brief mention of findings from research on infant cognition serves to illustrate that even at the youngest ages, the individual's interactions with the environment stem from organized systems of thought: "The structures of physical cognition are of a piece; they constitute a unified organization of one fundamental form – functions. Similarly, logico-mathematical cognitions take one fundamental form – operations" (Langer, 1981b, p. 16). It is proposed, therefore, that thought is characterized by systems of organization in which the elements or parts are subordinated to the laws of the whole (Piaget, 1970c; Turiel, 1978a). However, it should be clearly noted that all aspects of thought do not constitute one general system of organization. Even during infancy distinctions are drawn between physical cognition (means–ends activities that are goal-directed; functions) and the precursors to logical-mathematical cognitions, which entail rudimentary forms of classification and seriation in part–whole transformations. Moreover, distinctions are drawn between aspects of knowledge that form organized systems and those that do not. (More will be said shortly in this chapter about the boundaries of systems of organization, which is a major topic of this volume with regard to social cognition.) It is also proposed that development entails systematic sequential changes in the organization of thinking within domains. As indicated, the cognitions of the sensorimotor period are the antecedent structures of later constructions of physical and logical cognitions.

A developmental sequence represents qualitative changes in ontogenesis from simpler to more complex forms of organization. The child's interactions with the environment are based on the existing organizations of thought (stages or levels of development). That is, relations between the individual and the environment are interactional in the sense that events are interpreted through the individual's structures of thought. One example of how this is manifested comes from the multitude of findings showing that children at different developmental levels respond to the same intellectual tasks in very different ways. It has also been found that level of development even sets limits on the child's comprehension of input from the physical and social (e.g., in the form of communications or instructions) environments. Examples come from experiments on children's moral judgments (Rest, 1973; Rest, Turiel, & Kohlberg, 1969). In these experiments measures were obtained of children's comprehension of presented solutions to problems that corresponded to levels different from their own. The degree of comprehension shown by a child was related to the match between his or her own level of thinking and the level of the communication. Children were able to comprehend communications at levels below their own and at their own level. For the most part, they were unable to comprehend communications at levels above their own. In fact, in many cases higher-level communications were reinterpreted to resemble the child's own level of thinking or, especially when the communication was discrepant with the child's position, to resemble levels *less* advanced than the child's own.

Perhaps the most striking examples of how the individual's existing modes of thinking have a powerful influence on the interpretation of new information come from research having an attribution-theoretic perspective. One example comes from an experiment by Lord, Ross, and Lepper (1979), who examined how adults deal with empirical evidence that is confirming and disconfirming of strongly held beliefs. Confirming and disconfirming evidence was presented to subjects who had expressed either the belief that capital punishment was a deterrent to potential murderers or that it did not serve as a deterrent. A complicated experimental design was used that may, for present purposes, be summarized as follows. Participants in the experiment were told about the results and methods of two studies (made up by the experimenters) on the deterrent effects of capital punishment. The two methods provided were (1) comparisons of murder rates before and after states had adopted capital punishment, and (2) comparisons between states with and without capital punishment. For some people one type of method (say, method 1) was combined with results supporting their original position on capital punishment, and the other method (method 2) was combined with results contradictory to their position. For other participants in the experiment method 1 was combined with results in contradiction with their position on capital punishment, and method 2 was combined with results supporting their position. The findings of the experiment showed clear cases of the assimilation of evidence to the preexisting positions. Participants in the experiment consistently found the "data" supportive of their position much more convincing than the disconfirming data. Regardless of how the methods and results were paired, the disconfirming studies were criticized and the confirming studies were viewed as superior.

From the attribution perspective of the researchers who conducted this experiment, the assimilation of new information to existing theories is termed "belief perseverance" (Nisbett & Ross, 1980). Belief perseverance is another way of stating that individuals have coherent systems of thought that serve to structure their interpretation of new information and evidence. Accordingly, similar types of structuring of information or environmental input has been documented in social psychological experiments with adults and children. Other related phenomena central to a structural approach to development have been documented by attribution analyses (Ross, 1977), as well as by the work of cognitive psychologists (Kahneman & Tversky, 1972, 1973; Tversky, 1977; Tversky & Kahneman, 1974). Starting with Piaget, an important means for understanding children's thinking has been the analysis of their conceptual errors. The best-known example, but it is only one example, is Piaget's analyses of young children's judgments of nonconservation of number, length, and weight. On a variety of tasks (classification, seriation, transitive relations, chance), children's errors in their solutions of tasks provide a data base for descriptions of levels of cognitive operations. The formulation of a developmental sequence includes both analyses of earlier levels of thought and their relation to the more adequate, more powerful conceptualizations of later levels of thought. Similarly, with regard to adult judgments, research by Ross (1977) has revealed errors in psychological attribution, and research by Kahneman and Tversky has focused on systematic errors in scientific and statistical inferences. Although the tasks used in the research with adults are of greater difficulty and complexity, the patterns of analysis are similar to the developmental research in that judgments are (1) analyzed for underlying strategies, and (2) compared with normative standards (in this case, of scientific inference).

Stages, developmental synchrony-asynchrony, equilibration

Several researchers working in a structural tradition have described sequential changes in the organization of thought. The sequences generally consist of stages or levels meant to demarcate qualitative changes. It is proposed that, within a sequence, movement from one stage or level to the next entails reorganization of a form of thought into a new form. The concept of a sequence of stages or levels, which is part of Piaget's formulations and is used by several others (e.g., Damon, 1977; Furth, 1978; Kohlberg, 1969; Langer, 1980; Selman, 1976; Turiel, 1978a; Youniss & Volpe, 1978), has recently been a topic of controversy. Given the controversies over the stage concept, it may be useful, at this point, to describe its characteristics.

Criticisms have been leveled at the stage concept by some whose own theoretical predilections are diametrically opposed to a structural viewpoint, such as those maintaining associationistic (e.g., Brainerd, 1978), learning-behavioristic (e.g., Bandura, 1977), or personality-trait (e.g., Kurtines & Greif, 1974) positions. It would appear that those criticisms are aimed at striking at the heart of structural theory in order to demonstrate its lack of validity, because the critics make the (somewhat misleading) assumption that the stage concept is the most fundamental aspect of the theory. Criticisms have also come from some (e.g., Flavell, 1982; Rest, in press) whose orientation is at least partly compatible with a structural viewpoint but who have disagreements with the stage concept and maintain that the concept is not supported by the empirical evidence.

There is consistency on certain points in the way the different critics have characterized the presumed structural-developmental use of the stage notion. Those characterizations are, of course, the bases for the critical analyses. However, these characterizations are not always accurate. There are important inconsistencies between (1) the way critics have characterized the structural-developmental use of the stage notion, and (2) the structural-developmental characterization and application of the stage notion – at least, as I interpret it. Comparisons between the critics' interpretations of structural sequences with how they have been used by its proponents (especially Piaget) would serve to clarify principles of development and their use in the analyses presented in subsequent chapters.

We can begin with a consideration of the features critics have attributed to stage-sequence formulations that they have regarded as inadequate or empirically unjustified. The features to be considered come not from two or three specific critics but represent a compilation of points made by several commentators. Typically, their overriding assumptions are that structural theorists are proposing that developmental stages are, in some sense, autonomous, self-contained units manifested independently of the subject's prior experiences, regardless of the type of task involved and across domains of knowledge. This general assumption, it will be argued, is an incomplete and basically inaccurate characterization of structural theory. Yet, the assumption is derived from some of the theoretical parameters of the structural position. Three aspects of structural theory have led the critics to propose theoretical implications and concomitant empirical tests:

1. *Structuralists have proposed that thinking is not a copy or internalization of environmental content.* Critics conclude that the structuralist claim is that cognitive development is minimally influenced by experience. They maintain that if the claim were correct, then the same stages of development would be observed regardless of the child's experiences. In turn, the structuralist position is faulted for paying insufficient attention to environmental influences, especially the social environment, on the child's development.

2. *Structuralists have proposed that thinking forms systems of organization.* Critics conclude that the structural claim is that there is general consistency or unity in the individual's thinking at each stage of development. They maintain that if the claim were correct, then thinking should be characterized by homogeneity. In that case, an individual's stage should be apparent across most tasks and situations. Further, it is maintained that the research findings show that thinking is not the same across tasks and situations and that, therefore, the stage hypothesis is not supported by the evidence.

3. *Structuralists have proposed that developmental changes in organized systems of thought involve a process of internal regulation and equilibration.* Critics conclude that the structuralist claim is that stage transitions are abrupt or saltatory, rather than gradual; when a new cognitive operation is acquired, it will be rapidly applied to a large variety of tasks. The critics maintain that if the claim were correct, then transitions would be observed as abrupt shifts with synchronous emergence of the new stage in a variety of tasks and conceptual domains. It is maintained that the research evidence shows that changes are gradual and asynchronous.

Have the critics adequately characterized the structural-developmental positions? The validity of their conclusions regarding the empirical evidence is contingent on the adequacy of the interpretations of structural propositions (if the reading of the empirical evidence is correct, which is still another matter). If we consider a more comprehensive version of the elements of structural theory, including some of the features already discussed, it becomes evident that the proposed empirical tests are based on a less-than-accurate account of the theory.

1. *Experience.* Although structural theorists have proposed that thought or knowledge are not copies of reality or experience, they have also maintained, as detailed earlier, that development stems from the child's interactions with the environment, that is, from experience. Portraying stages as autonomous units whose emergence is independent of prior experiences is more in accord with innatist or maturational structural theories (e.g., Chomsky, 1980) than with interactional-constructivist structural theories. The interactional proposition is that knowledge is formed through the subject's actions upon events, tasks, and problems, as well as through reflections upon actions (Piaget, 1976, 1980b). It follows, therefore, that the child's experiences would influence the type of thought or knowledge constructed (Nucci & Turiel, 1978; Turiel, 1975). The nature of events or tasks, as well as the child's familiarity with them (the extent to which the child has acted and reflected upon them) should have a bearing upon type and level of thinking. However, there is an interaction between experiential variables and stage of development. Similar experience would be expected to influence children at different stages in different ways.

What is Logical-mathematical knowledge?

Most important, the interactional-structural model implies that there are systematic relations between the nature of environmental events experienced and development. Fundamental differences exist in the types of events experienced by young children, and these differences contribute to the construction of distinct domains of knowledge (Turiel, 1979, in press). As an example, it has been proposed (Piaget, 1970b, 1976) that a distinction exists between experiences of a physical-empirical nature, which are closely related to the development of physical concepts, and logical-mathematical experiences entailing the coordination of actions, which are closely related to the development of logical-mathematical cognition.

The relation of experience and social cognitive development is dealt with in some detail in this volume. Analyses of how different types of social events and interactions are related to the development of distinct domains of knowledge is considered in Chapter 3. The relation of social judgments to prior familiarity with tasks and issues is considered in Chapter 4.

2. *Homogeneity and heterogeneity of thought.* The structural proposition that thinking forms organized systems does imply consistency of thinking across tasks and situations. However, it is not necessarily the case that the stage notion implies that all forms of thinking are part of the *same* system of organization. At least two alternative propositions can be made regarding the boundaries of systems of organization. It may be proposed that thought is organized in such a way that it encompasses all areas, all tasks and domains, that it encompasses the mind as a whole. Or it may be proposed that thought is organized within narrower boundaries and in accordance with domains. As stated in Chapter 1, one of the aims of this volume is to explicate a domain-specific model of the development of social concepts. The proposition is that social knowledge is organized within domains (the moral, societal, and psychological) and not across domains. Additional sources of heterogeneity in thought stem from the differences between social-informational knowledge and social-conceptual knowledge.

What amounts to domain distinctions have already been mentioned with regard to nonsocial cognitive development, as well. In his earliest work Piaget (1923, 1929, 1932) did hypothesize structural relations among varied aspects of thought (this issue is considered in Chapter 7). However, this hypothesis, which may imply that a stage encompasses wide boundaries, was subsequently displaced by Piaget. His conception of genetic epistemology is based on a concern with the epistemology of domains of knowledge in analyses of cognitive development. In Piaget's research, the development of logical-mathematical knowledge is distinguished from concepts about the physical world. We have already seen that this kind of a distinction is evidenced in infancy through the differences between means–ends and part–whole transformations (Langer, 1980). Further and not insignificant distinctions are made between conceptual-transformational knowledge (based on cognitive operations) and informational knowledge derived from the figurative activities of imagery (Piaget & Inhelder, 1971), imitation (Piaget, 1951), perception (Piaget, 1969), and memory (Piaget & Inhelder, 1972).

From a structural viewpoint, therefore, there is both homogeneity and heterogeneity in cognition. The homogeneity expected from a stage or level of development is restricted to thinking within narrowly defined conceptual domains. Variations in an individual's thinking would stem from domain differences and from the intersections of informational and conceptual knowledge.

3. *Developmental synchrony or asynchrony.* The proposition that thought is organized within domains is inconsistent with the idea that developmental transitions reflect abrupt changes across tasks and domains (general developmental synchrony). It is proposed, instead, that developmental transitions, which are hypothesized to be internally regulated (equilibration), occur within domains. Again, at least two propositions can be made regarding the nature of such within-domain transitions. One is that transitions are abrupt, involving an immediate shift from one stage to the next. An alternative proposition is that transition entails a dual process of self-correction of one form of thinking and the emergence of a new form and is, therefore, gradual.

The interpretation of the developmental process in concepts of social convention (see Chapter 6) is that transitions include a phase of negation of a system of thought, through criticalness of its structure, followed by the construction and affirmation of a more advanced set of concepts. This interpretation is consistent with the cross-sectional and longitudinal findings. It is also consistent with longitudinal and experimental findings in research on moral judgments (Damon, 1980; Turiel, 1974, 1977) and on nonsocial cognitive development in childhood (Inhelder & Sinclair, 1969; Inhelder, Sinclair, & Bovet, 1974; Strauss, 1972) and adolescence (Langer, in press). Indeed, a consensus can be said to exist among all these researchers that developmental transitions are gradual.

Moreover, all these findings are consistent with the principle of equilibration (Langer, 1969, in press; Piaget, 1977, 1980b; Turiel, 1969, 1974). The hypothesis is that the process of change from one stage to the next is regulated by equilibration: Development is continually directed toward increasing equilibrium, so that each stage is a more equilibrated state than the previous one. Equilibrium, however, does not simply mean adjustment or conformity to external pressures. There are two interrelated aspects to structural equilibrium. One refers to the equilibrium or coherence of a system of thinking. The second refers to an understanding of the environment in the most powerful, comprehensive, and effective way. That is, each stage of development represents a more equilibrated means of understanding the environment than the previous stage. When new information, evidence, or propositions are assimilated, the coherence of cognitive organization is maintained. It is disequilibrium, which is characterized by conceptions of inadequacies, contradictions, and inconsistencies in the existing way of thinking, that can result in activities producing new information leading to the reorganization of thought. If the child's existing way of thinking inadequately handles encountered events, the result may be disequilibrium that can precipitate a gradual process of reorganization into a form of thought that more adequately coordinates the child's previous conceptions with the novel, discrepant events.

Therefore, a structural state constitutes the basis for environmental interactions that may lead to inconsistencies and contradictions. As has been shown by longitudinal research with subjects identified as undergoing transition (Turiel, 1974, 1977), change involves conflict over two types of concepts, those of the prior stage and those of the emerging stage. Put in this form, transitions constitute an identifiable phase and cannot be said to occur in sudden, abrupt fashion. The portrayal of a developing child who shifts abruptly from one stage to another does not accord with structural analyses of conflicts, nor with the discrepancies and contradictions that are proposed to be essential components of the equilibration process.[1] Nor does it accord with the frequently observed phenomenon, labeled "U-shaped behavioral growth" (Strauss, 1981, in press), of the appearance of a behavior at a certain age, its disappearance sometime later, and its reappearance at a still later age. Some phases in development that seem to reflect a lesser achievement than that of an earlier phase actually represent conceptual conflicts and cognitive advance.

Domains of knowledge and partial structures

Cognitive structures are partial in that they encompass delimited domains of knowledge; thinking is organized within the boundaries of fundamental categories (e.g., logical-mathematical thinking, moral judgment). Development within a domain entails reorganizations of thought, so that separate developmental sequences can be identified for each domain. One basis for the proposition that concepts are organized within domains rests upon the idea that they are constructed through the individual's interactions with the environment. Conceptual knowledge is constructed through an interactive process, but it is not causally determined by the environment. Because such constructions originate from the individual's interactions, they are influenced by the environment. It follows,

[1] Piaget's formulations of stages of cognitive development include the specification of substages within each stage. For instance, six substages have been identified within the stage of sensorimotor development (Piaget, 1936/1963). With the inclusion of substages in each of the stages of cognitive development, Piaget proposed a gradual process of development because the shift from the start of one stage to the start of the next stage involves progress through several phases.

therefore, that interactions with fundamentally different types of objects and events should result in the formation of distinct concepts.

From the perspective of partial structures, therefore, stages or levels of development *are not* autonomous, self-contained units manifested across tasks and situations. The proposition is that there is neither a general structure of mind as a whole to be identified nor are there so many domains of knowledge that we are left with a series of elements but no systems of organization. A program of research, therefore, requires identification and definition of the boundaries of conceptual domains.

The analyses presented in this volume deal with domains in social knowledge, on the assumption that social concepts are not all of one kind. Several interrelated tasks are involved. The first task is to identify and define the domains under investigation. In Chapter 3 morality and social convention are defined further and criteria are presented to delineate their boundaries. A second task is to examine the experiential sources of development. The domain criteria provide a basis for studying the types of social experiences that stimulate development within each domain, as is also discussed in Chapter 3. Two other types of investigation stem from the proposition that morality and social convention constitute two distinct structural and developmental systems. One type is designed to test if the distinction is made by subjects of different ages and to determine the criteria that they use in their judgments about each domain. A series of such studies is discussed in Chapter 4. Insofar as valid domains are identified, developmental analyses would focus on sequential changes in the organization of concepts within each domain. The development of each type of concept is considered in Chapters 6 and 7.

Methods of research

As with any program of research, various methods have been used in studies of structural development. These have included observational studies, controlled experiments, and a type of interview labeled the clinical method (Piaget, 1929). The primary methods used in the studies of social cognitive development discussed in this volume were systematic observations and variations of the clinical interview method. Some of the studies were conducted in the everyday or naturalistic contexts of the children's lives, such as schools or playgrounds, and others were conducted in the context of the "laboratory." In this case, laboratory simply means that the researcher administered a given procedure to the subject in a separate room (e.g., in the child's school) set apart at the time for the purpose of conducting the research.

The use of the laboratory or the naturalistic context depended on the purposes of the research and the questions addressed. For instance, studies of the relations of children's social interactions to domains of social knowledge (as discussed in Chapter 3) have been conducted in naturalistic contexts in which the social interactions occur (e.g., preschools, elementary school classrooms, and playgrounds). By contrast, most of the studies of children's social reasoning were conducted in the laboratory context so as to enable close and detailed gathering of data. One of the potential disadvantages of the laboratory context is that the subject's familiarity with the events or stimuli presented may not be as great as with those encountered in naturalistic contexts. This means that it is necessary to control for the familiarity of stimuli through procedures that provide the researcher with its independent assessment, as was done in some of the studies discussed in Chapter 4.

It should be noted that there is a sense in which the distinction between natural and laboratory contexts is artificial – depending on the topic of the investigations. In research on the structure of thought the distinction is not valid, because reasoning about problems or events occurs naturally in and out of the context of ongoing social interactions. The type of reflective thinking that occurs in the research laboratory setting is no less real or natural than reflective thinking that occurs in many nonresearch settings.[2]

Specific research methods are detailed in the context of the discussions, in later chapters, of particular studies. The remainder of this chapter is devoted to discussion of the rationale and features of interview methods used in research on structural development. The reasons for amplifying on the clinical interview are twofold. First is its significance for structural-developmental research and, especially, its widespread use in studies of social cognition. The second reason is to clarify the aims and uses of the method, especially with regard to the differences between the clinical interview and so-called standardized testing in the psychometric tradition.

A major question regarding assessment and scoring in the clinical method pertains to the standardization of interviewing and the objectivity of response scoring. An incorrectly presumed lack of standardization of assessments and objectivity of scoring has sometimes led to attempts to translate the procedures into "tests" that do not require the interviewing of subjects and that are scored mechanically. In addition, confusions about method and theory are evident in efforts to evaluate (e.g., Kurtines & Greif, 1974) the clinical method and associ-

---

[2] The methods of assessing reasoning in natural and laboratory contexts are not in opposition and should be seen as complementary. There are methodological advantages and disadvantages to each method. The laboratory methods allow for specification and control of variables, as well as experimental manipulations to pursue predetermined questions or hypotheses. The laboratory methods also provide data on reflective thinking, which can then be used in the study of thinking in naturalistic settings. Although naturalistic settings are not often amenable to the control of variables, they do provide stimulus events that are not readily reproducible in the laboratory. Naturalistic settings also provide data on thinking in the situational context, which can then be used in the study of reflective thinking in laboratory settings.

ated theoretical frameworks through the use of what is referred to as psychometric criteria (Campbell, 1960; Cronbach & Meehl, 1955).

A basic difference between the two methods of assessment is that clinical interviews are aimed at describing the organization of thought and, therefore, are designed to obtain data on processes of reasoning and not just on conclusions or products (Kohlberg, 1969; Langer, 1969; Luria, 1976; Piaget, 1928, 1929; Turiel, 1969; Werner, 1937), whereas psychometric measures are designed to elicit responses reflecting a pass or fail on test items that can be scored mechanically, without any interpretation on the part of the scorer. Consequently, it must be asked: If one begins with the theoretical assumptions that there are underlying structures or organizations of thought that are related in something other than a one-to-one correspondence to answers to problems or conclusions on tasks (e.g., of the pass–fail variety), then is it methodologically reasonable to replace the interview method with psychometric tests or to apply psychometric criteria in assessments of validity? The answer to this question, it will be argued, is No! This does not mean that there are no restrictions on the standardization or objectivity of the clinical method or that there are no criteria for assessment of validity. Quite to the contrary, standardization and objectivity have always been motivating goals of the users of the clinical interview, and there are criteria to assess the validity of the methods and the related theory. However, the criteria are somewhat different from psychometric criteria and closer to general scientific criteria of hypothesis testing and theory validation. Accordingly, a brief description of the clinical method is provided (for more extensive discussion see Cowan, 1978; Damon, 1977; Piaget, 1929), followed by discussion of the reasons why tests with mechanical scoring methods are not appropriate replacements of the clinical method and why psychometric criteria are inadequate for evaluation of structural theories.

The interview method

The process of formulating methods of research cannot be dissociated from the topics of investigation or the type of information that one intends to uncover. To be productive, the investigator's methodologies must be related to hypotheses and theoretical propositions. If one begins with a set of propositions requiring exploration but fails to use methods that are adequately adapted to the task or that are insufficiently powerful to tap the proposed phenomena, then the proposed phenomena will, essentially, go uninvestigated and related hypotheses will remain untested. As an obvious example, the proposition that an understanding of cognition is necessary for explanations of the psychology of human functioning is incompatible with radical behavioristic methodology of the sort that would be based on the assumption that cognition is irrelevant to psychological investigation (Watson, 1924).

Summary
of model

Structural-developmental theorists have proposed, as already discussed, that thinking is most adequately explained by describing its organizing principles, that its development is not a continuous accumulation of content, that development involves qualitative changes forming a systematic sequence, and that phases of transition entail conflict and contradiction. The clinical interview is one of the methods originally designed (Piaget, 1927/1960, 1928, 1929) and subsequently refined (e.g., Inhelder & Piaget, 1958, 1964; Piaget, 1952) specifically to provide a means for eliciting data that would inform these structural propositions. In particular, the clinical method is designed to ascertain how an individual thinks about particular issues and not just what he thinks or how correctly he solves problems.

Research findings confirm the need for methodologies that examine process in addition to products. It has been shown that children's solutions on a task or problem or their correct or incorrect answers to questions are not complete indicators of type or level of conceptualization (Karmiloff-Smith & Inhelder, 1975; Kohlberg, 1963; Piaget, 1928; Sugarman, 1979; Turiel, 1969, 1974, 1977). Perhaps the clearest and most striking demonstrations of the inadequacy of solely analyzing products are the repeated observations of U-shaped behavioral growth (Strauss, in press). According to Strauss, the phenomenon of a disappearance of an earlier behavior, which actually reflects an advance in underlying performance, has been found in several areas, including language acquisition, artistic expression, conservation of quantities, and motor skills. Another example comes from the experimental work of Karmiloff-Smith and Inhelder (1975). They observed that younger children (4½- to 5½-year-olds) appeared to be more successful in solving a balancing-blocks problem than were older children (5½- to 7½-year-olds). Analyses of the children's strategies revealed that the younger children were using a trial-and-error procedure that was simpler than the hypothesis-testing procedure of the older children (which led them to the incorrect solution).

As a means of obtaining information relevant to analyses of processes of thought, the clinical method consists of a set of tasks pertaining to a domain (such as number, classification, seriation, or morality) and a closely associated interview, which includes a series of predetermined questions and probes based on specific hypotheses. In some cases, the subject is presented with a task of the sort that has objects and transformations of objects to observe and/or manipulate. The subject is instructed to both solve the task and answer questions that pertain to the ways the task-related objects and transformations are conceptualized and to the mode of reasoning involved in solving the task. In some cases, particularly in research on social cognition, verbally presented problems (e.g., in story form) are solved and the questions pertain to the conceptualization of the elements of the problem and mode of reasoning. Concrete tasks, verbally posed problems, and the associated questions should each be carefully designed to yield information relevant to specific issues addressed by the researcher. In a properly constructed interview the questions are not random or unrelated to proposed hypotheses and the aims of the investigation.

A feature of the clinical method is that the interviewer decides during the course of the interview which probing questions to ask. In an adequately constructed interview with a well-trained interviewer the probes are also systematically determined. One type of probe is straightforward and predetermined in the interview schedule. Alternative sets of probing questions are contingent on the response given by the subject. That is, one type of response could require one set of probes, whereas a different response would require a different set of probes (or perhaps no probes).[3]

Other types of probes are not always predetermined in the interview schedule but represent questions introduced in the course of the interview to obtain adequate responses relative to the objectives of the investigation. Such probes are used for two interrelated reasons. One is that a question on the interview schedule may be misinterpreted by the subject. Probes serve to clarify questions, so that the subject understands the question as it is meant by the researcher and responds accordingly. The other reason for probing questions stems from the assumption that subjects interpret questions and do not merely react to them as stimuli. Remember that central to structural theory is the proposition that the stimulus-response relation is reciprocal: The individual interprets stimuli on the basis of type or level of thinking. Probes are, therefore, deemed necessary in order to determine how the subject is interpreting the task and the questions. Probing questions of a systematic nature are one of the ways to control for the different meanings that can be attributed to the same stimuli.

It should be apparent that the administration of a clinical interview is conducted in accordance with strict guidelines. Therefore, interviewers must be well-trained in several respects. An interviewer must be well-versed in structural theory and in the specific hypotheses and aims of the particular interview administered. Furthermore, the interviewer must be adept at stimulating the subject to deal with the task or problem presented and to respond to questions. Interviews that produce more information from the subject yield richer and more reliable data. Indeed, a well-trained interviewer is one who comprehends the experimental nature of the method. As Piaget maintained (1929, p. 8), "The clinical method is experimental in the sense that the practitioner sets himself a problem,

[margin note: Structuralism like in L.t.]

---

[3] A useful technique in clinical interviews is what Piaget termed "countersuggestions." In a countersuggestion the subject is presented with a judgment differing from the one he has given (in the form of, for example, "another child told me that...."). Countersuggestions test the limits of the certainty with which the judgment is maintained and provide a stimulus for further exploration of reasoning. In some of the studies discussed in Chapters 3, 4, and 5 the idea of countersuggestions was translated and expanded into systematic procedures for obtaining data on specific issues.

makes hypotheses, adapts the conditions to them and finally controls each hypothesis by testing it against the reactions he stimulates in conversation."

Just as the theoretical premises and research aims are related to the methods used in data gathering, so too are they closely related to methods of data interpretation. Because the aim of gathering data through the clinical method is to obtain information about the organization of thought and sequential transformations, it follows that methods for coding responses would include descriptions of such systems and a basis for distinguishing them sequentially. Therefore, procedures for coding responses are aimed at describing, in as detailed and precise a fashion as possible, the relevant elements of thought and their interrelations. A coding procedure attempts to characterize thought through criteria for classifying responses and descriptive categories that can be used by trained coders. The coding procedures are part of the theoretical framework in that the categories are descriptions of organizations of thinking. Coders, too, must be well trained so as to understand the theoretical framework and the technical details of the categories; to be able to interpret the bases for discriminating between responses that are and are not germane to the domain of the investigation;[4] and to be able to objectively interpret responses and apply the coding system.

The clinical method and psychometric measures compared

We can now return to the standardization and objectivity of the clinical method as compared with psychometric modes of assessment. Because the clinical interview allows for probing questions, whose use is dependent on the subject's responses and which may vary somewhat from one subject to another, it has been claimed that it lacks standardization (e.g., Enright, Franklin, & Manheim, 1980; Kurtines & Greif, 1974). Because the scoring procedures are not mechanical and require an understanding of the coding system as well as judgment in its application, it has been claimed that they are not objective (Kurtines & Greif, 1974). In turn, it is claimed that psychometric measures are more precise because of their standardization (i.e., the same questions are administered in exactly the same way to all subjects) and objectivity of scoring (i.e., scoring is mechanical, requiring no interpretation on the part of the scorer).

To evaluate these claims it would be useful first to consider a concrete example of a psychometric measure. Psychometric measures of intelligence provide a good example, because the clinical method was originated by Piaget (1928, 1929) as a way of ameliorating, given his theoretical orientation, what he re-

---

[4] In clinical interviews a subject may provide responses that do not correspond to any of the coding categories. Responses that cannot be scored are only a problem if the coding procedures do not have clear criteria for distinguishing responses relevant to the domain of judgment from those that are not. Coding procedures with such criteria obviate the necessity for coding all responses, when some of them are not germane to the topic under investigation.

garded as their methodological shortcomings. Typically, psychometric measures of intelligence contain a series of items (problems, tasks, and questions) designed so that the responses can be recorded as correct or incorrect. A tally of the number of correct responses produces a score that constitutes the basis for comparison with standardized norms. The tests are calibrated to age norms in that items vary according to their difficulty. However, test items are not calibrated to type of intelligence or knowledge. Intelligence tests, such as the Stanford-Binet (Terman & Merrill, 1937), contain items pertaining to a variety of areas, including number, logical inferences, classifications, vocabulary, information (e.g., naming the days of the week), and motor skills. All items are scored on a pass–fail dimension and are weighted equally.

The intelligence-testing tradition, too, illustrates that methods of study are closely related to a set of theoretical propositions. In this tradition intelligence is defined as a trait or capacity possessed by individuals. Therefore, intelligence is defined quantitatively; it is an amount of the trait or capacity possessed by an individual, relative to others in comparable groups (for some theorists the amount can shift with experience, but for others it is primarily fixed by inherited factors). Insofar as additional theoretical issues regarding intelligence are considered, it is through proposed relations of the capacity to other variables (what Cronbach & Meehl, 1955, have termed the "nomological network"). In itself, intelligence is operationalized as the capacity measured by intelligence tests.

The contrasting structural position is that "intelligence" is a topic of direct investigation in the formulation of theories of thought and knowledge. The study of intelligence is the study of cognitive development. In the study of cognitive development, the sorts of logical, mathematical, and physical tasks found in intelligence tests would be presented to children through the clinical method in order to investigate their forms of reasoning. This entails obtaining more than solutions to the problems, as is well illustrated by Piaget's (1928) adaptation, in his early work, of items from the Binet-Simon (1916) tests of intelligence. For instance, the Binet-Simon test included a set of "absurd sentence" items of the following sort (as cited in Piaget, 1928, p. 63):

(a) A poor cyclist had his head smashed and died on the spot; he was taken to hospital and it is feared that he will not recover.
(b) I have three brothers: Paul, Ernest and myself.
(c) Someone said: If ever I kill myself from despair I won't choose a Friday, because Friday is a bad day and would bring me ill luck.

In the Binet-Simon version, the subject's statement of what is absurd or wrong with each sentence is scored as correct or incorrect. Piaget used these same items to study elements of thought by examining how children understand the logical contradictions and reciprocal relations (e.g., in the brothers example) in the sentences. By explaining how children reason about these items, Piaget focused on cognitive activities like reciprocal relations, on the use of premises, deductions, hypothetical propositions, and on discriminations between empirical and logical necessity. This is just one example representing the early work on development from concrete forms of inference to formal thought. This example illustrates the difference between the purposes of the clinical and psychometric methods. Psychometric methods are designed to obtain test scores reflective of a quantitative assessment of a capacity or trait, whereas clinical methods are aimed at gathering data for analyses of qualitative and developing characteristics of thought processes.

The example also highlights that the two approaches lead to differing strategies regarding standardization of assessment and objectivity of scoring. Moreover, the methods of each approach are judged as lacking in standardization and objectivity, if they are viewed through the lens of the opposing theoretical perspective. Therefore, the perceived degree of standardization is not a purely methodological issue but is related to theoretical perspectives.

In the psychometric approach standardization is achieved by eliminating or drastically reducing the role of the tester. The uniformity of the assessment instrument is considered free of bias as long as the items are presented in exactly the same way to all subjects on a sheet of paper (to a subject who reads them) or in the tester's words (to a subject who hears them). The elicited response is simply recorded by the subject (if in written form) or by the tester (if in oral form). Insofar as a tester deviates from the questions to elicit other responses (e.g., through probes), it is assumed that bias is brought into the study (Enright et al., 1980; Kurtines & Greif, 1974). This realist conception of standardization follows from (1) the assumption that the subject's response to stimuli is unilateral and not interpretative, and (2) an attempt to assess a quantitative dimension of a phenomenon (e.g., intelligence) that is presumably tapped at the level of content.

The realist conception of standardization, however, does not follow from the structural-developmental theoretical propositions. Therefore, it does not follow that users of the clinical method should accommodate to the psychometric conception of standardization. At the simplest level the argument can be put as follows: If one proposes that a stimulus is interpreted by the subject and that the interpretations may vary among subjects in systematic ways, then the methods used, if they are to be adequate to the task, will account for the subject's interpretations of the stimulus and not solely for the subject's noninterpretative reaction to it. This is a simple, logical point! Accordingly, it is not reasonable to claim that the method is inadequate because it allows for the subject's interpretation of the stimulus or that it should be replaced by a method that solely records and tallies responses to stimuli.

It is certainly reasonable, however, to argue that the theoretical premises that lead to the clinical method are inadequate. However, on the assumption that structural theory may be correct, it is apparent that psychometric measures are not the only means of attaining adequate levels of standardization and objectivity. In fact, from the structural perspective psychometric measures are sources of inaccuracy and are lacking in controls in that they fail to account for the subject's interpretations, for differences between the content of responses and underlying structure, for varying means of arriving at correct responses and making errors, and for different types of knowledge. Moreover, subjects are susceptible to momentary influences because their responses are left unmonitored.

As can be seen, both standardization and objectivity are goals of the clinical method – as they should be. In the clinical method, however, standardization is sought through specification of the parameters of the stimuli (task, question) and the subject's interpretations of stimuli. It is presumed that the goal of standardization is furthered by extensive questioning and probing in a given interview. The adequacy of standardization can be assessed in two ways. One is through measures of test–retest consistency over short periods of time. It has been demonstrated that the clinical method can have high test–retest reliability (Damon, 1980; Colby et al., in press; Selman, 1980). The second way of assessing standardization is through the replicability of findings. If a measure yields similar results in studies by different researchers, it can be concluded that the measure is stable. Studies on social cognitive development based on the clinical method have shown high replicability (e.g., Damon, 1977; Kohlberg, 1976; Selman, 1980; and the studies reported in this volume). The replicability of research on nonsocial cognitive development by Piaget and others has, as put by Cowan (1978, p. 64), "yielded some of the most replicable results in the field."

Correspondingly, objectivity of scoring procedures is a goal of the clinical method. However, objectivity is not regarded as synonymous with mechanical methods of scoring. If it is proposed that thinking forms organized systems, then it follows that its adequate characterization would require nonmechanical, complex, and interpretative forms of coding. It is for this reason that coding procedures need to consist of precisely defined systems of classification and categories of judgment. In this context, it is neither plausible nor desirable to eliminate scorer judgment. A scoring procedure is sufficiently objective if it can be used with consistency by independent (but trained) coders. There is no question that coding procedures developed through the clinical method can be objective, as evidenced by the high interrater reliabilities reported by several researchers (e.g., Broughton, 1978a; Damon, 1980; Kohlberg, 1969; Selman, 1980; Turiel, 1966; and as described in Chapter 6 of this volume).

Evaluation of structural theory by psychometric criteria

Misunderstandings of the aims and procedures of the clinical method, therefore, have resulted in misconceptions about standardization and objectivity. These misconceptions have been further compounded by translation of some general propositions of structural theory into psychometric criteria, with resulting misconceptions of both the theoretical propositions and the research findings. In addition to test standardization and mechanical scoring requirements, psychometric criteria include *predictive* validity and *construct* validity (Cronbach & Meehl, 1955). These criteria, as used psychometrically, are specific to the validation of tests. As stated by Campbell (1960, p. 546), "Test validity and test reliability are not concepts belonging to the philosophy of science. Instead they are concepts which have developed in the course of mutual criticisms of test constructors and test users, concepts which relate to the implicit and explicit claims of test constructors and test salesmen."

Psychometric criteria were designed to provide ways of assessing the scientific status of tests and related theoretical propositions. The importance of evaluating any empirically based theoretical framework and the necessity of testing hypotheses is, of course, consensually accepted. However, the special terms of psychometric criteria, like predictive and construct validity, are specifically germane to the evaluation of psychological tests. Most important, the overriding feature of the rules of psychometric validation distinguishes it from the usual norms of evidence for assessing the adequacy of a theoretical framework: With psychometric criteria, the test stands at the core, as a source of quantitative assessment, constituting the standard to which a set of propositions (the nomological network) relate. The test scores do not represent descriptive or explanatory propositions. In structural theory, by contrast, descriptions of stages or levels of development are in themselves theoretical propositions designed to explain phenomena, such as logical inferences or moral judgments. The descriptions of the organization or types of thinking constitutes one element of a theory that may be related to other elements through additional theoretical explanations. As examples, theoretical formulations may explain relations between types of thinking and behavioral decisions, or the ways in which individuals pass through a developmental sequence. In such a case, a comprehensive theory would include explanations of thought processes, of behavioral decisions, of movement in a sequence, as well as the interrelations among these elements.

It is important, therefore, to distinguish between test validation, on the one hand, and the use of empirical evidence, on the other. Nevertheless, psychometric criteria have been applied to structural theories by those who characterize a clinical method and related structural descriptions simply as a psychological test. One of the most extensive and perhaps most influential efforts at applying these psychometric criteria to structural-developmental research was made by Kurtines and Greif (1974) in their purported evaluation of Kohlberg's (1963, 1969) theory and research on moral judgments.[5] The many misconceptions and confusions in the Kurtines and Greif evaluation have been carefully and insightfully discussed elsewhere (Broughton, 1975, 1978b). For the present purposes, their analyses provide concrete examples of how the notions of predictive and construct validity are misapplied to structural theory.

The notion of predictive validity reflects a behavioristic bias in that one of the requirements of a test is that it be predictive of behavior. This is because psychological tests are usually designed to provide consumers with a means to predict performance. Many intelligence tests are designed for use in educational settings to predict academic performance. Personnel-selection tests are designed to make predictions about occupational success. This model was adopted by Kurtines and Greif in their assertion that the validity of Kohlberg's methods of assessing moral judgments depended, in part, on the extent to which they were predictive of moral behavior. Moreover, a rather stringent test of predictability was imposed. A one-to-one correspondence between stages of moral judgment and behavior was expected, so as to demonstrate the discriminative validity of the measure.

However, like other structural analyses of social cognition, Kohlberg's methods were designed not to predict behavior but to describe judgments. The judgment–action issue is one that requires explanation. The explanation of relations between thought and action, and especially their developmental relations, is a problem that can be approached through a range of hypotheses. At one pole, it would be possible to hypothesize that moral judgment and moral behavior are largely unrelated. For instance, it may be proposed that moral judgments serve real and significant functions separate from those served by behavioral systems. Whatever the proposed reasons for the discontinuity, if the hypothesis were correct, then valid descriptions of judgment would not be predictive of behavior.

Determining the relations of thought and action is a complex and difficult problem in psychological theory that is not reducible to prediction or correlation. Chapter 9 considers social behaviors and their relations to domains of social judgments. It is proposed that moral judgment is only one component in the process of coordinating different domains of judgment in behavioral decisions. In such a case, the absence of a strong empirical association between moral judgment and behavior would not indicate a lack of validity of the assessment of moral judgment.

---

[5] Kurtines and Greif mistakenly assumed that Kohlberg's method was a projective test. The differences between projective methods and the clinical interview are unambiguous. Projective tests are highly unstructured stimuli; responses to them are presumed to reflect personality characteristics and unconscious dynamics largely inaccessible through direct methods. The clinical interview is structured, task-oriented, and presents the subject with concrete problems to solve.

Similarly, the criterion of construct validity fails to account for explanations of the relations among different variables in a theoretical framework. Construct validation is meant for test scores that are not descriptive of an underlying construct (Cronbach & Meehl, 1955, p. 282) but that are used in relation to scores on other measures. Therefore, construct validation is also a predictive notion. It is used to assess the adequacy of test scores in predicting other variables or other test scores.

To evaluate the construct validity of a structural assessment it is necessary to transform it into a test score that supposedly predicts other variables. In an arbitrary fashion, Kurtines and Greif established, as one test of the construct validity of the assessment procedures, the proposition that the moral judgment stages described by Kohlberg form a unidirectional and invariant sequence. In other words, the validity of the hypothesis that children progress through the stages step-by-step in the prescribed sequence and without regressions was one of the ways of determining if the descriptions of moral judgments were valid. Again, the relations among different components of a theory were misinterpreted as predictive variables. Alternative hypotheses can and have been proposed regarding the assessment of types of thought and processes of change. It may be proposed (Werner & Kaplan, 1963), for instance, that regressive changes are necessary for progressive changes within a sequence. Still other developmental hypotheses are plausible within the context of a particular assessment and description of forms of thinking (cf. Flavell, 1982).

The theoretical task is to explain the structures of knowledge and the processes of development. Components of a theoretical framework are not static constructs that validate or invalidate a central testing instrument. Rather, they are explanations of phenomena and of the interrelations among variables. The differences between test validation and assessments of the validity of psychological theory were recognized by Campbell (1960) in his rebuttal to Bechtoldt's (1959) critique of the topic of construct validity. Campbell's counterargument was simply that Bechtoldt's critique was directed at philosophy-of-science issues and that the scope of construct validation is delimited within the narrow confines of test validation (1960, p. 546):

While not denying the presence of a serious philosophical disagreement nor its relevance to psychology, this paper will emphasize the common ground implicit in psychology's tradition of test validation efforts. The philosophical disagreement will remain, but it need not produce a lack of consensus about desirable evidence of test validity. Bechtoldt's argument is indeed more against the role of construct validity in discussions of philosophy of science and psychological theory, rather than an objection to specific statements of desirable evidence of test validity contained under that rubric.

3   Social experience and social knowledge

Two propositions regarding the child's interactions with the environment were presented in the previous chapter: that interactions are reciprocal and that qualitatively different types of events experienced by the child produce distinct domains of thought. Responses are not unilaterally determined by stimuli and, therefore, knowledge does not stem directly from experiences. The child gains knowledge by acting upon and abstracting from events. In addition to experiencing events, individuals select, interpret, and systematize elements of their experiences. However, social experiences are systematically related to the development of social concepts. Just as social concepts are not all of one kind, social experiences too are not all of one kind. There exist different forms of social experiences associated to development within domains of social knowledge. The research discussed in this chapter examines elements of social interaction as they relate to the formation of moral and social conventional concepts.

Before considering these studies, it is necessary to provide working definitions of the domains under investigation and the criteria that delineate their boundaries. One of the definitional problems in the social domains is that similar terminology is often used to mean different things. In everyday discourse, the same label, including the labeling of events as moral or conventional, may be applied in different ways and with different implications. Terms that are associated with moral discourse, such as "good," "should," and "ought," are also frequently used in nonmoral senses. In a philosophical essay on morality, Harman (1977) provided an informative example of how the term "should" can be used in moral and nonmoral ways. A moral use of the term might be, "The thief should not steal." Moral reasons would then be given to support this prescription. It could also be stated, without endorsing the action of stealing, that "in carrying out the robbery, the thief should wear gloves." In the latter case, means–ends reasons of efficiency would be given for why the thief should wear gloves.

Consider other examples of uses of the term "should" that can pertain to either morality or social convention. The following statement could represent a moral use of the term:

33

He should not kill innocent children!

In its moral sense, the statement is *not* contingent on group membership or societal standards. We would not say that if he wants to be part of the group, he should not kill innocent children; nor that it would be permissible for him to kill innocent children if he did not wish to be part of the group. By contrast, the following uses of the term are contingent on group membership or societal standards:

> If he wants to be a member of our group, he should wear a yellow jacket.
> If he wants to play baseball with us, he should play as hard as he can.

In these statements the term "should" is used in a nonmoral sense. The behavioral requirement is directly related to group membership or participation in attainment of the goals of the activity. It would be acceptable for him to wear a brown jacket if he did not wish to be part of the group. There is no requirement that one be part of the group or engage in the activity of playing baseball.

Morality and social convention

Definitions of morality and social convention consistent with the two examples of the use of the term "should" have been presented previously (Nucci & Turiel, 1978; Turiel, 1979, in press). In reviewing those definitions, they will be expanded somewhat in relating them to corresponding philosophical conceptions. Indeed, the definitions were highly influenced by some detailed and extensive philosophical treatments of morality. In addition, a number of issues or problems raised by the separation of social categories will be discussed.

In previous work, convention and morality have been defined as follows:[1]

Social conventions are...behavioral uniformities which coordinate interactions of individuals within social systems. Individual members of the society have shared knowledge about conventions....Consequently, conventions (e.g., modes of greeting, forms of address) provide people with means of knowing what to expect of each other and thereby serving to coordinate interactions between people....Conventions involve coordinations at the level of social organization; they are uniformities that coordinate the stable interactions of individuals functioning within a social system and the ends are social organizational.

Social-conventional acts are symbolic of elements of social organization. As such, the acts, in themselves, are arbitrary and alternative courses of action can serve similar functions. That is, by virtue of their shared knowledge, a given conventional uniformity in one social system may serve the same symbolic function as a different uniformity in another social system....Conventions are validated by consensus and, therefore, are

---

[1] The terminology does not necessarily correspond to general, nonsocial scientific usage of the labels "convention" and "morality." Clear or systematic patterns of general use of the labels would be difficult to discern. As labels, the terms are often used interchangeably or even inconsistently; sometimes they correspond to the definitions provided here and sometimes they are inconsistent with them. The terms and their definitions are being used here with regard to forms of social reasoning that do correspond to the definitions.

relative to the societal context. In addition to the variability of conventions from one social system to another, they may be altered by consensus or general usage within a social system.

The individual's concepts of social convention are, therefore, closely related to his or her concepts of social organization. In contrast with convention, moral prescriptions are not perceived to be alterable by consensus. This is not to say that morality is fixed and unalterable. We know, for instance, that historical changes have occurred with regard to such matters as slavery. However, the bases for those changes are not perceived as shifts in the general consensus or in social organization, but on the intrinsic merits, from the moral point of view, of one type of action over another. Again, in contrast with convention, in the moral domain actions are not arbitrary, and though moral prescriptions form part of social organization, they are not defined by social organization nor is their rationale based on their status as implicit or explicit regulations. The individual's moral prescriptions (e.g., regarding killing and the value of life) are determined by factors inherent to social relationships, as opposed to a particular form of social organization. An individual's perception of an act such as the taking of a life as a transgression is not contingent on the presence of a rule, but rather stems from factors intrinsic to the event (e.g., from the perception of the consequences to the victim). This means that moral issues are not perceived as relative to the societal context. The moral theories formed by individuals are based on concepts regarding the welfare of persons, the rights of persons, and justice, in the sense of comparative treatment of individuals and means of distribution. [Turiel, in press, pp. 38–40]

A concern with the differences between moral judgments and conventionality is evident in many philosophical treatises. It goes back, at least, to Aristotle's distinction between natural justice and conventional justice:

There are two forms of justice, the natural and the conventional. It is natural when it has the same validity everywhere and is unaffected by any view we may take of the justice of it. It is conventional when there is no original reason why it should take one form rather than another and the rule it imposes is reached by agreement after which it holds good. . . . Some philosophers are of opinion that justice is conventional in all its branches, arguing that a law of nature admits no variation and operates in exactly the same way everywhere – thus fire *burns* here and in Persia – while rules of justice keep changing before our eyes. It is not obvious what rules of justice are natural and what are legal and conventional, in cases where variation is possible. Yet it remains true that there is such a thing as natural, as well as conventional justice. [Aristotle, *Nicomachean Ethics*, as cited in Winch, 1972]

Without relying on the idea of *natural* justice, in more recent (e.g., J. S. Mill, 1863/1963) and contemporary times (e.g., Dworkin, 1978; Gewirth, 1978; Rawls, 1971), other philosophers have made distinctions between moral imperatives and the standards, conventions, or practices of social organizations and institutions. This position is exemplified by the philosopher Alan Gewirth in his recent work on *Reason and Morality* (1978, p. 24): "Judgments of moral obligation are categorical in that what persons morally ought to do sets requirements for them that they cannot rightly evade by consulting their own self-interested desires or variable opinions, ideals or institutional practices."

Gewirth's propositions are useful not only as a statement of the inadequacy of substituting institutional practices for moral obligation. More important, he has provided a basis for deriving criteria applicable to research on moral judgments. Consider a fuller set of propositions regarding the nature of morality (Gewirth, 1978, p. 1):

A morality is a set of categorically obligatory requirements for action that are addressed at least in part to every actual or prospective agent, and that are concerned with furthering the interests, especially the most important interests, of persons or recipients other than or in addition to the agent or the speaker. The requirements are categorically obligatory in that compliance with them is mandatory for the conduct of every person to whom they are addressed regardless of whether he wants to accept them or their results, and regardless also of the requirements of any other institutions such as law or etiquette, whose obligatoriness may itself be doubtful or variable. Thus, although one moral requirement may be overridden by another, it may not be overridden by any nonmoral requirement, nor can its normative bindingness be escaped by shifting one's inclinations, opinions or ideals.

A set of criteria for the moral domain may be inferred from Gewirth's orientation (as well as that of some others). Moral prescriptions are *obligatory*. They are *universally applicable* in that they apply to everyone in similar circumstances. They are *impersonal* in that they are not based on individual preferences or personal inclinations. Furthermore, moral prescriptions are determined by criteria other than agreement, consensus, or institutional convention. Agreement regarding moral obligations often exists among a group of people. However, the existing agreement does not constitute the grounds or justification for what is considered morally right or wrong (see also Dworkin, 1978). For example, it would not be said that killing innocent children is wrong just because everyone agrees that it is wrong.

Moreover, the nonexistence of agreement over an issue and its nonpractice does not mean that it does not involve moral obligations. Dworkin provides the illustrative example of a vegetarian who might argue that killing animals is morally wrong. The vegetarian's claim, according to Dworkin, is that in spite of a lack of consensus and irrespective of its widespread practice, it is wrong to kill animals for food: "He wants to say, not simply that it is desirable that society rearrange its institutions so that no man ever has the right to take life, but that in fact, as things stand, no one ever does have that right. Indeed, he will want to urge the existence of a moral duty to respect life as a reason why society should have a social rule to that effect" (Dworkin, 1978, p. 53). Dworkin's example can be adapted to the historically relevant issue of slavery. Suppose that during the early 1800s, one had asserted that slavery was wrong – meaning that even though widely practiced, slavery was wrong from a moral point of view and, therefore, it would be desirable that everyone regard it as wrong. The intent of the statement would not have been that only a change in the consensus would be necessary to transform slavery into a morally wrong practice. Likewise, today one would not say that slavery was morally right in the 1800s but morally wrong now simply because of a change in the consensus.

In contrast with morality, general agreement is one of the criteria for convention. Conventions are determined by the social system, and institutionalized practice does constitute one of the grounds for adherence to conventions. Hence, conventions produce uniformities in the behavior of members of ongoing social systems. However, the definition of convention does not rest upon observations of behavioral uniformities or what appears to be performed in specified ways by large numbers of people. It is not sufficient, as a way of describing convention, to say that it reflects what is generally practiced or even what is customary in one's society. Many actions that upon observation appear uniform, habitual, or customary do not necessarily owe their existence to group consensus. Consider as an example the use of a tool like the screwdriver. Observation of the way people tighten screws would, no doubt, reveal widespread uniformity in its application to this task. In this sense, the mode of using screwdrivers is customary and may be the way people have always done it. Nevertheless, uniformity in the use of a screwdriver would not be considered an example of a social convention. The uniform use of screwdrivers is not determined by consensus but by the utility of a particular method of putting a screw in place. The method is the most effective means to the end of tightening screws. It could be argued that some people do, in fact, use screwdrivers in a particular way because it is the way everyone else does it. Although this may account for one's first use of the tool, it is likely that after some experience the utility of the practice will be understood.

Uniformities in actions like the use of tools arise from the knowledge of efficient means to achieve physical ends. Behavioral uniformities reflective of social conventions originate in social procedures that are related to social ends. One of those social ends is the coordination of interactions among individuals participating in a social system. The coordination of interactions, however, is not strictly synonymous with convention. There are ways that interactions are coordinated for physical ends that do not necessarily involve conventions. Again, the screwdriver example illustrates the point: Two people might work together to tighten a screw (if it cannot be accomplished by one person) and will coordinate their activities in order to accomplish the goal. Conventions, in serving to coordinate the social aspects of interactions, are part of the structure of social organizations. The individual's knowledge of social conventions is organized through his understanding of the social system.

In linking social conventions to social organization, it is being proposed that they are part of the definition of social systems. Therefore, social conventions can be regarded as forming what Searle (1969) has referred to as a *constitutive* system. Constitutive systems are characterized as follows (Searle, 1969, pp. 33–34):

Constitutive rules do not merely regulate, they create or define new forms of behavior. The rules of football or chess, for example, do not merely regulate playing football or chess, but as it were they create the very possibility of playing such games. The activities of playing football or chess are constituted by acting in accordance with (at least a large subset of) the appropriate rules. Regulative rules regulate a preexisting activity, an activity whose existence is logically independent of the rules. Constitutive rules constitute (and also regulate) an activity the existence of which is logically dependent on the rules.

It should be emphasized that it is the notion of a constitutive system, and not that of rules, that is useful for understanding social convention. Conventions are not strictly rules, but they are constituted within social units to define a class of social interactions. Searle's terminology differs from the way the term "rule" is used in this volume. Searle used the term in a broad sense, with reference to elements of systems (e.g., linguistic systems). The term is used here in its more restricted sense of rules (or regulations) that are explicit statements about behavior effected by the appropriate agent in a social unit. Rules of this sort can apply to constitutive and nonconstitutive systems, as will be discussed in the following chapters. In fact, Searle did recognize the ambiguity of his use of the term:

Constitutive rules are likely to strike us as extremely curious and hardly even as rules at all. Notice that they are almost tautological in character, for what the 'rule' seems to offer is part of a definition of "checkmate" or "touchdown". That, for example, a checkmate in chess is achieved in such a way can appear now as a rule, now as an analytic truth based on the meaning of "checkmate in chess". That such statements can be construed as analytic is a clue to the fact that the rule in question is a constitutive one. [Searle, 1969, p. 34]

Games and their rules represent one kind of constitutive system. Game rules are defined mainly within a circumscribed context, and usually with the clearly stated goal of winning a competition. Conventions are part of a broader system of social organization with varied and abstract goals. Nevertheless, there are aspects of the organization of social systems that are designed to specify behaviors that contribute to the definition of the social system. The reasons for those behaviors are in the makeup of the social system and not in other considerations. It is in this sense that conventional acts are arbitrary. They become nonarbitrary once they have the status of a conventional expectation in that they coordinate interactions and form part of the definition of the constituted system. Outside of the context of the constituted system, the acts are arbitrary in that there is no compelling reason for behaving one way or the other. The meanings and functions of conventions, then, are contextual; they are closely related to the social system in which they occur. From the viewpoint of a constitutive system, conventions are relative to the context in which they exist. In a differently constituted system, a particular convention (or set of conventions) may not exist or may exist in another form. Even within a social context, conventions are regarded as changeable insofar as the system is redefined in certain ways, with resulting changes in the nature of the constitutive system.

It was stated earlier that moral prescriptions are not determined by consensus or defined by social organization. Thus, the notion of a constitutive system of social organization is not applicable to the moral domain. Moral prescriptions are not arbitrary acts that become definitional of types of social interactions. Moral prescriptions, which are based on concepts of justice, welfare, and rights, are analytically independent of systems of social organization that coordinate interactions. This is not to say that moral considerations do not apply to social organizations. It is to say rather that moral prescriptions are based on grounds other than the makeup of the social system. In this sense, morality is not determined by a constitutive system that defines the behavior, as suggested by Gewirth and Dworkin in their separation of morality from institutional practices.

The conceptual separation of morality and social organization requires some clarification, lest it appear that what is being claimed is the exemption of systems of social organization from moral considerations. Stating that morality is based on concepts separable from the makeup of specific social contexts does not imply that morality does not apply to social organization. It is assumed that aspects of the way a social system is organized may be, and normally are, guided by moral prescriptions. Indeed, the philosophical perspectives cited earlier (i.e., those of Gewirth, Dworkin, and Rawls) are, at least in part, directed to justice and rights in social institutions (as discussed in Chapter 5, Dworkin's concern was with moral principles in the formation and interpretations of laws, as well as their part in judicial decisions).

An interesting example of the application of independently formulated moral principles to the structure of social institutions can be seen in the work of Rawls (1971). His *Theory of Justice* was meant to apply to institutions and to societies, as he explicitly stated early in the volume (p. 7): "The primary subject of justice is the basic structure of society...." However, as in the positions taken by Gewirth and Dworkin, Rawls's conception of justice is neither defined nor determined by social organization, in its constitutive sense. A priority is given to principles of justice, which serve as a guide for how society is regulated (rather than the converse).[2] The following statements indicate that, for Rawls, moral obligations cannot be evaded by resorting to institutional practices and that the question of justice is distinct from the claims of coordination and efficiency:

Laws and institutions no matter how efficient and well-organized must be reformed or abolished if they are unjust. Each person possesses an inviolability founded on justice that even the welfare of society as a whole cannot override. [p. 3]

Some measure of agreement in conceptions of justice is, however, not the only prerequisite for a viable human community. There are other fundamental social problems, in particular those of coordination, efficiency, and stability. [p. 6]

[2] Rawls's concepts of the original position and veil of ignorance are indicative of the separation of justice and existing societal arrangements in his formulation. Briefly put, Rawls proposed the procedural notion that in choosing moral principles for a social contract or society, individuals would assume an original position in which they are ignorant of their personal qualities, tastes, talents, power, or status in the social system.

The linkage of justice and social organization is one of application – the application of independent principles to the actual arrangements of society. It may be argued, however, that despite philosophical definition, there is a closer link in the minds of the members of society in that they regard adherence to institutional practices or societal rules as morally obligatory. In other words, people may not separate adherence to the existing social system from the issues of fairness or justice. To some extent, this is an empirical issue that is addressed by several studies discussed in this and the following chapter. It is an issue that pertains to how morality and social organization are conceptualized during the course of individual human development. The research indicates that, across ages, adherence to institutional rules, authoritative directives, and existing societal expectations is generally recognized as involving different considerations from those implied by a concern for justice, harm, and rights. This research is discussed after a consideration of the experiential sources of development and some hypotheses regarding the relations of actions and events to domains of social reasoning.

Social interactions

Investigation of the relation of experience to development has been based on the structural proposition that development is a function of individual–environment interactions. Most theories of development have been concerned, in one way or another, with the influence of experience on development. It is often assumed that social experiences, usually in the form of the actions of socializing agents, are the causal antecedents of the child's acquisition of social judgment and behavior (these approaches are dealt with in Chapter 8). Because the structural hypothesis states that the child is in reciprocal interaction with the environment, it is assumed that the study of experiential sources of development requires analyses of both the nature of social events and the ways events are interpreted.

From the perspective of an equilibration model, research into experiential sources entails the difficulty of translating what is a long-term process of individual–environment reciprocal interaction into an empirical analysis of appropriately narrow scope and adequate precision. A series of observational studies of children's social interactions has provided a beginning for the exploration of this complicated issue. The first task was to delineate systematically the characteristics of social events. If the process of interaction is a reciprocal relationship, rather than a unilateral imposition of the environment on the child, then it is to be expected that the nature of a social event will have a bearing on how it is interpreted by the child and how it influences conceptual development. The definitional criteria for morality and social convention provide a basis for characterizing naturally occurring social events. The starting point for this analysis is the proposed features of the intrinsic consequences of moral transgressions and the arbitrariness of social-conventional acts. The following two illustrative events (taken from Turiel, in press), each involving prescriptions and prohibitions, can serve as examples of the significant distinguishing features between moral and conventional acts.

Event A
A number of nursery school children are playing outdoors. There are some swings in the yard, all of which are being used. One of the children decides that he now wants to use a swing. Seeing that they are all occupied, he goes to one of the swings, where he pushes the other child off, at the same time hitting him. The child who has been pushed is hurt and begins to cry.

Event B
Children are greeting a teacher who has just come into the nursery school. A number of children go up to her and say "Good Morning, Mrs. Jones." One of the children says "Good Morning, Mary."

Each of these events is social in nature and may occur in a young child's life. Within a nursery school setting, for example, each event may even constitute a breach of explicit regulations or norms. Furthermore, both children and adults might spontaneously respond to transgressions (e.g., "you should not hit him," "you should not call the teacher by her first name"), but adults will be more likely to transmit explicit instructions or directions regarding how a child should behave in these situations. The transmission of such instructions, however, does not completely account for the way social events are interpreted, or their influence is felt, by the child. It is necessary to go beyond a level of analysis that considers only the presumed accommodations to instructions, directions, and regulations transmitted to the child by others (e.g., parents, teachers) or by the system (society, culture). The child's interpretations of the total event and, most important, those features of the interactions that occur between people must be considered, so that the event itself is not excluded from the purview of the child's interactions.

Although both of these events are social, there are important differences that can be clarified with reference, again, to the notion of a constitutive system. In Searle's formulation, constitutive systems are associated with what he referred to as "institutional facts," which are contrasted with "brute facts." Brute facts refer to events, especially physical events, that do not require knowledge of the institutional context. Events that are part of a constitutive system are referred to as institutional facts because they are understood only "against the background of certain kinds of institutions." Events occurring during a marriage ceremony, for example, are institutional facts, whose meaning is associated with the constitutive system of the marriage ceremony.

The distinction between brute and institutional facts, however, requires a further distinction in order to account for the differences between moral and conventional events. Conventional events (such as Event B) are akin to institutional facts because their meaning comes from their place in a system of social organization. Neither the notion of a brute fact nor that of an institutional fact quite captures the characteristics of events (such as Event A) in the moral domain. At least three categories are needed: (1) events with direct and sensed consequences (akin to brute facts), (2) events with intrinsic consequences leading to inferences, and (3) arbitrary acts that are part of an institutional context (akin to institutional facts).

The need for these three categories can be further illustrated by examining one of Durkheim's (1924/1974) propositions regarding what he referred to as "moral facts." Durkheim made a distinction that corresponds to the brute–institutional fact distinction (pp. 40-43):

The first question that confronts us, as in all rational and scientific research, is: By what characteristics can we recognize and distinguish moral facts?. . .

To achieve any result at all in this research there is only one method of proceeding. We must discover the intrinsic differences between these moral rules and other rules through their apparent and exterior differences, for at the beginning this is all that is accessible to us. We must find a reagent that will force moral rules to demonstrate their specific character. The reagent we shall employ is this: We shall put these various rules to the test of violation and see whether from this point of view there is not some difference between moral rules and rules of technique.

The violation of a rule generally brings unpleasant consequences to the agent. But we may distinguish two different types of consequence: (i) The first results mechanically from the violation. If I violate a rule of hygiene that orders me to stay away from infection, the result of this act will automatically be disease. The act, once it has been performed, sets in motion the consequences, and by analysis of the act we can know in advance what the result will be. (ii) When, however, I violate the rule that forbids me to kill, an analysis of my act will tell me nothing. I shall not find inherent in it the subsequent blame or punishment. There is complete heterogeneity between the act and its consequence. It is impossible to discover *analytically* in the act of murder the slightest notion of blame. The link between act and consequence is here a *synthetic* one.

Such consequences attached to acts by synthetic links I shall call *sanctions*. I do not as yet know the origin or explanation of this link. I merely note its existence and nature, without at the moment going any further.

We can, however, enlarge upon this notion. Since sanctions are not revealed by analysis of the act that they govern, it is apparent that I am not punished *simply because* I did this or that. It is not the intrinsic nature of my action that produces the sanction which follows, but the fact that the act violates the rule that forbids it. In fact, one and the same act, identically performed with the same material consequences, is blamed or not blamed according to whether or not there is a rule forbidding it. The existence of the rule and the relation to it of the act determine the sanction.

For Durkheim, the act of killing has consequences only if it is connected to an institutional system of rules and sanctions (moral facts are institutional facts). Therefore, the intrinsic features of an act are defined narrowly to include only direct perception of consequences upon violation (consequences to the self resulting directly and mechanically from a violation). Durkheim's scheme, however, does not take into account the relatively simple inferences that can be made about an act like killing. If the individual's inferential capacities are included, then the act of killing is neither arbitrary nor dependent on an institutional or constitutive system. It is an event with intrinsic features, whose observation is likely to lead to inferences – to the construction of moral judgments.

The perception of acts with intrinsic consequences is not, in itself, the moral judgment. Moral judgments do not spring automatically or mechanically from the experience; but the construction of moral judgments is based on such experiences. Moral judgments pertain to social events and involve inferences about social relations (in contrast with the prudential considerations stemming from the violation of a rule of hygiene). A different type of social inference results from social interactions that involve arbitrary acts and institutional contexts. From the child's cognitive perspective, Events A and B, despite some similarities, differ from each other in significant ways. First consider Event A as an example of a moral transgression. For the child to regard the act in Event A as wrong or as a transgression, it is not necessary to be told by others that it is wrong, or that he or she model others, or to perceive the act as a rule violation. Rather, the child can generate prescriptions through abstractions from the experience itself (either as an observer or participant). Important elements in the perception of such an event would be the pain experienced by the victim and the reason for the offender's act. By coordinating these different concepts, the child can generate prescriptions regarding the event. For instance, the child will connect his or her own experience of pain (an undesirable experience) to the observed experience of the victim. In turn, this will be related to the perceived validity of the child's motive for harming the other person. Moreover, when the child is the victim, the perception of the undesirability of the offender's act is even more direct and vivid.

One of the ways children form judgments of moral necessity regarding actions of the type depicted in Event A would be through a comparison of the performance of the act itself with its opposite. In the case of the act described in Event A, its negation (in the child's mental activities) would result in a comparison of its occurrence with its nonoccurrence. If the constructed consequences of its nonoccurrence (the victim is unharmed) are judged to be more desirable than the consequences of its occurrence (the victim is harmed), then inferences will be made regarding how people *should* act under those circumstances (e.g., people ought not to hit each other). In attempting to understand their social experiences, children form judgments about what is right or wrong and fair or unfair. Such judgments evolve from the child's experiences but are not latent in the experiences themselves.

The source of morality, therefore, is not the standards of the group or society. On the contrary, the source of convention is in understandings of the characteristics of the social system. Consider the characteristics of Event B. For a child to regard calling a teacher by his or her first name as a transgression, the act would have to be viewed as a violation of an implicit uniformity or an explicit regulation within the social system (e.g., the school). There is no intrinsic prescriptive basis for a requirement in a school that children refer to teachers by their titles. Uniformity of regulations regarding forms of address (or other conventions) is determined by the social system and their functions are related to the way the system is organized. Consider again the child's comparison of the performance of the act with its opposite. As far as the act itself is concerned, referring to a teacher by a title is not likely to be regarded as more desirable than using a first name. It is social organizational factors, such as consensus, rules, and authority, that provide meaning to the act. It is by starting to conceptualize the social context in which they are embedded that the child forms an understanding of conventions. Consequently, the act of referring to a teacher by a first name would not be spontaneously regarded as wrong by a child, unless the child had some understanding of the status of the use of titles as a socially determined regularity. In the conventional domain, an event like this one would not be regarded as a transgression unless it were recognized as part of a constituted system and, thereby, a violation of social regulations, authoritative commands, or general expectations.

It is proposed that systems of social action correspond to the features of moral and conventional events just outlined. Children experience social events that are moral, entailing intrinsic consequences, and social events that are conventional, entailing institutional systems of rules, authoritative expectations, and organization. Thus, the constellation of social interactions associated with moral events would differ from that associated with events of a conventional nature. Furthermore, it is proposed that there is a coordination of these systems of action with systems of social judgment; that is, the types of judgments made about social events are related to the types of social interactions that occur.

A series of observational studies was conducted primarily to examine the types of social interactions experienced by children, and secondarily to ascertain the relation between judgment and social action. The main foci of these studies were social events, in the form of transgressions (such as Events A and B), and the network of interactions among children and adults in the context of these events. The first of these studies (Nucci & Turiel, 1978) was conducted in preschool settings (in ten different preschools that varied in group size, the social class backgrounds of the children, and the teachers' instructional practices).

Two interrelated measures of systems of social interaction were obtained. One was a measure of social transgressions. At each preschool, descriptions were recorded of naturally occurring events that exemplified transgressions in the moral (e.g., inflicting harm, taking the possessions of another) and conventional (e.g., behavior inconsistent with uniformities in dress or modes of eating) domains. Transgressions were chosen as the unit of analysis because they provide public, observable displays of social interactions, highlighting the prescriptions and uniformities that exist among a group of people. Transgressions create occasions for communications among children, and between children and adults, regarding social standards. Such communications provide feedback to the transgressing child and constitute events that can be observed by others who are not participants in the specific event. The definitions of the domains provided a means for classifying social events. Transgressions were recorded and classified as moral or conventional through the use of a systematic coding procedure (there was 93% agreement between two independent coders).

The second measure obtained was for the types of social interactions generated by each type of transgression. The reactions and interactions stimulated by the transgressions (among the children and the teachers) were recorded by means of a standard list of response categories. Two general types of behaviors were observed in the children's reactions to the transgressions. One pertained to the intrinsic consequences of actions and occurred mainly in the context of moral transgressions. These reactions included statements regarding the pain or injury experienced by a victim of an act, expressions of emotion, explanations of the reasons for an action, and physical reactions toward the transgressor. The second general type of response pertained to the organizational features of the situation and occurred usually in the context of conventional transgressions. These reactions included statements about social order or disorder, specification of rules and sanctions, and direct commands.

In this study, the patterns of responses by children differed somewhat from those of the adults. Children rarely initiated responses to transgressions of social conventions but they frequently responded to transgressions of morality. Consequently, a good deal of spontaneous child-child interaction regarding moral issues was observed. These interactions generally occurred proximate to the actions themselves. In some cases, children responded to others' transgressions with physical reactions and expressions of emotional states. Frequently, the children also responded by pointing up the consequences of actions, such as the pain experienced or loss incurred. Children's responses to moral transgressions did not focus on social organizational features. For instance, children did not invoke rules or sanctions as reasons for objecting to moral transgressions. Teacher reactions to the children's moral transgressions were similar, in form, to the responses of the children; that is, they did not revolve around rules, sanctions, or social order. The teachers most often responded in two ways: They pointed out to the transgressor the effects of his or her actions upon the victim (or they encouraged the victim to do so); or they provided children with reasons for objections to the behaviors.

Although the children generally did not spontaneously respond to transgressions of social conventions, the teachers frequently did. In the observations made in this study, therefore, most of the interactions of children involving conventional transgressions were with adults. These interactions revolved mainly around the social order of the school (that is, the constituted system). Teachers responded to social-conventional transgressions by invoking school rules, sanctions, and prohibitions regarding norm-violating behavior. It can be seen, then, that two distinct forms of social interaction occurred: The interactions among children and between children and adults that related to moral events took a different form from the interactions that related to social conventions. Within the moral domain, the behaviors of both children and adults were in correspondence with each other and were consistent with the definition of morality presented earlier.

Few observations were recorded by Nucci and Turiel of children's reactions to conventions, though the interactions they did experience in the adults' responses were consistent with the way convention has been defined. This particular study, however, focused on conventions related mainly to the organization of the school. Therefore, the finding that children did not react spontaneously to social-conventional transgressions should not be taken to suggest that children are unaware of social conventions. Two other studies have demonstrated that children do react to social-conventional transgressions when the conventions pertain to patterns of social interaction among children. In one of the studies (Much & Shweder, 1978) the children were about the same age as those in the Nucci and Turiel study, but somewhat different procedures were used. Linguistic analyses were conducted of spontaneous verbal interactions resulting from transgressions of school regulations, conventions, and moral precepts. In their observations of nursery school and kindergarten settings, Much and Shweder found that a characteristic way of responding to social transgressions is to make accusations of the transgressor. In turn, accusations produce counter-responses, or what Much and Shweder refer to as "accounts." Here are some examples of the types of dialogues recorded by Much and Shweder. The first two are about conventional transgressions, and the third concerns moral transgressions.

Some nursery school children have gotten their clothes wet and are changing into extra pairs of trousers kept by the school. They are in a dressing area with a double door that opens separately above and below. Gary, Abel, and Edith stand around the open top of the door. Edith stands on a chair looking through the door. Gary and Abel peek over the top.

Vickie: You silly dummies. . . you're all peeking. We're getting dressed.
Teacher (approaching): What's wrong? Are you changing clothes?
Vickie: Yes.
[Teacher closes the door]
Edith (to Gary): Keep that locked. Now don't open it.
Vickie: Don't look, now, don't look! [P. 21]

The teacher has greeted Fred as he came in the door. Fred did not respond. The teacher walks over to Fred.

Teacher: Fred, Fred, Fred, you were so busy you didn't hear me say "Hi, Fred." [She takes Fred's chin in hand] Just say "Hi," then I'll know we saw each other.
[Note: the teacher's "accusation" contains an account "you were so busy..."] [P. 27]

Tammy and Nina are washing the table where brownies were mixed. Agnes comes to help.

Tammy: I'm sorry but you can't help.
[Alice comes over from her painting and intervenes]
Alice: She can help. You don't have to be just rude.
[Tammy begins to cry]
Teacher (approaching): What's the matter?
Tammy: She pinched me.
Teacher (to Alice): Why?
Alice: She wouldn't let Agnes help.
Teacher: That's not your business. I told Tammy to clean the table. I'm angry that you hurt Tammy.
[Alice cries. The teacher kneels down and comforts her until she stops] [P. 28]

Children in the nursery school, as well as in the kindergarten, recognized and responded to social transgressions. In many cases, children initiated accusations; that is, they responded by pointing out the transgression, as in the above examples. The children responded mainly to conventional and moral transgressions, whereas the majority of responses to transgressions of school regulations were made by adults. The number of responses to conventional transgressions were divided equally between the children and adults. Responses to moral transgressions were made by both children and adults, though a greater frequency of child responses was observed.

The dialogues that occurred in the nursery school and kindergarten settings varied with the domain of the transgression. That is, the accusations made by children or adults, as well as the ways in which children defended themselves against accusations, depended upon whether the transgression was moral or conventional. The discussion of conventional transgressions dealt with the social context and rules (what Much & Shweder refer to as a legalistic orientation), whereas discussions of moral transgressions dealt primarily with the actions themselves.

The other study that demonstrates that children's social interactions include conventional systems was conducted by L. Nucci and M. Nucci (in press). Their investigation was conducted in playgrounds where groups of children interacted outside of the school context and without adult supervision. Groups of children ranging from 7 to 10 and 11 to 14 years of age engaged in play activities, while observed by using procedures adapted from the Nucci and Turiel study. A substantial number of conventional and moral transgressions occurred that produced reactions on the part of the children. Even in the playground context, children's responses to conventional transgressions pertained to social organizational features of their interactions.

The generality of the phenomena observed in these studies is demonstrated further by two other investigations. One was a replication of the Nucci and Turiel study in a setting outside of the United States (Nucci, Turiel, & Gawrych, 1981). Results similar to the Nucci and Turiel findings were obtained through observations of preschool children in rural and urban settings on St. Croix in the Virgin Islands. In the other study (L. Nucci & M. Nucci, 1982), which was conducted in the United States, the observations were of social interactions in second-, fifth-, and seventh-grade classrooms. In each grade, the forms of social interaction observed were the same as in the other studies. There was, however, a tendency for children in these grades to respond to conventional transgressions more frequently than the preschool children (although the majority of such responses to such transgressions were still initiated by teachers).

In all the contexts studied, children responded to moral events. In their peer interactions, preschool and school-age children also function with conventional systems. Furthermore, as children get older, there is an increasing involvement in the conventional regulations of the institutional context of the school. These observational studies have shown that there are coherent systems of social interaction corresponding to different types of social events. Systems of action, as reflected in children's social interactions, are of a kind within each domain but they differ between domains. Correspondences were observed between actions (as reflected in the transgression), observations of and reactions to actions, and communications (from child to child and from adult to child). Moreover, systems of actions are coordinated with systems of thought. The observed reactions of the children reflected both action and judgment. The type of reaction to a given transgression included evaluations of the actions and a conceptualization of the event involved (e.g., statements about rules, order, harm).

Further and more explicit evidence of the coordination of action and judgment comes from another assessment made in some of the studies (in Nucci & Turiel, 1978; Nucci & Nucci, 1982; Nucci, Turiel, & Gawrych, 1981). Selected children were administered a brief interview about transgressions immediately after the events had occurred (and had been witnessed by a child). The child was asked whether the act just witnessed would be wrong if there had been no rule in the school pertaining to the act. The results were as follows: In the majority of the cases (over 80%), the children, when questioned about conventional events, said that the act would be right if no rule existed in the school, but when questioned about moral events, they said that the act would be wrong even if no rule existed. The following two responses by preschool children in St. Croix are typical:

(DID YOU SEE WHAT JUST HAPPENED?) Yes. They were playing and John hit him too hard. (IS THAT SOMETHING YOU ARE SUPPOSED TO OR NOT SUPPOSED TO DO?) Not so hard to hurt. (IS THERE A RULE ABOUT THAT?) Yes. (WHAT IS THE RULE?) You're not to hit hard. (WHAT IF THERE WERE NO RULE ABOUT HITTING HARD, WOULD IT BE RIGHT TO DO THEN?) No. (WHY NOT?) Because he could get hurt and start to cry.

(DID YOU SEE WHAT JUST HAPPENED?) Yes. They were noisy. (IS THAT SOMETHING YOU ARE SUPPOSED TO OR NOT SUPPOSED TO DO?) No. (IS THERE A RULE ABOUT THAT?) Yes. We have to be quiet. (WHAT IF THERE WERE NO RULE, WOULD IT BE RIGHT TO DO THEN?) Yes. (WHY?) Because there is no rule.

It is apparent from these reactions that children draw inferences about the intrinsic relations between acts and their consequences and that they recognize the contingency of arbitrary acts in relation to institutional contexts. More extensive analyses of these kinds of social judgments are considered in the next chapter.

4   Dimensions of social judgments

The series of observational studies discussed in the previous chapter provides a picture of several interrelated components in the interactions among children, as well as between children and adults. The data obtained in these studies indicate that certain types of social interactions constitute coherent systems revolving around a particular social domain. Domain is the organizing component for actions, in the form of transgressions, reactions to those actions, communications, and dialogues. As we have seen, types of reactions, communications, and dialogues in the contexts of moral and conventional transgressions form a consistent pattern and are coordinated with social judgments.

The findings from the observational studies also provide information regarding the early sources of social concepts. Again, a pattern of interrelated components is evinced. As was discussed in the previous chapter, events likely to stimulate moral concepts differ from those likely to stimulate concepts of social convention. The analyses presented in Chapter 3 regarding elements of each type of event (with Events A and B as prototypical examples) were given empirical support by the observational studies. Young children experience each type of event and begin to construct distinctly different kinds of judgments corresponding to each domain (as evidenced by findings from the interview procedures in the Nucci & Turiel and Nucci et al. studies). Therefore, the research indicates that young children do make inferences about experienced events. It follows from the proposition that individual–environment interactions are reciprocal, and not just one-way, that the nature of the event has a bearing on what is abstracted from them by children.

The research has also shown that domain-related patterns of social interactions occur across ages and settings. Similar patterns of social interaction were observed in the preschool, kindergarten, elementary school, and junior high school classrooms, and in playgrounds free of adult supervision. The findings suggest that there are distinct courses of development for each domain of judgment and that the origins of thought are to be understood through domain analyses. This means, for example, that children begin at an early age to form distinctively

50

moral judgments through their social interactions and that with age those judgments may become transformed into qualitatively different, but still moral, judgments. Analyses of the development of a domain of judgment requires specification of both constant dimensions and changing features.

Another interpretation of the findings from the observational studies could be made. In place of the proposition that morality and social convention represent basic categories of social judgment constructed out of the child's social interactions, it could be proposed that it was the behavior of adults and communications from them that determined the children's behaviors and judgments. Because the research showed a correspondence between children and adults in the differential responses to the two domains, it may be that children acquired the measured responses as a consequence of what had been transmitted by the adults. It could be argued further that the adult responses reflect a culturally specific way of distinguishing among social events. Alternative ways of classifying events as moral or conventional may exist in other cultures, which would be transmitted to children and learned by them. In other words, Ruth Benedict's proposition that the individual accommodates to the standards handed down by the community explains the findings of our observational studies.

Cross-cultural issues are raised by this type of argument, and they are considered in the concluding chapter. There are, however, developmental issues applicable to non–cross-cultural findings in the argument just outlined. First, it is claimed that the type of distinction made between morality and convention by children in this culture is also made by adults. Second, it is claimed that the children learned a particular way of making the distinction from the adults. The second (developmental) aspect of the argument does not necessarily follow from the first. An observed correspondence between child and adult judgments does not necessarily mean that the children learned to make those judgments *because* adults make them. If morality and convention are basic social-conceptual categories that children begin to construct at an early age, it can be expected that adults will also understand those categories. In order to evaluate the relative merits of the alternative hypotheses, it is necessary to consider closely the types of interactions experienced by children and the nature of their judgments. On the basis of only an observed correspondence between adult and child responses, it can be supposed either that the correspondence reflects a process of adult transmission or that it reflects the development of fundamental epistemological categories.

It should be noted first that the types of adult and child social interactions observed were not of the sort reflective of adult attempts at socialization or training. For the most part, they involved explanations of domain-relevant considerations. In turn, the children's responses were spontaneous reactions that revealed an understanding of morality and convention. One aspect of the developmental analyses, therefore, pertains to the forms of social interaction and types of social event that constitute the sources of development within each domain. In addition, an assessment of the validity of the cognitive and developmental propositions requires detailed analyses of judgments made at different ages. If children accommodate to a distinction provided by adults in the socialization process, then it follows that they would simply discriminate between issues on the basis of severity or importance. By contrast, if children form basic categories of social judgment, it is expected that they would display complex conceptualizations regarding the identification, sources, and functions of social domains.

Criterion judgments, justification categories, and social events

The dual proposition that categories of social judgment are organized within domains and that development involves transformations in those forms of organization implies that there are two aspects of the individual's social concepts requiring specification and empirical analysis. One of these aspects will be referred to as *criterion judgments* and the other as *justification categories*.

Criterion judgments pertain to the categories used by individuals in the identification and classification of the parameters of a domain of knowledge. In examining criterion judgments, the researcher formulates a set of criteria based on the definitions of the domain as a means of determining the subject's construction of the parameters of domains. Therefore, criterion-judgment analyses address the question: Which judgments made by subjects delineate the identifying features of a domain of knowledge (e.g., how does an individual judge whether a problem is a moral issue, a question of logic, or a mathematical task)? In turn, criterion-judgment analyses provide a way of demonstrating the boundaries of a given domain. Moreover, comparative analyses of criterion judgments make it possible to ascertain whether or not, and in what ways, domains are distinguished.

The criterion judgments examined in the research on morality and social convention stemmed from the definitions considered in the previous chapter. Several of these studies, which will be reviewed in this chapter, together provide a comprehensive set of findings regarding criterion judgments for morality and convention. The research examined subjects' judgments in the following criterial dimensions: obligatoriness, impersonality, alterability, universality, relativism, social consensus, and institutional status (i.e., rule contingency and authority jurisdiction). Because the criterion judgments represent the definitional parameters of a domain, it was expected that criterion judgments for morality would differ across ages from those for convention.

Not all types of judgments, however, are constant across ages. The second and equally important aspect of social concepts, as mentioned earlier, is the form of reasoning within a domain of knowledge. The forms of reasoning are the categories used in justification of a course of action. The justification categories (e.g., those pertaining to justice, harm, and rights or to the elements of social system coordination) are proposed to form organized systems of thinking within domains. It is the forms of organization of the justification categories that are hypothesized to undergo age-related transformations.

Forms of reasoning were dealt with only secondarily in the research discussed in this chapter (the topic is considered more extensively in Chapters 6 and 7). The primary concern of this chapter is criterion judgments. The usual procedure of the research was to present subjects with stimulus events – identified as moral or social conventional in accordance with the definitions – and then to pose a series of questions designed to elicit judgments regarding each criterion. Consequently, this procedure assumes that the relation between the stimulus event and criterion judgments is nonarbitrary. That is, there is a subject matter for each domain, so that a nonarbitrary relation exists between how one reasons and what one reasons about (cf. Gewirth, 1978).

The nature of the relation between conceptual domains and events is not proposed to be one of straightforward, direct correspondence and does, therefore, require clarification and some qualification. In proposing that a nonarbitrary relation exists between reasoning and events it is assumed, of course, that the individual's orientation to moral and conventional events is not derived entirely from one's culture. It has been maintained by some, for instance, that insofar as distinctions between moral and conventional understandings exist, they are formed at the cultural level and communicated in either tacit or explicit ways to individuals (Shweder, 1981). Although one culture may treat some issues as moral (i.e., as obligatory, impersonal, unalterable) and others as conventional (i.e., as alterable and specific to the social context), the specific issues associated with each domain will vary from culture to culture. According to this view, the content of what is reasoned in a moral or nonmoral way stands in an arbitrary relation to the individual's criterion judgments, because the substance of a social domain is externally determined. Accordingly, issues pertaining to, as examples, dress codes or inflicting harm (e.g., veiling one's face, beating a certain class of persons) may be moral injunctions established through consensus in one culture but not in another. There is no conceptually based relation between the content of moral prescriptions or conventional norms and processes of judgment; there is only a culturally determined relation.

The interactional-constructivist view of development implies a different kind of relation between conceptual domains and social events. Social concepts and associated contents are not prepackaged units transmitted to the individual, but are constructed through a developing process. Social concepts, the events that stimulate the formation of those concepts, and events that are the objects of those concepts, once constructed, all constitute interrelated components. As already discussed, moral concepts are formed through the child's experiences with interpersonal actions that have intrinsic consequences, whereas conventional concepts are formed through experiences with social system elements and related coordinative events of an arbitrary nature. The concepts formed through such experiences pertain to classes of social interactions, so that there is a subject matter for each domain of knowledge. That is, moral concepts pertain to the subject matter of justice, rights, and welfare and conventional concepts pertain to social organization.

Therefore, the nature of social events is not only relevant to the developmental sources of social concepts. The concepts that are formed implicate how one reasons about experienced events. A person's social concepts provide a basis for recognizing differences between the intrinsic and the nonintrinsic. Furthermore, events that do bear on social coordinations but not on justice, welfare, or rights will be reasoned about differently from events that involve justice, welfare, or rights, but not social coordinations.

It should be stressed that the proposed relation of concepts and events is interactive and does not stand in a relation of one-to-one correspondence. Although components of events are likely to evoke one kind of concept or the other, the activity is interpretative. The primary focus of analysis is on how events are conceptualized by the subject. Therefore, stimulus events should not be viewed merely as means of eliciting responses or as ways of predicting the subject's concepts. An interactive process makes it necessary to examine the ways subjects reason about events. This focus on conceptualizations may lead one to suppose that the determining factor is the subject's reasoning and that moral or conventional judgments can potentially apply to any event. Reasoning, however, does not occur in a vacuum, and the structure of an environmental event does place some constraints on the concepts applied to it. (As an illustrative example of the constraints placed upon reasoning by the nature of an event, consider the implausibility of applying social concepts to events involving physical causality.) Although it is quite possible that some variations will exist in different subjects' domain interpretations of similar events, adequate investigation of social concepts requires delineation of the structure of the event, as well as the structure of the subject's concepts.

Nevertheless, it may be thought that an invalid distinction is being drawn because we know that there are many events that are not exclusively moral or conventional; or it may be thought that the identification of events including both moral and conventional components would invalidate the proposed distinction. Not necessarily! It does not logically follow that the combination of domains in events invalidates the conceptual or stimulus distinction. Suppose for the moment that there is a fundamental domain distinction; it would still be the case that two components could be combined in a given situation. The presence of more than one function in a sequence of interrelated events does not mean that different principles cannot be identified for each function. Situations in which aspects of morality are related to aspects of convention present the subject with a coordination task – the problem of coordinating two conceptual categories.

Indeed, different types of identifiable domain combinations will be described in Chapters 6 and 9. In Chapter 6, research on how subjects coordinate (or fail to coordinate) domains of judgment is considered. Chapter 9 deals with coordination of judgments in relation to behavioral decisions. For now, it suffices to note the types of combinations. One type involves a straightforward mixture of domains (in conflict or in synchrony) requiring that both moral and conventional considerations be taken into account. Perhaps the most common examples are those in which moral decisions are in contradiction with social-organizational functions of coordination and efficiency. Another type of domain combination can be seen in issues that are ambiguously multidimensional, so that significant discrepancies exist in their domain attribution by different people. A good example of this kind of combination, to be discussed in Chapter 9, is the issue of abortion.

It may also be true that established conventions sometimes take on a moral significance. A third type of combination is one in which the violation of another's conventions is considered morally wrong insofar as those adhering to the convention experience psychological hurt by virtue of the violation. Such transformations of conventional uniformities into symbolic moral significance represent a *second-order* phenomenon. It is necessary first to determine the primary functions served by the conventional uniformity and the individual's primary conceptual justification for it. Although the uniformity may be regarded as primarily conventional, it may also be thought that in particularistic ways its violation can have moral implications.

As noted earlier, the existence of overlap, mixture, or ambiguity does not invalidate the distinction. The first step is to explore domain distinctions. If the domains are indeed distinct, then mixtures and second-order phenomena cannot be understood without first knowing the principles governing thought in each domain. The strategy of the research considered in this and the next chapter was to present subjects with prototypical examples of events in each domain as a means of investigating domain-specific criterion judgments.

Research on criterion judgments

The studies exploring criterion judgments are summarized in Table 4.1. Included in this table are three studies discussed in the previous chapter. Two of the other studies listed (Turiel, this volume, Chapter 5; Dodsworth-Rugani, 1982) dealt explicitly with rules and prohibitions, which is the topic of the next chapter. The rest were designed to investigate one or more criterion dimensions. As shown in

Table 4.1. *Studies of criterion judgments*

Study	Ages	Criterion dimensions	Type of questions posed to subjects
L. Nucci & Turiel (1978)	4-5	Rule contingency (see Chapter 3)	Would act be wrong if no rule? (regarding observed transgression)
L. Nucci, Turiel, & Gawrych (1981)	4-5	Rule contingency (see Chapter 3)	Would act be wrong if no rule? (regarding observed transgression)
L. Nucci & M. Nucci (1982)	7-12	Rule contingency (see Chapter 3)	Would act be wrong if no rule? (regarding observed transgression)
Smetana (1981a)	3-4	Rule contingency	Is act (transgression) wrong in absence of rule?
		Generalizability	Is act okay in a different context?
L. Nucci (1981)	6-19	Rule contingency	Is act (transgression) wrong in absence of rule?
		Impersonality	Is act a personal decision?
Smetana (1980)	10-20	Rule contingency	(1) Is act wrong in absence of rule (for transgressions)?
			(2) Is act right in absence of rule (for positive acts)?
		Impersonality	Is act a personal decision?
Weston & Turiel (1980)	5-11	Institutional practice (authority power)	Is act right or wrong when permitted by practice of a social institution and its authorities?
Davidson, Turiel, & Black (in press)	6-10	See Table 4.4	See Table 4.4
Turiel, this volume, Chapter 4	6-10	Importance in interaction with: rule and authority contingency	Is act wrong in absence of rule, as eliminated by authority?
		Generalizability	Is act okay in different country with no rule?
Turiel, this volume, Chapter 5	6-16	See Chapter 5	See Chapter 5
Dodsworth-Rugani (1982)	7-13	See Chapter 5	See Chapter 5

the table, there are both overlap and differences in the criterion dimensions assessed in the various studies. One study (Davidson, Turiel, & Black, in press) included a comprehensive set of criterion dimensions and attempted to account for children's prior familiarity with specific moral and conventional issues. Although the major emphasis in all of these studies was on criterion judgments, assessments of forms of reasoning were not excluded. Exploratory analyses of justification categories were included in the Nucci (1981) and Smetana (1980) studies and, especially, in the Davidson et al. (in press) study.

The methodology used in this set of studies represents a variation of the clinical method discussed in Chapter 2. Whereas the clinical method is most often used to systematically obtain responses that can be applied to analyses of the forms of reasoning, the clinical method was adopted to test hypotheses in the studies on criterion dimensions. Typically, subjects were presented with stimulus events and questions designed to represent specific criterion dimensions. The subject's responses were analyzed in relation to predetermined hypothesized orientations to each criterion dimension. This method, however, can be readily combined with questions designed to obtain responses on forms of reasoning.

The results of the studies listed in Table 4.1 provide specification of the criterion dimensions used in the moral judgments and in the judgments about convention of subjects at different ages. In addition, the findings point to the types of events associated with each domain. The youngest subjects thus far studied were the 3- to 4-year-olds in Smetana's (1981a) study. The observational studies discussed in the previous chapter did include a brief assessment of the rule contingency dimension in the judgments of 4- and 5-year-olds. Smetana's study provides further confirmation that very young children judge moral events as noncontingent.

The subjects of the study were presented with depictions of a series of transgressions and asked first to rate the seriousness of the act (the moral transgressions included causing physical harm to others and taking another's belongings; the conventional transgressions included deviance from group activities and failure to put objects and clothing in designated places). The ratings of transgressions were accomplished with such young children through the use of drawings and a 4-point scale (of seriousness) represented by pictures of frowning faces. As expected, the moral transgressions were evaluated as more serious than the conventional transgressions. In addition, subjects stated that moral transgressions were deserving of a greater amount of punishment than conventional transgressions.

The differences in thinking about moral and conventional transgressions among 3- and 4-year-olds were not limited to assessments of seriousness or punitiveness. As indicated in Table 4.1, subjects were also posed two criterion-dimension questions referring to rule contingency and generalizability. For the purposes of these analyses subjects were divided into two age groups: those from 2¾ to 3¾ years old and those from 3¾ to 4¾ years old. Both groups of subjects treated the moral events as noncontingent as to rules. It was generally stated that moral transgressions would be wrong even if no rule existed; the young children focused on the intrinsic features of the actions, so that their moral judgments were not based on the presence or absence of an external rule.

The older group of subjects also regarded morality as generalizable in that they said that the transgressions would still be wrong in a different context. By contrast, the younger group of subjects did not demonstrate an understanding of the generalizability of moral judgments. Their responses to the generalizability questions reflected a lack of comprehension of the issue. It appears, therefore, that noncontingency is an earlier-developing dimension of moral judgment than generalizability. Moral transgressions were considered non–rule-contingent by all the subjects, whereas the children under four years of age did not use the generalizability dimension.

The findings of the Smetana study also indicated that children of 3 to 4 years of age have not yet formed stable understandings of the types of conventional transgressions presented in the study. The findings regarding rule contingency for conventions were equivocal, though clearly in the predicted direction. Although a majority of subjects stated that the conventional acts would be all right if no rule existed, it was not a majority large enough to attain statistical significance.

However, clear-cut results for the dimensions of rule contingency and impersonality were obtained with older subjects by Nucci (1981). Nucci's subjects, who ranged from 7 to 19 years of age, were also presented with a series of moral and conventional transgressions as stimulus events (they arc listed in Table 4.2). Subjects were also presented with several events that, in this culture, are likely to be considered the realm of personal jurisdiction (also listed in Table 4.2). The inclusion of "personal" events provided a means of measuring the criterion dimension of impersonality (i.e., Is the act considered a personal decision or is it independent of personal desires?).

Rule contingency and impersonality were assessed by the following procedures. Each subject was presented with the entire list of acts and instructed to group together those acts considered wrong regardless of the presence or absence of a rule for each act (this is a measure of rule contingency similar to that used in the Smetana study). After sorting the acts on the basis of rule contingency, the subject was again presented with the entire list and instructed to group together those acts considered the "person's own business" and that should not be governed by a rule.

The results from these two procedures are reproduced in Tables 4.2 and 4.3. Table 4.2 shows that, at each of the ages represented in the sample, only the moral transgressions were judged as wrong regardless of the rule. These findings

Table 4.2. *Number of subjects out of 16 at each grade level sorting actions as "Wrong even in absence of rule"*

Action	Grade				
	2	5	8	11	College
Moral					
Lying[a]	16	16	—	—	—
Stealing	16	15	15	16	16
Hitting	16	16	16	15	16
Selfishness	16	15	15	14	16
Athlete throwing game[b]	—	—	16	15	16
Damaging borrowed property[b]	—	—	16	16	16
Social convention					
Chewing gum in class[a]	2	0	—	—	—
Addressing teacher by first name	2	0	0	0	0
Boy entering girls' bathroom	1	2	1	0	0
Eating lunch with fingers	0	0	0	0	0
Eating in class[b]	—	—	1	1	0
Talking without raising hand[b]	—	—	2	1	0
Personal					
Watching TV on a sunny day[a]	1	0	—	—	—
Keeping correspondence private	1	0	0	0	0
Interacting with forbidden friend	0	0	0	0	0
Boy wearing long hair	0	0	0	0	0
Smoking at home[b]	—	—	0	0	0
Refusing to join recreation group[b]	—	—	0	0	0

Note: Eight subjects would be expected to sort an action as "wrong even in absence of rule" by chance; $p < .01$ or greater when fourteen or more subjects sort an action as "wrong even in absence of rule" using χ^2 goodness-of-fit test.
[a]Actions sorted by subects in grades 2 and 5, but not grades 8, 11, or college.
[b]Actions sorted by subjects in grades 8, 11, and college, but not grades 2 or 5.
Source: Nucci (1977).

are consistent with the Smetana findings, showing that across a wide age range (3 to 19 years), evaluations of moral issues are not based on the presence or absence of social rules. Table 4.3 shows that moral acts are considered impersonal (i.e., not solely the "person's own business"). None of the moral transgressions were classified as actions that should be the person's own business.

The sorting of the conventional transgressions under each instruction demonstrates some of the salient dimensions of social-conventional thinking. On the one hand, subjects' evaluations of conventional transgressions were contingent on the presence or absence of a rule (Table 4.2). On the other hand, conventions were not regarded as legitimately based on personal inclination (Table 4.3). The most plausible interpretation for the combination of rule contingency and imper-

Table 4.3. *Number of subjects out of 16 at each grade level sorting actions as "Should be person's business"*

Action	Grade				
	2	5	8	11	College
Moral					
Lying[a]	0	0	—	—	—
Stealing	0	0	0	0	0
Hitting	0	0	0	0	0
Selfishness	0	0	0	0	0
Athlete throwing game[b]	—	—	0	0	0
Damaging borrowed property[b]	—	—	0	0	0
Social convention					
Chewing gum in class[a]	0	0	—	—	—
Addressing teacher by first name	0	0	0	0	0
Boy entering girls' bathroom	0	1	2	3	0
Eating lunch with fingers	5	5	8	8	9
Talking without raising hand[b]	—	—	0	0	0
Eating in class[b]	—	—	0	0	0
Personal					
Watching TV on a sunny day[a]	13	16	—	—	—
Keeping correspondence private	12	12	13	13	13
Interacting with forbidden friend	12	13	13	13	13
Boy wearing long hair	13	12	15	15	13
Smoking at home[b]	—	—	12	12	12
Refusing to join recreation group[b]	—	—	12	12	13

Note: Eight subjects would be expected to sort an action as "should be person's business" by chance; $p < .05$ or greater when twelve or more subjects sort an action as "should be person's business" using χ^2 goodness-of-fit test.
[a]Actions sorted by subjects in grades 2 and 5 but not grades 8, 11, or college.
[b]Actions sorted by subjects in grades 8, 11, and college, but not grades 2 or 5.
Source: Nucci (1977).

sonality is that the status of conventions can vary in accordance with their role in the social system. Within the cultural context of the subjects of the study, the conventional transgressions would be acceptable if not governed by regulations, but at the same time they are legitimately considered under social jurisdiction. Unlike actions with intrinsic consequences, arbitrary acts are judged by their societal context.

In conjunction with criterion judgments, domains are distinguished by forms of reasoning. The Nucci study provided evidence of the relationship between domains and reasoning through an additional set of findings. Subjects were instructed to rank the list of actions according to their degree of "wrongness" (from most to less to least wrong) and to explain their reasons for the rankings.

The ranks corresponded directly with the domain of the act. At all ages acts in the moral domain were ranked as more wrong than conventional ones, which were in turn ranked as more wrong than the personal actions (these differences were statistically significant). There were no differences between the rankings of subjects at different ages. The analyses of explanations for the ranking yielded a coding system of the types of justifications, which were closely linked to the rankings. That is, different justifications were associated with the acts ranked less wrong. The justifications for the ranking of moral transgressions produced reasons of justice, harm, and rights; the ranking of conventional transgressions was justified on social-organizational grounds; the reasons given for ranking acts as least wrong were that they are of a personal nature and only affect the actor.

The Nucci study was replicated by Smetana (1980) with the addition of another type of stimulus event. In all the studies mentioned thus far the stimulus events presented to subjects were put in the form of transgressions. However, not all social actions relevant to morality take the form of transgressions. Actions of a positive nature, such as helping others, can have moral components. Conventional transgressions generally have their counterparts in the opposing act that affirms the convention (e.g., dressing in the prescribed mode or using titles as a form of address). In the Smetana (1980) study judgments about positive actions were compared with transgressions, using the procedures from the Nucci study. The findings demonstrated that criterion judgments apply to both transgressions and positive actions.

One other study (Weston & Turiel, 1980) examined the criterion dimensions of institutional practice, which is closely related to rule contingency, and jurisdiction or power of authority. The procedure was to present hypothetical stories about schools in which it was the policy to permit certain actions. Four actions were specified, and only two of them were classified as moral or conventional: hitting another child and undressing in the playground. (One story described a school in which children are allowed to hit and even hurt each other; the other, a school in which children are allowed to wear no clothes.) In each story, subjects were asked to evaluate the school's policy of permitting the act and to predict an authority's (i.e., a teacher's) response to a child who engaged in the act.

The purpose of the procedure used in the Weston and Turiel study, therefore, was to ascertain how children relate the policies of the institution and of those in authority to their own judgments of the actions. Subjects were asked, in a concrete way, about cases in which the policy of the institutional authorities permits the actions. Subjects at all the ages, it was found, did not accept the legitimacy of the policy regarding hitting, an act in the moral domain. The majority (86%) were critical of a school policy that would allow people to hit and hurt one another, saying that it was wrong because this could result in harm to persons. By contrast, the majority (68%) at all ages accepted the legitimacy of a policy that would allow children to be undressed. Before being presented with the hypothetical situation, most of the children had stated that it would be wrong to remove one's clothes in school. Nevertheless, in this domain of behavior, it was assumed that the policy could legitimately be determined by the school authorities.

Some examples of children's responses to the questions posed in the Weston and Turiel study illustrate their use of the criterion judgments of institutional policy and authority power. The following excerpts, from a 5-year-old (David) and an 11-year-old (Jane), were in response to each of the stories:

David: (THIS IS A STORY ABOUT PARK SCHOOL. IN PARK SCHOOL THE CHILDREN ARE AL-LOWED TO HIT AND PUSH OTHERS IF THEY WANT. IT'S OKAY TO HIT AND PUSH OTHERS. DO YOU THINK IT IS ALL RIGHT FOR PARK SCHOOL TO SAY CHILDREN CAN HIT AND PUSH OTHERS IF THEY WANT TO?) No, it is not okay. (WHY NOT?) Because that is like making other people unhappy. You can hurt them that way. It hurts other people, hurting is not good. (MARK GOES TO PARK SCHOOL. TODAY IN SCHOOL HE WANTS TO SWING BUT HE FINDS THAT ALL THE SWINGS ARE BEING USED BY OTHER CHILDREN. SO HE DECIDES TO HIT ONE OF THE CHILDREN AND TAKE THE SWING. IS IT OKAY FOR MARK TO DO THAT?) No. Because he is hurting someone else.

[Before specifying the school rule David was told about a boy who took his clothes off because he was warm from running around and asked if that was all right.] No, because it's a school and other people don't like to see you without your clothes on. It looks silly. (I KNOW ABOUT ANOTHER SCHOOL IN A DIFFERENT CITY; IT'S CALLED GROVE SCHOOL...AT GROVE SCHOOL THE CHILDREN ARE ALLOWED TO TAKE THEIR CLOTHES OFF IF THEY WANT TO. IS IT OKAY OR NOT OKAY FOR GROVE SCHOOL TO SAY CHILDREN CAN TAKE THEIR CLOTHES OFF IF THEY WANT TO?) Yes. Because that is the rule. (WHY CAN THEY HAVE THAT RULE?) If that's what the boss wants to do, he can do that. (HOW COME?) Because he's the boss, he is in charge of the school. (BOB GOES TO GROVE SCHOOL. THIS IS A WARM DAY AT GROVE SCHOOL. HE HAS BEEN RUNNING IN THE PLAY AREA OUTSIDE AND HE IS HOT SO HE DECIDES TO TAKE OFF HIS CLOTHES. IS IT OKAY FOR BOB TO DO THAT?) Yes, if he wants to he can because it is the rule.

Jane: (IS IT ALL RIGHT FOR PARK SCHOOL TO SAY CHILDREN CAN HIT AND PUSH OTHERS?) No. You could break somebody's neck and nobody would care. You won't get in trouble, but still I think that's not right. She might really get hurt, might even die and that person might not even care. (SUE HITS A CHILD, ETC. IS IT OKAY FOR SUE TO DO THAT?) No, she should wait her turn or ask someone else to ask that person.

[Before specifying the school rule Jane was asked if it was all right to go undressed in school.] No, I don't like streaking. It's weird, strange. I just don't like it. (IS IT ALL RIGHT FOR GROVE SCHOOL TO SAY CHILDREN CAN TAKE THEIR CLOTHES OFF IF THEY WANT TO?) I don't know. (IF YOUR SCHOOL SAID THAT, WHAT WOULD YOU THINK?) I wouldn't go to that school because I don't like to see everybody streaking. It just isn't right. But if they want to, it's up to them. (BETTY TAKES HER CLOTHES OFF. IS IT OK FOR BETTY TO DO THAT?) It is really. They say you can, but I don't like it. (WHY?) Because I don't like to see people streaking.

David, the 5-year-old, expressed it clearly: Some rules should apply to all situations and the existing policy does not alter that assessment; other rules need not apply across situations. The justification for the belief that a school could not legitimately allow children to hit each other was the idea that it is not good to harm people ("It hurts other people, hurting is not good"). For David, therefore, the authority for moral prescriptions is neither in the dictates of specific persons nor in the group structure; for him the authority behind moral prescriptions comes from inferences that can be made about actions and their consequences to persons. By contrast, the authority behind conventions is in persons and their positions in the social system. Furthermore, the children's expectations of how an authority would respond to the permitted actions differed according to domain. Significantly more subjects expected teachers to contravene policy and reprimand a child who hit another than expected teachers to reprimand a child who took off his or her own clothes.

Criterion judgments, justification categories, and familiarity with the issue

One of the conclusions that may be drawn from the studies just reviewed is that children begin to form social concepts at an early age, which is evident in their criterion judgments that are maintained as definitional features of domains across a wide age range. However, in conjunction with constancy across ages in criterion judgments, age variations would be expected in the organization of reasoning within a domain. Furthermore, the structural proposition that experience influences development implies that the children's previous familiarity with a task or issue should influence their judgments.

Davidson, Turiel, and Black's (in press) investigation of criterion-judgment dimensions was combined with research about age-related changes in forms of reasoning and experiential sources of variation. There are three main differences between the Davidson et al. study and the others already described.

First, several criterion-judgment dimensions were assessed for the same subjects. The procedure was to present the subject with a brief hypothetical story and then pose a comprehensive set of questions pertaining to criterion judgments. (The types of questions are listed in Table 4.4, as well as five general criterion dimensions in which questions may be grouped for purposes of statistical analyses.) The dimensions tapped in the study included authority, punishment, rule alterability, and consensus. To these are added two dimensions – subordinate jurisdiction and objective-subjective responsibility – that are directly related to propositions made by Piaget (1932) regarding what he referred to as young children's heteronomous orientation to morality. Among other things, Piaget proposed that, in contrast with judgments made in late childhood and early adolescence, young children do not have an understanding of equality in peer relations and they judge by consequences (objective responsibility) rather than

Table 4.4. *Criterion judgment dimensions and questions*

Criterion judgment dimensions	Questions posed
Subordinate jurisdiction over rule	Who do you think made this rule? Could the children have made this rule? Could the children get it changed?
Acceptance of absolute authority power	Is it all right for authority figure to give/withhold punishment arbitrarily? (If yes) Is this because of authority role, or other reason? Is infraction all right if directed by authority? Can authority figure abolish this rule?
Punishment orientation in evaluation of the act	Is act all right, if punishment is expected? (if no) Is this because of punishment, or other reason? Is act all right, if no punishment expected? (If no) Is this because of absence of punishment, or other reason?
Rule change and consensus/ generalizability	Is it all right to change this rule (unspecified change)? Is it all right to change an arbitrary detail of the rule? Is it all right to change the rule by group consensus? Is the act all right, if rule has been changed by group consensus?
Objective- subjective responsibility	Is act wrong if well-intentioned? Should actor be punished if well-intentioned? Did well-intentioned or ill-intentioned actor do worse?

Source: Adapted from Davidson, Turiel, and Black (in press).

intentions (subjective responsibility). Findings pertaining to these two dimensions are considered in Chapter 7, where Piaget's theory and research on moral judgments are discussed at length.

The second difference between the Davidson et al. study and the others is that assessments were made of the child's previous familiarity with the moral or conventional event presented. A set of 12 stories, each dealing with either a moral or a conventional issue, were constructed. Some of the stories involved issues thought likely to be familiar to children, whereas others were designed so as to present what were likely to be unfamiliar issues. (The study included three

Table 4.5. *Descriptions of stories in the Davidson, Turiel, and Black study*

Story	Domain	Frequency of use	
		Familiar	Unfamiliar
1. *Physician's Duty*. An emergency room surgeon leaves his post due to boredom although there is no one there to relieve him.	Moral	3	46
2. *The Bully*. A boy bullies a group of children on the playground, pushing one off the top of a slide.	Moral	37	0
3. *The Dollar*. A student steals a dollar which another boy had earned by doing chores for his mother.	Moral	14	1
4. *The Embezzler*. A trusted employee cleverly embezzles money from the company he works for.	Moral	2	10
5. *The Scapegoat*. A crowd is incensed at not being able to catch a thief, and punishes the man's innocent brother.	Moral	5	1
6. *The Toy*. A student takes advantage of his teacher's trust and steals a toy belonging to the school.	Moral	1	0
7. *Table Manners*. A girl eats dinner with her fingers, knowing this is not allowed in her family.	Conv.	43	0
8. *Marriage Surname*. A couple gets married and the husband adopts the wife's surname, contrary to custom.	Conv.	1	31
9. *Teacher's Title*. A student addresses his teacher by a first name, knowing that title (Mr., Mrs., Ms.) plus surname is the required form.	Conv.	11	19
10. *School Uniforms*. A boy wears clothes of his own choosing in a school where students are expected to wear uniforms.	Conv.	3	6
11. *Greetings*. A girl greets her friends by bowing rather than by the customary greeting.	Conv.	1	3
12. *Uniforms in Sports*. A baseball player decides not to wear the team uniform to a game, and wears a different color.	Conv.	2	0

age groups, each with 20 subjects: 6-, 8-, and 10-year-olds.) By using the pool of stories and a standard way of assessing and coding the subject's familiarity with the event, it was possible to obtain responses to four types of events combining domain and level of familiarity: familiar moral, unfamiliar moral, familiar conventional, and unfamiliar conventional. A table from the study containing a list of the stories is reproduced here (see Table 4.5) to provide additional examples of events classified as moral or conventional. The table includes summary descriptions of the stories and the number of times they turned out to be familiar or unfamiliar events for the 6- to 10-year-old subjects.

A third feature of the study is that in addition to assessments of criterion judgments, subjects were systematically probed for responses that could be analyzed for justification categories. A coding system describing the different categories used in reasoning about the events was formulated from analysis of a portion of the protocols and then applied to the remainder. Summary descriptions of the reasoning categories are presented in Table 4.6.

Comparisons were drawn on both criterion judgments and justification categories for domain and familiarity of event. The major findings were that responses differed in accordance with domain, that familiarity with the event had some influence – especially on the responses of the youngest children – and that there were age-related differences in justification categories. If the responses to familiar moral and conventional events are considered alone, the judgments on the criterion dimensions are consistent with those in the other studies discussed. It was found that the authority and punishment dimensions were relevant to judgments about conventional practices, but not to moral prescriptions. In the case of conventions, a person in authority (e.g., parent, teacher, principal, police chief) could, in the judgments of the children, legitimately withhold punishment for an infraction, or even direct others to violate or eliminate a rule. Similarly, the absence of a punishment was judged to bear on the severity of an evaluation of conventional but not of moral transgressions.

Children associate authority and punishment with the existing social organization. This implies that children recognize the possibility of other kinds of social arrangements, accepting that variations can coexist with regard to nonmoral issues. The children's responses to direct questions about the alterability of rules indicate that children do indeed comprehend variations in social arrangements. When asked straightforward questions about whether a given rule could be changed, most children said that rules pertaining to conventional issues could be changed, but not those pertaining to moral issues. In turn, consensual agreement was regarded as part of the conventional aspect of social organization.

The influence of the child's prior familiarity with an event was not as straightforward as might have been anticipated in that responses to familiar and unfamiliar events were not always different. The best way to summarize the findings on the familiarity variable is to say that the distinction between unfamiliar moral events and unfamiliar conventional events was not made as frequently by the youngest subjects, the 6-year-olds, as it was by the older subjects. Yet on some dimensions the 6-year-olds did respond similarly to unfamiliar events and to familiar ones. There is evidence, therefore, from the Davidson et al. study that children's prior experiences do have an influence on the formation of judgments.

Table 4.6. *Justification categories*

Category	Description of responses included in category
Custom or Tradition	Appeal to personal and family customs ("Our family doesn't do it, so why should they?") as well as social customs and traditions ("Because it's polite"; "Because you always do it when you marry").
Appeal to Authority	Appeal to the approval of specific authority figures ("If his coach gives him permission, I guess it's all right") or to the existence of rules ("Because if they make the rules you should abide by them").
Punishment Avoidance	References to negative reactions of other persons toward the actor, including social condemnation as well as explicit punishment ("It's not okay because she could get into trouble").
Prudential Reasons	References to nonsocial negative consequences to the actor, such as personal comfort or health ("Because it may be hot enough and so maybe he could get some fresh air"; "Because if your hands aren't clean, you might get germs or something").
Personal Choice	Appeal to individual preferences or prerogatives ("She should be able to say it; people who want to say one thing they can say it and people who want to say the other thing can say that"; "Because she thought it looked like fun").
Social Coordination	Appeal to the need for social organization or for maintaining a system of shared expectations between persons ("Because, another teacher of the same name, you'd get mixed up"; "If everybody took walks and not obeyed their jobs, then there'd be nothing get done").
Others' Welfare	Appeal to the interests of persons other than the actor ("Because somebody could have gotten hurt, or you know had to go to hospital or emergency"; "Nobody wants to get their money taken because they like to have lunch").
Appeal to Fairness	References to maintaining a balance of rights between persons ("I don't think it would be fair, where if someone earns some money and the other guy would take it and keep it for himself when he didn't do anything, he didn't earn it").
Obligation	References to feelings of obligation, including personal conscience ("Because my conscience would bother me") as well as to personal duty ("You should keep your promises"; "He should do it for him because they are friends").

Source: Davidson, Turiel, and Black (in press).

By the ages of 8 or 10 years, however, there is an increased ability to abstract elements from unfamiliar events, identify issues, and apply domain-specific judgments. Nevertheless, 6-year-olds did apply their judgments to unfamiliar events, though not as extensively as older children. It appears that experience influences conceptual development in conjunction with the child's ability to abstract from events and reflect upon them. These differences between the 6-year-olds and the older children also help explain some of the inconsistent results from studies on young children's judgments (see Pool, Shweder, & Much, in press). In several studies it was found that young children (3 to 6 years old) distinguished between morality and convention, but this distinction was not found in some other studies. It is likely that variations in young children's familiarity with the events used in the different studies account for the inconsistent results.

The evidence from all the studies discussed thus far is that, as children grow older, there is a fair amount of stability in the ways they apply criterion judgments to social events. Differing responses across ages, to some extent, are accounted for by the ways judgments are applied in contexts unfamiliar to the child. Other age differences were accounted for by the categories used to justify courses of action, as is suggested by additional results from the Davidson et al. study. In their reasoning about moral issues, subjects most often used three of the categories listed in Table 4.6: welfare, fairness, and obligation. Moral prescriptions were justified with reasons that appealed to the interests of others, avoidance of harm, or a balance of rights and duties or obligations to others. The welfare category was the one used most frequently by children of all ages. However, as illustrated by Figure 4.1, fairness and obligation responses increased with age for familiar events. The earlier appearance of an understanding of harm and welfare also manifests itself in an increased use of the welfare category by older children in their reasoning about unfamiliar events.

The relationship between age and the justification categories associated with conventional events was not as clear-cut. The first six categories (and not welfare, fairness, or obligation) of Table 4.6 were associated with conventional issues. There were trends in the data indicating that the punishment categories decreased with age, whereas the prudential and personal-choice categories increased with age. Although this study did not provide adequate characterizations of changes in conventional reasoning categories, more extensive research on levels of development is discussed in Chapter 7. The Davidson et al. research does, however, point to both continuities (criterion judgments) and discontinuities (justification categories) in development.

Discontinuity or continuity in the domain distinction

The evidence suggests separateness in moral and conventional thinking for several aspects of both criterion judgments and justification categories. At the same

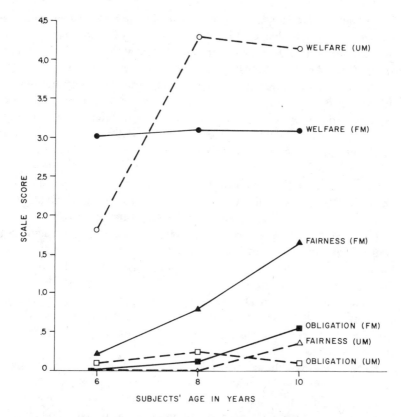

Figure 4.1. Age changes in type of justification given for familiar moral (FM) and unfamiliar moral (UM) issues. (From Davidson, Turiel, and Black, in press.)

time, however, there is evidence of an empirical correspondence between the quantitative dimension of attribution of importance and moral-conventional reasoning differences. Studies that assessed the attribution of importance to rules (Turiel, 1978b) or the seriousness of transgressions (Nucci, 1981; Smetana, 1980, 1981a) have found that, across ages, moral rules are rated as more important than conventional rules and moral transgressions are considered more serious than conventional transgressions.

The association that has been found to exist between attribution of importance and domain can be interpreted in two ways. One interpretation holds that moral categories are usually perceived to be more important than conventional categories. And, for the most part, subjects do regard moral transgressions as more serious than conventional transgressions. However, the perceived importance can also be influenced by other factors – the severity of consequences, the extent of deviance from established practice, or the degree of disruption of social organization. Importance, therefore, can vary within each of the domains; that is, one moral transgression may be perceived as more serious than another moral transgression, or one conventional transgression may be considered more serious than another. Underlying the continuous, quantitative dimension of importance are the discontinuous, qualitatively different conceptual categories.

An alternative interpretation may be that variations along the quantitative dimensions of importance or seriousness of transgressions produce the observations of differences in moral and conventional thinking. The distinctions in reasoning actually reflect the quantitatively derived continuum of importance. The implication of such an interpretation is that the research described earlier may have confounded the domain of event or transgression with quantitative variations, such as the severity of consequences or the deviance from established practice. That is, the results actually reflect the use of moral events that were more serious transgressions than the conventional transgressions.

These two hypotheses can be tested through an assessment of judgments about conventional transgressions that are rated as more serious or important than moral transgressions (C > M). The first hypothesis states that it is to be expected that the same reasoning distinctions found in the other studies (C differs from M) would apply to conventional and moral transgressions, when conventional transgressions are rated as more serious than the moral transgressions. The second hypothesis implies that reasoning varies in accordance with the seriousness of the transgression.

To test these hypotheses, the following four transgressions were used in research with first- and fifth-grade children: the theft of five dollars (M_1); the theft of an eraser (M_2); a boy wearing a dress to school (C_1); a child wearing pajamas to school (C_2). The two conventional transgressions (C_1 and C_2) were chosen because they are, in a quantitative sense, very deviant from expected (or actual) behavior and would likely produce much ridicule and disruption of social order in the school. By contrast, the act of stealing an eraser represents a moral transgression with minor consequences. The other moral transgression (stealing $5) was included so as to compare reasoning about two similar moral acts, where the magnitude of the consequences of the acts varied.

Children's attributions of relative importance to each of the four acts was not assumed to be based merely on the magnitudes of consequences, disruption, or deviance. Measures were obtained of subjects' ratings of each act, along with assessments of criterion judgments and justifications. The study included 24 subjects (12 boys and 12 girls), of which 12 were in the first grade (age range of 5 years, 4 months, to 7 years, 3 months) and 12 were in the fifth grade (ranging from 10 years, 9 months, to 11 years, 7 months). Importance ratings were obtained by asking subjects to rate each transgression on a 4-point scale (1 = Very important, 2 = Important, 3 = Only a little important, 4 = Not important at all). The use of the scale was explained to subjects and it was understood by them. They were then asked to rate each transgression according to how important it was to avoid the action (e.g., how important is it *not* to steal $5?).

In addition, the subjects were asked questions that assessed the criterion-judgment dimensions of authority and generalizability. To assess the dimension of authority, subjects were asked whether it would be all right to engage in the act if the governing rule were abolished by the principal of the school. ("Suppose the principal decided that there is no rule in the school against ———.") To assess the dimension of generalizability, subjects were asked whether it would be all right to engage in the act in a country where no rule prohibited it. Through probing of the subject's evaluation of the transgressions and his or her judgments on authority and generalizability, responses were obtained that were coded for use of justification categories (the coding system from the Davidson et al. study was used for the purposes of coding justification categories).

Consider first the results of the importance ratings. It turned out that attribution of importance is not solely or directly determined by the quantitative features of the magnitude of the transgression. Instead, attributions of importance are interactively influenced by the magnitude of the transgression, its domain, and the age of the subject. These interactions were evident in differences between the first- and fifth-grade subjects. It was found that 9 of the 12 first-grade children attributed greater importance to one of the conventional transgressions (for some subjects it was "wearing pajamas to school," and for others it was "a boy wearing a dress") than to the moral transgression of stealing an eraser. But only 1 of those 9 subjects attributed greater importance to a conventional transgression than to stealing $5 ($C_2 > M_1 > M_2 > C_1$). The other 8 subjects attributed equal or more importance to stealing $5 than to one of the conventional transgressions ($M_1 \geqq C_1$ or $C_2 > M_2$). The remaining 3 subjects attributed greater importance to both moral transgressions than to the conventional transgressions (M_1 and $M_2 > C_1$ and C_2). The average ratings for the group of first-graders were consistent with the patterns for individual subjects: stealing $5 = 1.08$; wearing pajamas to school $= 1.92$; stealing an eraser $= 2.17$; a boy wearing a dress $= 2.67$ ($M_1 > C_2 > M_2 > C_1$).

The first-graders, therefore, made importance ratings that in part corresponded to differences in magnitude of transgressions. A minor theft was generally not considered as important as one or the other of the conventional transgressions. By contrast, the importance attributions of the older subjects were primarily determined by the domain of the transgression. Nine of the 12 fifth-grade subjects attributed greater importance to each of the moral transgressions than to the conventional transgressions (M_1 and $M_2 > C_1$ and C_2). The remaining 3 subjects attributed as much or more importance to a conventional transgression as to stealing an eraser ($M_1 > C_1$ or $C_2 > M_2$). The average importance ratings of the fifth-grade group showed a linear progression from moral to conventional

Table 4.7. *Negation of rule by authority (percentage of subjects stating that it is all right or not all right to engage in the act)*

Age		Transgression			
		Stealing $5 ($M_1$)	Stealing an eraser (M_2)	Boy wearing dress (C_1)	Wearing pajamas to school (C2)
Grade 1	Yes	8	8	50	67
	No	92	92	50	33
Grade 5	Yes	0	0	64	55
	No	100	100	36	45

Note: Tests of statistical significance: No age differences for each transgression. No differences between the two transgressions within each domain (M_1 vs. M_2; C_1 vs. C_2) grades combined. Significant differences between domains (M_1 vs. C_1, M_1 vs. C_2, M_2 vs. C_1, M_2 vs. C_2) grades combined. McNemar tests each $p < .02$.

Table 4.8. *Generalizability: absence of rule in another country (percentage of subjects stating it is all right or not all right to engage in the act)*

Age		Transgression			
		Stealing $5 ($M_1$)	Stealing an eraser (M_2)	Boy wearing dress (C_1)	Wearing pajamas to school (C2)
Grade 1	Yes	17	17	82	67
	No	83	83	18	33
Grade 5	Yes	0	0	100	91
	No	100	100	0	9

Note: Test of statistical significance: No age differences for each transgression. No differences between the two transgressions within each domain (M_1 vs. M_2; C_1 vs. C_2) grades combined. Significant differences between domains (M_1 vs. C_1, M_1 vs. C_2, M_2 vs. C_1, M_2 vs. C_2) grades combined. McNemar tests each $p < .01$.

transgressions: stealing $5 = 1.00$; stealing an eraser $= 2.00$; a boy wearing a dress $= 2.92$; wearing pajamas to school $= 3.25$ ($M_1 > M_2 > C_1 > C_2$).

Before interpreting the differences between the importance ratings of the two age groups, it is necessary to consider the criterion judgment and justification category findings. Although the results with the fifth-grade subjects have a bearing on the hypotheses that the study was designed to explore, it is only the findings obtained with the first-graders that can be used as a direct test of the hypotheses. This is because only the first-grade subjects provided data on conventional transgressions that were attributed greater importance than moral transgressions. The findings on criterion judgments and justifications confirmed the hypothesis that the importance of the issue does not determine the domain characteristics of the reasoning. The relevant results are presented in Tables 4.7 (authority dimension) and 4.8 (generalizability dimension). As can be seen in these two tables, responses on authority and generalizability differed according to domain. Most subjects said that the minor theft of an eraser or the greater theft of $5 would be wrong in either circumstance (negation of rule by authority or absence of rule in another country). In response to the authority and generalizability questions, subjects most frequently used the *welfare* justification category for both moral transgressions. The welfare category also predominated in the subjects' evaluations of the acts (most subjects stated that the act was not all right).

The pattern of responses to the conventional transgressions differed from the pattern of responses to the moral transgressions. The majority of the first-graders stated that wearing pajamas to school would be all right if this rule were negated by authority or if permitted in another country that did not have the rule. In the case of a boy wearing a dress, the first-grade subjects were evenly split as to whether the act would be all right if the rule were negated by authority. However, the majority (82%) stated that the act would be all right in another country that did not have such a rule. Justifications in response to the authority, generalizability, and evaluation questions for each of the two conventional transgressions were coded in the *custom, authority,* and *punishment* categories (welfare was not used).

As shown in Tables 4.7 and 4.8, there were no differences in criterion judgments between the two moral transgressions ($M_1 = M_2$), despite their quantitative discrepancy and differences in the subjects' ratings of their importance. The criterion-judgment differences between the moral and conventional transgressions (M_1 and $M_2 \neq C_1$ and C_2) were statistically significant, despite the overlap (e.g., C_1 or $C_2 > M_2$) in ratings of importance. The tables also show that there were no differences between the two age groups in their criterion judgments, even though there were differences in the patterns of ratings of importance. The one notable age difference in justifications was that, with regard to the conventional transgressions, fifth-grade subjects used the *personal choice* category more frequently than the first-graders.

It is apparent from this study that types of social concepts are not determined by the quantitative dimensions that reflect importance. Importance can vary within a domain, so that forms of reasoning are the same across events with different levels of importance attributions. Importance attributions can be similar across domains, so that forms of reasoning differ between events with the same level of importance attributions. Possible domain and importance combinations may be characterized as follows:

(1) Within a domain:
    (a) Variations in importance ($M_1 > M_2$; $C_1 > C_2$);
        similar forms of reasoning ($M_1 = M_2$; $C_1 = C_2$)
    (b) Similarity in importance ($M_1 = M_3$; $C_1 = C_3$);
        similar forms of reasoning ($M_1 = M_3$; $C_1 = C_3$)

(2) Between domains:
    (a) Similarity in importance ($M_2 = C_3$);
        different forms of reasoning ($M_2 \neq C_3$)
    (b) Variation in importance ($M_1 > C_2$; $C_2 > M_2$);
        different forms of reasoning ($M_1 \neq C_2$; $C_2 \neq M_2$)

An interesting and unexpected finding was that the fifth-graders, unlike the first-graders, attributed greater importance to the stealing of an eraser than to the conventional transgressions. It is not likely that the wearing of dresses or pajamas to school by boys is considered to deviate less from the social norms of the fifth grade, nor that erasers have more value for fifth-graders than for first-graders. The most plausible interpretation of the importance attributions of the fifth-graders is that the combination of domain with magnitude determines the importance. This is not to say that older subjects will always attribute greater importance to moral than to conventional transgressions. It is likely that there are other conventional transgressions of even greater deviance from what is expected or more disruptive of social order than those mentioned in the study, which would be attributed greater importance by older subjects than would some moral transgressions. The findings show, however, that importance is a result of the interaction of the relative magnitude to the relative importance attributed to the domain. The findings also illustrate that between-domain comparisons of importance are not as straightforward as within-domain comparisons.

This study enables us to say with more confidence that distinct conceptual domains can be characterized in qualitatively different terms. As shown by the Davidson et al. study, continuities and discontinuities in the development of social concepts are evident in the differences between criterion judgments and justification categories. It has also been shown that continuities in magnitude of consequences and deviance from expectations do not account for domain discontinuities.

5 Rules and prohibitions

Within social systems the promulgation of rules and prohibitions, as well as their enforcement with sanctions, serve as primary means for the exertion of control on the behavior of individuals. Undoubtedly, most children become aware of the existence of rules at a fairly early age. Parents, in one way or another, generally impose prohibitions and communicate rules regarding behavior for both in and outside the home. As soon as he or she is attending school, the child is also made aware of a series of classroom and schoolwide rules and prohibitions. It is therefore important to consider the role of rules in social development, assuming that their existence and enforcement do represent significant and pervasive aspects of the child's social environment. There are three interrelated aspects to this issue. The first pertains to the means by which social development occurs: Can it be said that social development is characterized as a process of learning to follow specified rules and avoid prohibited behaviors? The second pertains to the psychological mechanisms controlling the individual's social behavior: Is a significant aspect of social behavior adequately characterized as the individual's adherence to (or violation of) rules? The third aspect pertains to the relation of rules to moral and conventional judgments: Can rule-following behavior be the basis for defining either morality or convention?

Psychological research on children's thinking about rules or on their behavior vis-à-vis rules has not been extensive. Nevertheless, differing theoretical approaches, with implicit views on the nature or definition of rules, are apparent in the existing psychological research. However, consideration of the nature of rules and laws has been extensive in philosophical analyses, and some of the positions explicitly maintained by philosophers are helpful for an understanding of the psychological research. In particular, the differing positions maintained by Austin (1832/1954), Hart (1961), and Dworkin (1978) more or less parallel the three major views implicit in the research of psychologists.

Austin and Hart, whose positions are generally referred to as a form of legal positivism, make a strict separation between the rules of legal systems and other types of social rules and principles, particularly those of morality. Both viewed

75

the legal system as a distinct social institution based on criteria different from those applied to morality. However, Austin and Hart differed with each other in regard to the criteria held to define law. Austin's position is characterized by the idea that habitual obedience by the people to the commands of those in power is the essence of law. He proposed a concept of law as a set of rules designed to govern social order; they amount to general commands backed by threat that are generally obeyed. Commands are rules when they are given by a person or persons who have the power to enforce their adherence. In every community there is what Austin referred to as a sovereign (which may be one person or a group of persons), whose commands are habitually obeyed by most members and who does not obey anyone else. As summarized by Hart (1977, p. 19), Austin's position was that "law is the command of the uncommanded commanders of society – the creation of the legally untrammeled will of the sovereign who is by definition outside the law."

The idea that the authority of law rests on the threat of sanctions available to those with power has been disputed by Hart. Hart maintained that a rule, unlike a command, establishes a standard of behavior based not on sanctions or power but on a general acceptance of a system of rules and a set of procedures for their enactment and enforcement. Therefore, a rule derives its validity, in part, from the group's acceptance that it is binding upon its members and that its violation may legitimately result in the application of sanctions. The validity of rules may also be derived from established and accepted procedures (such as a constitution) for the promulgation of rules. Accordingly, it was maintained by Hart that the validity of laws is based entirely on the ways in which they are enacted and on their general acceptance within a group. For this reason, he argued that the rules of a legal system are separate and independent from other social prescriptions, such as those of moral principles. In other words, a system of law is based on acceptance of the authority of existing procedures for adopting and enforcing them and not on anything else. As stated by Hart (1961, pp. 7–8), "Theories that make this close assimilation of law to morality seem, in the end, to confuse one kind of obligatory conduct with another, and to leave insufficient room for differences in kind between legal and moral rules and for divergence in their requirements." In sum, legal rights and duties exist only when there are rules providing for such rights and duties and those rules are determined by accepted practices.

Dworkin's objections to legal positivism apply to both the Austin and Hart formulations. Whereas positivism maintains that the validity of laws has its basis solely in those laws adopted by specific social institutions, Dworkin argued that the validity of laws is based on factors that go beyond the system of rules. This position was succinctly summarized by Dworkin (1978, p. 22):

When lawyers reason or dispute about legal rights and obligations, particularly in those hard cases when our problems with these concepts seem most acute, they make use of standards that do not function as rules, but operate differently as principles, policies, and other sorts of standards. Positivism, I shall argue, is a model of and for a system of rules, and its central notion of a single fundamental test for law forces us to miss the important roles of these standards that are not rules. . . . I call a "policy" that kind of standard that sets out a goal to be reached, generally an improvement in some economic, political, or social feature of the community. I call a "principle" a standard that is to be observed, not because it will advance or secure an economic, political, or social situation deemed desirable, but because it is a requirement of justice or fairness or some other dimension of morality.

According to Dworkin, standards and principles are different from rules, which are aimed at stipulating specific behaviors. Among other aims, legal systems have the moral aims of securing rights and ensuring justice. The promulgation and enforcement of laws does not solely involve the maintenance of behavior that is specified by rules. Within legal systems rules can also be informed by moral principles in various ways. Moral principles serve as support and justification for certain rules (rules may also be informed by other considerations, such as economic and political ones). In turn, the interpretation of rules is guided by moral principles. For Dworkin, the role of moral principles in rule interpretation is most clearly demonstrated by the often-found situation in which the application of rules is ambiguous. Ambiguous situations require interpretations on the part of those applying law (e.g., lawyers, judges) that are based on the use of moral principles (see Dworkin, 1978, pp. 31–45). Therefore, rules are closely associated to principles, which are binding. The validity of rules is not solely determined by the fact that they were enacted by a legitimate institution and have general acceptance, but by their underlying principles as well.

Psychological explanations of the individual's orientation to rules parallel the different positions on legal philosophy. On the one hand, there are motivational approaches focusing on rule-following behavior corresponding to the legal positivism of Austin and Hart. On the other hand, cognitive approaches to the development of rule concepts are closer to the view proposed by Dworkin. In the motivational approaches (which are only briefly mentioned here and are considered again in Chapter 8), it is maintained that to a large extent, social development entails the learning of adherence to rules and prohibitions. Rules are viewed as functional for both the individual and the social system. Rule conformity is functional for the individual in that it provides order by constraining the wide variety of behaviors that are part of one's potential repertoire. In turn, rules serve to bring order to the social system by providing uniformity for the potentially wide variation in the behavior of its members.

Two types of motivational explanations have been posited. One explanation concerns the way obedience to rules is learned and maintained (e.g., Aronfreed, 1968; Parke & Walters, 1967). It is proposed that rules are learned or internalized, like other aspects of social learning, through the acquisition of habits of behavior. The child internalizes rules and prohibitions as a result of the disciplinary actions (e.g., rewards and punishments) of socializing agents. This proposition, then, is the psychological counterpart of Austin's view that a rule is the command of the commanders. The commands of commanders, such as parents, become the child's own, insofar as the training procedures are successful. Rule-following behavior is tantamount to Austin's "habit of obedience."

A second motivational explanation assumes that individuals possess a disposition for the acceptance of social rules ("man as a rule-following animal") (e.g., Hogan, 1973; Hogan & Mills, 1976). In some cases, such a disposition is described as partly natural and partly acquired (in the sense that it is a reaction to great diversity in the social world). In other cases, it is proposed that there is a biologically based predisposition toward rule-following behavior. The assumption regarding the nature of rules in this second motivational approach is akin to Hart's version of legal positivism. A system of rules in a social institution is treated as an autonomous entity that, by virtue of the social functions it serves, is naturally accepted by individuals as binding. The primary motivation for an adherence to rules is that they exist with social institutional backing.

These motivational approaches are not considered in detail until Chapter 8. For now, suffice it to say that Dworkin's comments on legal positivism apply to these motivational approaches. From a psychological perspective, as well, it is necessary to consider the ways individuals conceptualize rules. Some researchers (Lockhart, Abrahams, & Osherson, 1977; Piaget, 1932; Tapp & Kohlberg, 1971), approaching the study of rules from the viewpoint of how they are conceptualized by children, have proposed that the development of an understanding of rules is characterized by a shift from the conception, held by young children, that rules are fixed and absolute, to the conception that rules are alterable by general agreement or mutual consent. In these studies, however, rules associated with different domains and contexts (e.g., games, language, morality, convention) were all classified in the same way. For example, Lockhart et al. (1977) grouped together a variety of social uniformities and rules as representative of social conventions. The uniformities considered as examples of social conventions were the meaning of words, game rules, laws of the state (i.e., the law concerning the side of the road on which cars are driven), rules of etiquette (i.e., table manners), and moral rules (i.e., theft). Similarly, in an earlier study Piaget (1932) attempted to generalize from children's concepts of game rules to their concepts of moral rules. In fact, game rules are frequently regarded as prototypical examples of social rules: They are presumed to provide an illuminating analogy with the moral rules found in nongame contexts. It is thought that, especially in research with children, the clarity and familiarity of game rules makes them a useful stimulus. Therefore, children's judgments about game rules are examined as a means of understanding their other forms of social judgment.

Using rules from different domains and contexts implies that the individual has a unitary concept of rules. However, the research findings discussed in the previous chapter suggest the alternative proposition: that all rules are not treated alike by children and adolescents. Evaluations and judgments of rules, as we have begun to see, vary with the domain of the rule. An important aspect of an individual's thinking about a given rule is the action to which the rule applies. Rules, in themselves, are elements of the social environment: They can be regarded as socially given facts. That is, rules are explicit statements about how to behave (e.g., brush your teeth twice a day; fasten your seat belts during takeoff and landing; do not take another person's property). A rule is stated within a social context (e.g., family, school, or nation), put into effect by a person (a mother, a king) or group of persons (a state legislature), and enforced, often with sanctions, upon its violation. Knowledge of the existence of a rule constitutes a form of factual knowledge about the social environment. Children, therefore, will come to know, in an *informational* sense, the specific rules that exist within the various social units in which they participate.

Knowledge about rules involves much more than just knowledge about their status as codified elements of the social environment. In considering rules, the individual goes beyond the fact of the rule, as something to be obeyed or violated, and interprets them. The concepts applied to a given rule will depend on the type of act to which the rule pertains. Consequently, we can distinguish between concepts of a domain and the legislated rules that pertain to that domain. The conceptual domains are not dependent upon the existence of a legislated rule. Moral judgments, for instance, are made and can be put into practice without necessarily calling upon legislated rules. Moral prescriptions alone may tell us not to kill people or to give food to the hungry, regardless of the legislated rules. However, legislated rules that are closely associated with moral prescriptions may indeed exist (e.g., one that prohibits killing). Concepts of social convention, which are based on the coordination of interactions within social organization, can be put into practice by a group in the absence of legislated rules. Such practices, however, can also have the status of legislated rules.

The inherent limitations of an analysis that focuses solely on the existence of rules can be illustrated by some examples of rules that may be part of one's social environment but that specify opposing actions. For instance, a person may simultaneously be a member of (a) a society that legally requires parents to have medical care administered to their children when it is needed to prevent physical damage or death, and (b) a religion that prohibits administration of any medical drugs, even when they are needed to prevent damage or death. How does one choose between these conflicting alternatives? The choice is not necessarily based on a preference for one institution over another (i.e., the law or one's religion). The same person may very well choose the laws of one institution in some circumstances but choose the laws of the other in different circumstances. Consider the possibility that (c) the society has a law prohibiting people from eating potatoes, and (d) the religion has a commandment requiring people to eat potatoes on Monday. Quite conceivably, many would say (1) that in the first set of examples (a and b) the law should be followed and the religious commandment should not exist, and (2) that in the second set of examples (c and d) the law should not exist and the religious commandment can be followed. In the first case, the conclusions would be based on judgments about the worth of saving a life, regardless of existing regulations; in the second case, the conclusions would be based on concepts regarding the role of regulations about certain (arbitrary) acts in religious systems.

The meaning and function attributed to a given rule will be determined by both its status as a rule and the conceptual domain of the act that is prohibited or prescribed. Although the primary concern here is with rules that apply to actions in the moral and social conventional domains, the analyses can be clarified by also considering how they contrast with rules in games and rules pertaining to prudential considerations. First, consider game rules. The analogy that has been made between game rules and the rules in other contexts, particularly moral rules, has significant limitations. Game rules constitute a special case, whose features are fundamentally different from those of rules pertaining to moral issues. Normally, games are activities, voluntarily engaged in for purposes of amusement, that have a specified conclusion (in competitive games it is to determine a winner). The rules are particularistic – they apply to the specific game – and form an essential ingredient of the definition of the game itself. Unlike moral rules, the purpose of game rules is not to ensure that people will behave in certain desirable ways. Rather, their purpose is to delimit the actions of the participants, so that behaviors are consistent with the definition of the particular game. A modification of the set of rules of a game changes the definition of the game.

Unlike game rules, and like rules in the moral and conventional domains, prudential rules (e.g., sharp objects should be handled carefully; brush your teeth twice a day) are not definitional. Unlike moral and conventional rules, however, the basic justification and ultimate source of authority for prudential rules is *self-interest*. Prudential rules can be social in certain respects. For instance, parents may attempt to teach children to adhere to a prudential rule and admonish them for violations. Prudential rules may even take the form of legal statutes, such as one requiring that an automobile seat belt be fastened. Nevertheless, the primary reason for adhering to a prudential rule is to avoid illness or pain. The violation of such rules results in immediate consequences: A child who does not handle a sharp knife carefully may cut himself. For these reasons it could not be logically maintained that prudential rules are alterable by social consensus. The validity of a prudential rule is not changed if a group of people have agreed to a different rule. Insofar as changes do occur in prudential rules, they are based on changed estimations of the degree of harmful consequences of a practice (e.g., if it were determined that the use of seat belts results in more injuries).

Rules in the moral and conventional domains are primarily social and their basic justification is not that of self-interest. Moral and conventional rules, by virtue of having the status of rules, share the characteristics of being in effect and having sanctions imposed upon their violation. There are also similarities in the modes of evaluating the two types of rules in that both are judged by standards of legality and illegality. However, if the validity of a moral rule is related to the act to which it pertains, then its authority would be derived from concepts of fairness and justice. Given that conventional rules pertain to arbitrary acts, their validity would be in the existence of the system of rules. Therefore, the authority of conventional rules can reside in persons in authority, consensus, or the system in which the rule is embedded.

Research on concepts of social rules

Two studies, using formats similar to the research discussed in Chapter 4, have focused explicitly and directly on children's conceptions of rules (as stated in social contexts). In the first investigation, an attempt was made to obtain information regarding children's conceptions of a general sampling of rules, including those in the contexts of games, family, school, and the legal system. The second investigation (Dodsworth-Rugani, 1982) was aimed at children's understandings of rules in the social-institutional context of the school.

Because the first study has not been previously reported, the methods and results are presented in some detail. A total of 88 subjects (45 males and 43 females) participated. For purposes of analysis, these subjects were divided into the following six age groupings: 6- to 7-year-olds (15 subjects), 8- to 9-year-olds (14 subjects), 10- to 11-year-olds (13 subjects), 12- to 13-year-olds (18 subjects), 14- to 15-year-olds (14 subjects) and 16- to 17-year-olds (14 subjects). Each subject was individually interviewed with a series of questions about rules, which are summarized in Table 5.1. The listing of questions in Table 5.1 does not represent the order in which questions were posed; rather, it reflects a grouping based on the six question topics.

The interview included a few general questions, such as the definition of a rule (What is a rule?; see no. 1 of table 5.1) and adherence to rules (Should rules

Table 5.1. *List of questions posed regarding rules*

1. Definitional: general (What is a rule?)
2. Existence of rules
   2.1. Games (Do people in other countries play with the same rules?)
   2.2. Home (Do all families have those rules?)
   2.3. School (Do all schools have those rules?)
3. Origin of rules (How was the rule _____ made?)
   3.1. Games
   3.2. Moral (Stealing)
   3.3. Moral Home
   3.4. Conventional Home
4. Adherence/nonadherence to rules
   4.1. General-unspecified (Should rules always be followed?)
   4.2. Specific rules (Should the rule _____ be followed?)
       4.2.1. Games
       4.2.2. Moral (Stealing)
       4.2.3. Moral Home
       4.2.4. Moral School
       4.2.5. Conventional Home
       4.2.6. Conventional School
5. Alterability of rules (Can the rule _____ be changed?)
   5.1. Games
   5.2. Moral (Stealing)
   5.3. Moral Home
   5.4. Conventional Home
6. Relativity of rules (Evaluation of differences)
   6.1. Games (Suppose everybody in another country decided to play by different rules?)
   6.2. Moral (Stealing)
       6.2.1. Nonexistence of rule (Suppose that all the people in another country decided that in their country it is all right to steal. So they had no rules or laws about it. Would it be all right not to have a rule about it?)
       6.2.2. Act in context of 6.2.1 (Would it be all right to steal in that case?)
   6.3. Moral (Home)
       6.3.1. Families within country (Suppose there is a family down the block that does not have the rule. Would that be all right?)
       6.3.2. Families in another country (Suppose there is another country in which no families have that rule. Would that be all right?)
   6.4 Conventional (Home)
       6.4.1. Families within country (Suppose there is a family down the block that does not have the rule. Would that be all right?)
       6.4.2. Families in another country (Suppose there is another country in which no families have that rule. Would that be all right?)

always be followed?; see no. 4.1 of Table 5.1). Most questions, however, dealt with specific examples of rules. In most cases, subjects were questioned about rules that had been generated in the interview; thus subjects had prior familiarity with the rules. The procedure was to ask subjects to name rules in *games*, in the *home*, and in *school* with which they were familiar. Rules generated in this way were chosen as the basis for the interview. In the case of the home and school contexts, subjects were questioned about rules corresponding to the moral domain and rules corresponding to the conventional domain. Furthermore, all subjects were questioned about rules pertaining to stealing. Although the stealing rule was not generated by the subjects, it could be confidently assumed that they all would be familiar with it. Some questions were designed to tap the subject's informational knowledge of the rules: Subjects were asked about the extent to which the same rules are in effect across groups (No. 2 of table 5.1) and about the origins of rules (No. 3). The remainder of the interview questions were designed to elicit three types of evaluations of the rules: whether or not the rule should be adhered to (No. 4); the alterability of the rule (No. 5); and the relativity of the rule (No. 6). Responses were scored with a standard and reliable coding system. The agreement between two coders for each question type listed in Table 5.1 ranged from 73% to 98%.

Before considering the quantitative results of the study, the presentation of a few interview excerpts may provide a clearer idea of the nature of the inquiry as well as some examples of how the children responded. The first excerpts come from questions pertaining to game rules.

Charles (6 years, 10 months): (CAN YOU TELL ME A GAME THAT YOU PLAY THAT YOU KNOW THE RULES OF?) I don't know football very well, but I like football. (DO YOU KNOW ANY OF THE RULES IN FOOTBALL?) I know some of them. (CAN YOU TELL ME ONE?) Sometimes you're supposed to tackle somebody and you're supposed to run right over them and go get the ball. You have to tackle them and stop them and sometimes you go around them if you can't run over them. (DO THE RULES OF FOOTBALL HAVE TO BE FOLLOWED?) No, not really but if you want to play it right they should be. (LET'S SAY THAT ONE PERSON WANTS TO PLAY FOOTBALL DIFFERENTLY THAN EVERYBODY ELSE. SHOULD HE BE ABLE TO?) Yes, if he wants to make up a game with the same name but he can't make up the same game. So it just doesn't work out. And if most people want to play it their own way then they have to play it the way most people want to. (IF YOU AND YOUR FRIENDS DECIDED TO MAKE UP NEW RULES FOR FOOTBALL, WOULD THAT BE ALL RIGHT?) Well, it wouldn't be the same game. You'd have to make up sort of a different game so people would know which game you were playing. (COULD YOU DO THAT IF YOU WANTED TO?) Yes. (IF EVERYBODY IN ANOTHER COUNTRY DECIDED TO PLAY FOOTBALL BY DIFFERENT RULES THAN WE DO HERE, WOULD THAT BE ALL RIGHT?) Yes. Our way here is the way we have here and if they want to have a different way they could make it their way. So they could have it the way that they want. And we can have our way and the way that we want it.

Jim (7 years, 1 month): (CAN YOU TELL ME A GAME THAT YOU PLAY THAT YOU KNOW THE RULES OF?) Buckle-Buckle Beanstalk. (CAN YOU TELL ME HOW TO PLAY IT? TELL ME A COUPLE OF THE RULES?) Hide a little seed, and then you open the doors, and then some people try to find it. And when they find it they have to say "Buckle-Buckle Beanstalk." (LET'S SAY THAT YOU AND YOUR FRIENDS DECIDED TO PLAY BUCKLE-BUCKLE BEANSTALK IN A DIFFERENT WAY? AND YOU CHANGED THE RULES AND YOU MADE UP DIFFERENT ONES: WOULD THAT BE ALL RIGHT IF YOU AND YOUR FRIENDS WANTED TO DO THAT?) No. (THAT WOULDN'T BE? WHY NOT?) Because other people if they invited us over to their house and they wanted to play Buckle-Buckle Beanstalk, and then we played it the way we wanted to, then you just get all confused. (DO YOU THINK PEOPLE IN OTHER COUNTRIES PLAY THE GAME BUCKLE-BUCKLE BEANSTALK WITH THE RULES AS WE DO HERE?) No. (YOU DON'T? WHY DON'T YOU THINK SO?) Because they can make other rules. (OH, THEY CAN MAKE OTHER RULES IN OTHER COUNTRIES? IS THAT OKAY FOR THEM TO DO?) Yah. (WHAT MAKES THAT OKAY IF EVERYBODY IN ANOTHER COUNTRY WANTS TO DO IT? BUT IT'S NOT OKAY IF JUST YOUR FRIENDS WANT TO DO IT?) Because everyone in one country would be all right because everyone wants to change it in that country. But just my friends...just because I've got my friends, that doesn't mean you can change it. Only if a whole bunch in the country, if they wanted to do it in this country.

Thomas (8 years, 7 months): (CAN YOU TELL ME ONE GAME YOU PLAY THAT YOU KNOW THE RULES OF?) Baseball, that's my favorite sport. (GIVE ME AN EXAMPLE OF A RULE.) If someone hits the ball and you catch it they are out, but if you drop the ball when you catch it they are safe. (DO YOU KNOW HOW THE RULES OF BASEBALL WERE MADE?) I don't know because I wasn't born when baseball started. (SAY YOU AND YOUR FRIENDS AGREED TO CHANGE THE RULE, WOULD THAT BE ALL RIGHT FOR YOU AND YOUR FRIENDS TO DO?) Yes if we wanted to play a baseball game we would make up our own way. Yes we could do that. (SAY EVERYONE IN ANOTHER COUNTRY DECIDED TO PLAY BASEBALL WITH DIFFERENT RULES, WOULD THAT BE ALL RIGHT?) Yes if they wanted to play their own way they could play their own way. If they wanted to play baseball they could make their own way up and they can make their own game up. It's the same thing, only they have different rules and they call it baseball. (WHAT THEY CALL IT DOESN'T MAKE ANY DIFFERENCE? DO YOU MEAN THEY COULD CALL IT FOOTBALL IF THEY WANTED?) Yes, they could call it football, like baseball is a name for baseball, like if there wasn't the word baseball we could play baseball and what would you call it, you wouldn't call it anything you would just say come on let's go play.

Richard (16 years, 10 months): (DO YOU KNOW HOW THOSE RULES WERE MADE?) O wow...I really don't. I don't know enough about baseball history to know exactly how they were developed. (DO YOU THINK ADULTS OR CHILDREN MADE UP THESE RULES?) O yah, it was definitely adults. I don't know, I think somebody just picked up a bat and somebody picked up a ball and started messing around and then he tried to figure out a confining area that wasn't too confining but was decent enough to play in these little areas and I think they used to play just to have people, you know the pitcher if they're going to have a pitcher and a batter, have the pitcher come close and not just make him go after bad pitches all the time. And I think that's how they set up foul aw – you know three strikes. (DO THE RULES OF BASEBALL HAVE TO BE FOLLOWED?) They should be followed, to play the game right. (IF YOU FOLLOW THEM, WHY DOES THAT MAKE THE GAME RIGHT?) Well, if you follow the rules, you're playing the game right by the way of inventors of the game. The way they thought it should be played right. (WHAT IF ONE PERSON WANTS TO PLAY BASE-BALL DIFFERENTLY?) I think his idea should be heard. If he's got a good idea and they tested it out and it works for him and it works for everybody else, and no really stiff complaints about it. I think sure. Like Charles Finley with those orange baseballs, I didn't think they were really that good, but his idea came out and let him experiment with it and let everybody see about it. (SUPPOSE EVERYBODY IN ANOTHER COUNTRY DECIDED TO PLAY BY DIFFERENT RULES?) It would be interesting, it really would. Because that's like Cana-dian football compared to National. American football, it's the same game but it's just totally different. And, I don't know. I don't like all the rules. I mean some of them are pretty weird. (DO YOU THINK IT'S ALL RIGHT?) Yes. Sure, I mean if everybody is going to agree to play under those rules, why not?

Those excerpts indicate that children and adolescents regard rules in games as particular to their narrow context, as serving to fundamentally define the game, and therefore as legitimately determined by agreement. It was also stated that game rules could be legitimately changed by agreement and that such changes would merely serve to alter the nature or definition of the game.

These interviews can be contrasted with the following responses to questions regarding moral and conventional rules, which differed from each other.

John (6 years): People don't like it if you steal. It's their things, they need them. (SHOULD THAT LAW BE FOLLOWED?) Yes, because if somebody steals a dress and they need it for a party they can't go. (COULD THAT LAW BE CHANGED?) If the government wants to. (COULD THE GOVERNMENT CHANGE IT SO THERE WASN'T A LAW?) People should always follow the law; they should make a bell and it goes off. (SUPPOSE ALL THE PEOPLE IN ANOTHER COUNTRY DECIDED THAT, IN THEIR COUNTRY, IT IS ALL RIGHT TO STEAL. SO THEY HAD NO LAWS ABOUT IT: WOULD THAT BE ALL RIGHT?) If they want to, but if the people there don't like it they can move to another country. (DO YOU THINK IT WOULD BE RIGHT NOT TO HAVE A LAW AGAINST STEALING?) There should be a law. (WHY?) People wouldn't like that and call the police. (SAY THERE WASN'T A LAW, WOULD IT BE ALL RIGHT TO STEAL?) No, people should think not to steal. . . . (WHAT ARE SOME RULES AT SCHOOL?) No running because you can slip, no hitting with balls, no scaring people. (DO YOU HAVE ANY RULES IN CLASS?) No running in class, got to raise your hand. (HOW ARE THOSE RULES MADE?) The office people. (CAN THE RULES BE CHANGED?) If the office people want. (HOW ABOUT NOT THROWING THE BALL AT PEOPLE, COULD THAT BE CHANGED?) If it was I wouldn't like it. (WHY?) Because I don't want to get hurt. (HOW ABOUT RAISING YOUR HAND, COULD THAT BE CHANGED?) It should because the teacher's name is the same thing.

Jim (7 years, 1 month): (NOW, DO YOU KNOW HOW THE LAW AGAINST STEALING WAS MADE?) Like something. . . like when the. . . the time when people kinda started to take things. (DID THOSE LAWS AGAINST STEALING COME BY THEMSELVES?) No, some people made them up. (DO YOU THINK THOSE PEOPLE WERE ADULTS OR CHILDREN?) Adults and children. Because the children wouldn't like their toys being stolen and the adults, they wouldn't like their silverware stolen. (NOW, DOES A LAW AGAINST STEALING HAVE TO BE FOLLOWED?) If people don't want to follow it, they don't have to, but they should. (WHY SHOULD THEY?) Because it's a good law. Because people wouldn't want their things stealed all the time. (WHAT HAPPENS TO PEOPLE WHEN THEY HAVE THINGS STOLEN FROM THEM?) Sometimes, the people that stole them, they get in jail. (COULD THE LAW AGAINST STEALING BE CHANGED?) Nope. (WHY NOT?) Because that is a real good rule. (LET'S SAY THAT ALL THE PEOPLE IN ANOTHER COUNTRY DECIDED THAT IN THEIR COUNTRY IT'S ALL RIGHT TO STEAL. SO THEY DIDN'T HAVE ANY RULES OR LAWS ABOUT IT: DO YOU THINK THAT WOULD BE ALL RIGHT? DO YOU THINK IT WOULD BE RIGHT NOT TO HAVE A LAW AGAINST STEALING?) No. (WHY NOT?) Because some people wouldn't like to have things stolen. (IF THERE WASN'T A LAW AGAINST STEALING, DO YOU THINK IT WOULD BE ALL RIGHT TO STEAL?) No. (AND WHY NOT?) Because it's a real good rule to obey. (WHY SHOULD YOU OBEY THAT? IF THERE WASN'T A LAW AGAINST STEALING, AND LET'S SAY YOU WENT AND STOLE SOMETHING, YOU WOULDN'T BE THROWN IN JAIL OR ANYTHING WOULD YOU? SO, WHY SHOULD YOU FOLLOW THE LAW AGAINST STEALING?) Because it wouldn't be right. Because, maybe people didn't want their things stolen.

Thomas (8 years, 7 months): (ARE THERE ANY RULES AT HOME?) If there are guests you treat them like guests and they spend the night then they get to pick out the book that we are going to read. (YOU TREAT THEM LIKE GUESTS?) Yes sometimes. Like when my friend was over and he spent the night we slept outside and I asked him if he wanted to go down to the creek and if he didn't want to I'd go where he goes. One time my friend I didn't know he was being invited over. . .he came and I didn't know it. . .and he left messes and my mom says I was responsible and I didn't invite him so I didn't feel responsible for it. (IS IT A RULE IN YOUR HOUSE THAT YOU SHOULD BE RESPONSIBLE FOR YOUR GUESTS?) Yes, if I invite them and they make a mess and they don't clean it up and they leave and they don't do it then I have to do it. That's one rule that I don't like. (ARE THERE ANY RULES ABOUT FIGHTING WITH YOUR FRIENDS IN THE HOUSE?) I don't like to hurt people, I never kick people real hard. You can't fight in the house or at school. (SHOULD THE RULE ABOUT BEING RESPONSIBLE FOR YOUR GUESTS IF YOU INVITE THEM BE FOLLOWED?) Yes, if I invite them then I'm responsible for inviting them. If I invite them then they are my guests so my mom says I'm responsible. (WHY IS THERE THE RULE ABOUT NOT FIGHTING AT HOME?) Well I bet I know why. I don't want to get hurt and I don't want to hurt anybody. That never happens hardly; sometimes we get mad at each other. (CAN THE RULE ABOUT BEING RESPONSIBLE FOR YOUR GUESTS BE CHANGED?) My parents could change the rules. (COULD YOU?) No, because they won't let me; like if I changed the rule that I could leave my room that way they wouldn't let me. (HOW ABOUT THE RULE ABOUT FIGHTING, COULD THAT RULE BE CHANGED?) Yes, it can be, but I don't want it to change. I don't think they'd change it. (DO ALL FAMILIES HAVE THE SAME RULES?) No, not all families. (HOW DO YOU KNOW?) Because I've been at other families' places and when I went to other houses, like at Christopher's house, he has to feed his pets and I don't have that rule. But there are other rules in different families. All families can't be just exactly the same. (SHOULD THEY?) No, different families can have their own rules, that's what I think. (SAY A FAMILY DOWN THE STREET DOESN'T HAVE THE RULE ABOUT NOT FIGHTING SO AT HOME THAT FAMILY CAN FIGHT. IS THAT ALL RIGHT?) I don't want to have a fight in my house, but I don't know any other families that let their kids fight. (WOULD IT BE ALL RIGHT WITH YOU IF THE CHILDREN IN THAT HOUSE FIGHT?) I don't think anybody wants that rule. . .(DO YOU KNOW HOW THE LAW AGAINST STEALING WAS MADE?) Yes. This is one way I think it was made. People steal, other people probably didn't want them to because that's taking away their things. Like if they had money and the robbers took it all they wouldn't have money to buy stuff. (CAN THE LAW AGAINST STEALING BE CHANGED?) Yes it could because it's not impossible. (COULD YOU CHANGE IT SO THAT THERE WAS NOT A LAW AT ALL AGAINST STEALING?) No, because then people would just go crazy and everybody would be stealing. People will have all their things taken away and then they want their things back and they try to steal it probably. (SUPPOSE IN ANOTHER COUNTRY ALL THE PEOPLE THERE DECIDED THAT IT WAS ALL RIGHT TO STEAL?) That's all right because I don't live in that country. (WOULD IT BE ALL RIGHT NOT TO HAVE A LAW AGAINST STEALING?) I think that there should be a law but people who are poor and they want to steal they shouldn't be able to steal. But they should be able to have some money. (WOULD IT BE ALL RIGHT TO STEAL EVEN IF THERE WASN'T A LAW?) I don't want to steal. (WHY? NOBODY WOULD THROW YOU IN JAIL.) Because I would be taking away from some other people and I don't think it's fair; people that don't have anything should be able to have something but they shouldn't get it by stealing.

Ellen (13 years, 7 months): (DO YOU HAVE ANY RULES ABOUT FIGHTING WITH YOUR BROTHERS AND SISTERS?) I shouldn't hit my brother. (SHOULD THE RULE ABOUT NOT HITTING YOUR BROTHER BE FOLLOWED?) Yes, because it's not really right to hit my brother. He's younger than me, so he couldn't really hurt me, but I can hurt him. (SHOULD THE RULE ABOUT NOT TAKING CALLS AFTER NINE O'CLOCK BE FOLLOWED?) I don't like that. (WHY NOT?) Because I'm not the only one that uses the phone. So maybe I only get to talk once and then it is already nine o'clock. (HOW WAS THAT RULE MADE?) Because I was on the phone too much.

(WHY WAS THE NOT HITTING RULE MADE UP?) Well my mom didn't like us hitting each other too much. We could fight and not hit each other; she doesn't want me to hurt him because he's smaller than me. (IS ONE RULE MORE IMPORTANT?) Fighting with my brother. (WHY?) My brother is more important than the phone. (CCULD THE RULE ABOUT NOT HITTING YOUR BROTHER BE CHANGED?) Probably could if I told my mom that it was necessary if I hit him, but I don't think she would believe me, I don't think that one could be changed. (HOW ABOUT THE ONE ABOUT TALKING AFTER NINE, COULD THAT BE CHANGED?) Yes, I'd have to ask my mother, I could change it if I talked her into it, but I can't think of a reason why I should change it, but I could. (BUT YOU COULDN'T TALK HER INTO NOT HAVING THE NO HITTING RULE?) No, I don't think so. (DO ALL FAMILIES HAVE THE SAME RULES?) No. (SHOULD THEY?) No, it just depends on the family and what they do, I don't think it would be right to have the same rules, it would be weird. (SAY THERE IS A FAMILY THAT DOESN'T HAVE A NO FIGHTING RULE. IS THAT OKAY?) No, I don't think that it would be right. I think it would be the parents that were making a mistake by not telling them to do it. (SAY THAT SOME FAMILY DOESN'T HAVE A RULE ABOUT TAKING CALLS AFTER NINE: IS THAT OKAY?) Yes, because their mom might not even care. (SAY THERE IS ANOTHER COUNTRY AND NO FAMI-LIES HAVE THE RULE ABOUT NOT TALKING ON THE PHONE AFTER NINE, WOULD THAT BE OKAY?) Yes, I think it would be all right. (WHAT IF IN THAT COUNTRY NO FAMILIES HAD THE RULE ABOUT HITTING, WOULD THAT BE OKAY?) No. I don't think it's right to hit each other. It wouldn't be right. . . . (COULD THE LAW ABOUT STEALING BE CHANGED?) No, I don't think so. (WHY NOT?) Because if everyone was stealing, if it wasn't a law, then people would just be getting what they want instead of having to work for it and it wouldn't be fair to other people who wouldn't do it. They wouldn't work for what they want, they would just take it and I don't think that would be right. People would be taking things from anybody and like if they took something from me I wouldn't take from them. I wouldn't think it was right, but I wouldn't be able to do anything about it if it wasn't a law. (SAY ALL THE PEOPLE IN ANOTHER COUNTRY DECIDED THAT, IN THEIR COUNTRY, IT IS ALL RIGHT TO STEAL: SO THEY HAD NO LAW ABOUT IT: WOULD THAT BE ALL RIGHT?) No. If they did it, it would be their problem. They should know whether it is right or not. If they did change it then they would just have to face what they changed. (WOULD IT BE ALL RIGHT TO STEAL IF THERE WASN'T A LAW?) No. (WHY NOT IF NOBODY IS GOING TO THROW YOU IN JAIL?) I just think it wouldn't be right because nobody would want their stuff taken and if you had something you really liked a lot and they said that's mine and they took it nothing would really be yours.

Richard (16 years, 10 months); (DO YOU HAVE ANY RULES AT HOME?) Yes, you can't put your feet on the dinner table when there's company there or even when there isn't company there. Just general ethics. . . . (SUPPOSE THERE IS ANOTHER COUNTRY IN WHICH NO FAMILIES HAVE A RULE ABOUT STEALING. IS THAT ALL RIGHT?) I really wouldn't go for it. I think I would move. (WHY'S THAT?) Because, why buy something that somebody is going to rip off? Let everybody else buy it. Let them buy it and we'll rip it back. It doesn't make sense. (WHAT IF NOBODY HAD THE RULE ABOUT PUTTING YOUR FEET UP ON THE TABLE? WOULD THAT BE ALL RIGHT?) It might be. It's no big deal. I mean if everybody had it, that would be acceptable.

1. *Definitional and informational knowledge.* Asking subjects to define a rule through a general question like "What is a rule?" is not likely, in itself, to provide rich information if rule conceptions are related to knowledge of domains and contexts. Indeed, three general types of responses were provided to the defini-tional question. Most subjects in each age group defined rules in a straightfor-

ward way, stating that *rules dictate behavior and are to be followed or obeyed*. There were (statistically significant; $p < .02$) age trends of a not unexpected nature. More of the younger (6- to 9-year-olds) than of the older subjects defined rules solely by means of *concrete examples*. In turn, more of the older (10- to 17-year-olds) than of the younger subjects defined rules with reference to their *underlying functions* (e.g., to ensure well-being, rights, reciprocity).

Informational knowledge was tapped by questions on the existence of rules across social groups and on the origins of rules. The majority of subjects assumed that rule differences exist within each of the contexts of games, families, and schools (significant at $p < .001$). With regard to games, 54% stated that rules differ in other countries, 29% stated that they are the same, and 18% did not know. Similarly, a majority stated that all families (68%) and schools (76%) do not have the same rules. Although not statistically significant, interesting age trends were obtained. The often-made assumption that young children are more likely than older children to have a stronger belief in rule uniformity was not confirmed by this study. It was the youngest subjects who most frequently stated that rules differ from one group to another. For example, 86% of the 6- to 7-year-olds stated that people in other countries do not have the same rules in their games, whereas only 25% of the 16- to 17-year-olds stated that game-rule differences exist (58% of them assumed that people in other countries have the same game rules). Similar age trends were apparent in assumptions about cross-group similarities and differences in family and school rules. It may be that children begin with what is perhaps an intuitive assumption that rules do differ from group to group. With age, there may be an increasingly stronger assumption that rules are, in reality, similar from group to group. However, the validity of, and reasons for, this age trend cannot be ascertained from the study.

Table 5.2 presents the explanations given by subjects for the origins of rules. It can be seen that the patterns of response differed according to rule type. First, note that two types of responses were used infrequently: Very few subjects attributed the origins of these rules to religious sources, and very few believed that there was no concrete source to rules or that the rules have always existed. Furthermore, no age differences were found in explanations of rule origins. Rules in the home were viewed generally as having been made or introduced by specific persons – usually parents, but sometimes children. Subjects varied to a greater extent in their explanations of the origins of the rule pertaining to stealing. Some (32%) stated that the rule was not made by specific persons, but by people in general and that it may have developed over time. An example of this type of response can be found in the excerpt presented earlier from the interview with Thomas, an 8-year-old ("This is one way I think it was made. People steal, other people probably didn't want them to because that's taking away their things"). Fewer subjects attributed the sources of this rule to persons in a gov-

Table 5.2. *Origin of rules (in percentages)*

	Rule Type			
Response categories	Games	Stealing	Moral home	Conventional home
1. Unknown	19	26	—	2
2. No concrete source: always existed	1	1	9	—
3. Religious source	—	6	3	2
4. Generalized person source: originated by "people" or developed over time	45	32	2	2
5. Specific person or persons				
a. In governmental capacity	—	15	—	—
b. Nongovernmental source: parents, children	33	12	70	81
6. Decision-making process: legislative, community, family	1	18	16	12

Note: Response category differences are as follows. Games: $\chi^2 = 63.19$, $p < .001$. Stealing: $\chi^2 = 14.31$, $p < .01$. Moral home: $\chi^2 = 58.87$, $p < .001$. Conventional home: $\chi^2 = 111.66$, $p < .001$.

ernment capacity (15%) or thought that it came about through a decision-making process (18%). It was mainly the older subjects (12- to 17-year-olds) who located the source of the stealing rule in the decision-making process. A substantial number (25%) maintained that they were unaware of how the stealing rule originated.

An unawareness of the origins of game rules was also maintained by a number of subjects. As expressed by two of the subjects whose interviews were excerpted, the lack of knowledge of rule origins reflects an awareness of historical sources. Thomas (8 years) said he did not know how the rules of baseball were made because he "wasn't born when baseball started." Richard (16 years) put it a little differently: "I don't know enough about baseball history to know exactly how they were developed." Most subjects, however, were willing to attribute game-rule origins to either a general development over time or to specific persons, such as parents or children.

2. *Evaluative judgments.* The main analyses of questions on adherence, alterability, and relativity of rules were on subjects' positive or negative evaluations (i.e., the rule is or is not alterable, it is or is not legitimate for the rule to vary). All tests of statistical significance were performed on these positive-negative evaluation data. Justifications in support of evaluations that could be coded for reasoning categories are presented descriptively and for exploratory purposes only. Because the total number of justification categories elicited by a given question was usually large, relative to the number of subjects in an age group, tests of statistical significance were not done on those data.

Table 5.3. *Alterability of rules: all age groups combined (in percentages)*

	Rule type			
			Moral	Coventional
Response	Games	Stealing	home	home
Yes (rule can be changed)	86*	21	32	73**
No (rule cannot be changed)	14	79*	68***	27

Note: No statistically significant age differences were found.
  *Sign test, $p < .0001$.
  **Sign test, $p < .001$.
***Sign test, $p < .01$.

Asking whether a *particular* rule should be followed does not discriminate between rule types or age of subjects. The majority of subjects at all ages, when the question was put in this form, maintained that the rule should be followed. However, fewer subjects (though still a majority) responded affirmatively when a rule was not specified and the question was put in a general form (i.e., should rules always be followed?). In this regard, there was a difference between the younger (6- to 11-year-old) and older (12- to 17-year-old) subjects. The older subjects, unlike the younger ones, could imagine possible, though unspecified, situations in which rule violations might be legitimate. Rule violations would be legitimate, according to these subjects, if the rule were bad, if its adherence could result in greater harm than its violation, if the rule were inconsistent with personal principles, or if self-interest sometimes demanded it.

These reasons were rarely applied to the specific rules discussed, because nearly all subjects stated that they should be followed. Nevertheless, the difference in the categories used to justify adherence to game rules and moral rules are informative. The most frequent reason given for following game rules was that they serve to define the game and that violations would alter the definitional parameters. This reason was used only for game rules. The most frequently used reasons for adherence to a moral rule (stealing, home, school) were that it serves to benefit others or contributes to the general welfare (the welfare category discussed in the previous chapter), and that it serves interests of fairness. Categories pertaining to authority (used mainly by the younger subjects) and social disapproval (used mainly by the older subjects) were generally associated with conventional home rules.

Responses to the alterability and relativity questions showed that the bases for beliefs in the necessity for adherence to rules differ according to rule type. Subjects were questioned about the alterability of game rules, the rule about stealing, moral home rules, and conventional home rules. The findings were clear-cut, as is shown in Table 5.3. A large majority of subjects stated that game

Table 5.4. *Relativity of rules: all age groups combined (in percentages)*

Response	Games	Stealing rule	Stealing act	Moral home, within country	Moral home, other country	Conventional home, within country	Conventional home, other country
Yes	90*	24	19	48	49	65**	76*
No	10	76*	81*	52	51	35	24

Note: No statistically significant age differences were found.
  *Sign test, $p < .001$.
  **Sign test, $p < .01$.

and conventional rules could be changed, and a similar majority said that the stealing and moral home rules could not be changed. Moreover, there were no age differences in judgments of the alterability or nonalterability of each of these rules.

Judgments about the relativity of rules were generally consistent with responses on alterability. An exception is the judgments made about home rules, which appear to reflect considerations of the intersection of social context and domain. The findings are presented in Table 5.4. (Note that for home rules one relativity question dealt with other families within the country and a second question with families in another country.) As expected, the majority of subjects stated that game rules and conventional home rules could legitimately vary from country to country and that conventional home rules could vary from family to family within the country. By contrast, the majority of subjects took a nonrelativistic view of the rule pertaining to stealing, which corresponds to their judgments about the act of stealing. They stated both that the absence of a rule prohibiting stealing would be wrong and that it would be wrong to steal even if the rule did not exist.

Judgments about the relativity of moral rules in family contexts were discrepant with judgments regarding the stealing rule. Subjects were evenly divided as to whether the nonexistence of a moral rule in other families could be justified. One possible explanation for the home moral rule findings is that some subjects regarded the family as a personal unit of sufficiently small scale to deal with social interactions without (or with different) explicit regulations. Examples of this type of reasoning about moral rules within family units appear in the following interview excerpts. The first two excerpts feature subjects who believe that conventional home rules are different from moral home rules. In the remaining excerpts we see examples of how families are regarded as self-contained units.

John (13 years, 8 months): (SUPPOSE THERE'S A FAMILY DOWN THE BLOCK FROM YOU THAT DOESN'T HAVE THE RULE AGAINST STEALING. IS THAT ALL RIGHT?) No. They shouldn't.

Their parents haven't taught them not to steal anything and stuff like that. Because they're not going to be, as my parents would put it, accepted in society if they did stuff like that. (IT'S NOT OKAY THEN TO NOT HAVE THAT RULE AT HOME?) They'll have problems probably during their later life. (SUPPOSE THERE'S ANOTHER COUNTRY WHERE THEY DIDN'T HAVE THAT RULE. IS THAT ALL RIGHT?) I don't know. That's another country and we're set up a lot different from most countries. I guess then if everyone did stuff like that, from my standpoint it's not all right; from their standpoint, maybe. (WHY FROM YOUR STANDPOINT IS IT NOT ALL RIGHT?) Cause I've been taught that way. That's because. . .not to steal and stuff like that. (SUPPOSE THERE'S ANOTHER FAMILY DOWN THE STREET FROM YOU THAT DOESN'T HAVE THE RULE ABOUT HAVING TO PLAY UNTIL DARK. IS THAT ALL RIGHT?) Yeah, 'cause that's up to the parents' decision. (WHY IS THAT ALL RIGHT AS OPPOSED TO STEAL-ING?) That's not a thing that happens everyday, some parents make their kids stay out until dark, screw around and stuff like that. A lot of people have kids and they could care less if they watch TV for 3 hours after school or you go outside and play. I can't think of the word for it, they can do it if they want, their parents can teach them if they want. If they don't care if they watch TV that's their decision on their own, they don't have to do that. (SUPPOSE THERE IS ANOTHER COUNTRY THAT NONE OF THE FAMILIES HAVE THE RULE ABOUT COMING IN AFTER DARK. IS THAT ALL RIGHT?) Yes, that's another country still. If they rule the family they can make that decision.

Tom (16 years, 8 months): (SUPPOSE A FAMILY DOESN'T HAVE THE RULE ABOUT NOT FIGHT-ING, IS THAT ALL RIGHT?) Well I have nothing to do with it and I could say no fighting but if they want to continue without a rule set down it's all right. (DO YOU THINK IT'S RIGHT NOT TO HAVE A RULE?) I think it's a rule that should be followed. Kids shouldn't be fighting, but there's nothing I can do as long as I know it's a rule in our house. I don't think it's right. I don't think anybody who lives under the same roof should be fighting anyway. (SUPPOSE THERE IS ANOTHER COUNTRY IN WHICH NO FAMILIES HAVE THAT RULE. IS THAT OKAY?) The way I see it that rule should be set in every house anywhere and if it's not then all I can say is it should be and problems will occur if it's not. I don't think it's right for them not to have it. (SUPPOSE A FAMILY DOESN'T HAVE THE RULE ABOUT EXCUSING THEM-SELVES FROM THE TABLE. IS THAT ALL RIGHT?) Yes I guess that's all right; it's something that the parents teach the kids. It's by their own choice if they want to teach the kids manners they can; if not, it's Okay. (SUPPOSE THERE IS ANOTHER COUNTRY IN WHICH NO FAMILIES HAVE THAT RULE. IS THAT ALL RIGHT?) It's Okay, it's what the parents want their kids to be; if they want them to leave their house without this rule it's all right.

Betty (13 years, 7 months): (SUPPOSE ANOTHER FAMILY DOESN'T HAVE THE RULE ABOUT BORROWING OTHERS' STUFF, WOULD THAT BE ALL RIGHT?) Yes. (HOW COME?) Well if it's in that family. When they go to others' houses they have to ask. But if it's in the family that's the way they want to work it. (HOW ABOUT IF THERE WAS ANOTHER COUNTRY IN WHICH NO FAMILIES HAVE THAT RULE?) Fine as long as they're all happy and it's working. (SUPPOSE A FAMILY DOESN'T HAVE ANY RULE ABOUT THE KIDS MAKING THEIR BEDS, WOULD THAT BE ALL RIGHT?) If they don't want them to make their bed they don't have to. It's fine. (WOULD THE SAME GO IF THERE WAS ANOTHER COUNTRY?) Yes.

Ellen (13 years, 9 months): (SUPPOSE THERE IS A FAMILY THAT DOESN'T HAVE THE RULE ABOUT TAKING EACH OTHERS' THINGS, WOULD THAT BE ALL RIGHT?) For that family if they wanted to. It's none of my family's business, it's their problem not ours. (WOULD IT BE A GOOD THING FOR THAT FAMILY TO HAVE?) If they are used to it and their mom lets them get away with it just let them go ahead and do it, just so they don't take your things or go around stealing from house to house. (WHAT IF THEY DON'T HAVE THE RULE ABOUT CLEAN-

ING THEIR ROOM, WOULD THAT BE OKAY?) For that family, not for mine though. (SAY IN ANOTHER COUNTRY NO FAMILIES HAVE THE RULE ABOUT TAKING EACH OTHER'S STUFF. IS THAT OKAY?) For them as long as they didn't do it to me. (HOW ABOUT IF NOBODY IN THAT COUNTRY CLEANED THEIR ROOM, WOULD THAT BE OKAY?) For them; I wouldn't like it though. (SAY IT WAS THIS COUNTRY AND NOBODY HAD THE RULE ABOUT TAKING EACH OTHERS' THINGS, WOULD THAT BE OKAY?) No way. (WHY NOT?) 'Cause it's my country too and I wouldn't want people going around taking my stuff.

Ruth (15 years, 7 months): (DO YOU THINK ALL FAMILIES SHOULD HAVE THOSE RULES?) Depends upon how the house is run. (WHAT DO YOU MEAN HOW THE HOUSE IS RUN?) Everybody's family is different and so if you apply those same rules to every family then, just some of them are run different. They would have more trust in the members of their family and others have less trust. (SUPPOSE THERE'S A FAMILY THAT LIVES DOWN THE BLOCK THAT DOESN'T HAVE THE RULE ABOUT COMING INTO EACH OTHERS' ROOMS, SISTERS CAN GO WHEREVER THEY WANT. IS THAT ALL RIGHT?) I guess it is. (WHY?) I don't run their family and if they can get along with it, if their contentment is with that, then it's all right. (SUPPOSE THERE'S A FAMILY THAT LIVES DOWN THE BLOCK THAT DOES NOT HAVE THE RULE ABOUT CLEANING UP YOUR ROOM. IS THAT ALL RIGHT?) I suppose. (WHY?) If that's the way they want to live, maybe they clean their rooms automatically when they get up, then they wouldn't need that rule.

All these examples are from older subjects in the study. Their views are consistent with observed age trends – though not statistically significant – in response to both types of moral home questions. A majority of subjects under 10 years of age took a nonrelativistic position on the variability of moral home rules, whereas a majority of subjects over 10 years old stated that the rules could legitimately vary from one family to the next. This interpretation is offered tentatively, because the age differences were not statistically significant. It is plausible, however, that as children become older, they come to understand families as flexible and intimate social units that do not require the same types of regulations as broader social organizations, such as schools.

3. *Children's concepts of social structure and school rules.* The school is a relatively impersonal social unit with varied functions and a large number of participants, and an environment that children experience daily. Many rules exist in the school that are likely to be well-known to children and not infrequently enforced by teachers and administrators. For this reason, among others, Dodsworth-Rugani (1982) extended the research program on children's rule conceptions through a comprehensive investigation of classroom and schoolwide rules. Although the investigation narrowed the focus to a specific set of school rules, the analyses were broadened to include a series of questions designed to systematically assess criterion judgments, justification categories, and developmental changes in conceptions of the relations of conventional rules to social organization. In addition to rules corresponding to the moral (e.g., "Do not run with scissors") and conventional (e.g., "Do not leave the room without teacher's permission") domains, a third type, labeled task rules, was included in the study. Task rules

were defined as specific to activities and processes of learning (e.g., "Complete your homework on time").

The specific task rules, as well as the moral and conventional rules, were determined through discussions with a number of students (who were not subjects in the study) from the two schools in which the study was conducted. The subjects, who were from the second, fifth, and eighth grades (20 from each grade), were questioned about six rules (two of each type) identified as familiar and important to the students in the school.

The inquiry revolved around criterion-judgment questions and justification questions that provided responses for analyses of justification categories. The criterion-judgment dimensions assessed were: evaluation of the rule and of its necessity in the school, judgments of the act in the absence of a rule, evaluations of the absence of the rule in another classroom (i.e., would it be all right if the class next door did not have the rule?), in another school, and in schools in another country.

With the exception of a task rule in one grade, subjects evaluated the rules positively and deemed them necessary in their classes. No significant differences (across grades) were found in evaluations of the moral, conventional, and task rules, with subjects stating that they were good rules and needed in the class. Only eighth-grade subjects' evaluations of one task rule ("study for a test") deviated from this pattern; approximately half of the eighth-graders stated that the rule was not always necessary. For the most part, therefore, the rules were considered desirable and necessary elements in the school.

However, different roles and functions within the social system were attributed to each rule, as indicated by additional criterion-judgment findings and the justification category findings. The validity of conventional and task rules was judged, by subjects at three grade levels, to be part of the existing social system within the school. This is reflected in responses to four questions on the evaluation of the act in conjunction with the presence or absence of rules. The results are summarized in Figure 5.1. Figure 5.1 shows that, with regard to conventional and task rules, most subjects stated that the relevant acts would not be wrong in three situations: the absence of such a rule within their class, in a nearby school, or in schools in another country. Conversely, just about all the subjects maintained that the moral acts would still be wrong in each of these three conditions of rule absence (all the moral-conventional rules and moral-task rule comparisons reached statistical significance).

These results, therefore, provide further confirmation of a distinction between morality and convention on the criterion dimensions of rule contingency and relativism. One question, however, did not serve to discriminate as clearly between the rule types. Most subjects (with the highest proportion in the second grade) maintained that it would not be right for another class within their school

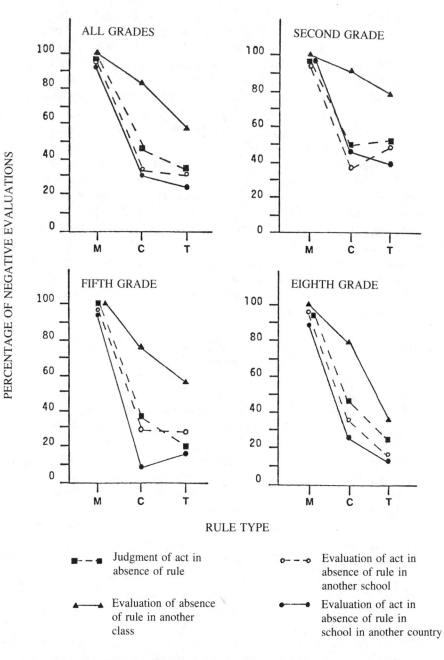

Figure 5.1. Percentage of subjects giving negative act and rule evaluations for moral (M), conventional (C), and task (T) rules. From Dodsworth-Rugani (1982).

to eliminate the conventional rules. A similar effect, though to a lesser extent, was obtained for task rules with the second- and fifth-grade subjects (see Figure 5.1). The discrepancy between responses to this question and the other responses shown in Figure 5.1 provides a good example of what was referred to in Chapter 4 as a second-order phenomenon whereby, under certain circumstances, moral implications obtain for what is primarily a conventional issue. On the one hand, the act was judged to be rule contingent and relative to the social contexts of other schools. On the other hand, when the rule is applied differentially within the same social unit, issues of fairness and equity arise.

The judgment that it would not be right to eliminate a conventional rule in another class represents a second-order phenomenon, because the primary justification for the rule is nonmoral. Although the criterion judgments provide some evidence for this interpretation, further and more direct supporting evidence comes from the analyses of justification categories. In the Dodsworth-Rugani study, subjects' justifications of judgments about the rules were coded through a modified version of the scoring system used in the Davidson, Turiel, and Black study (the scoring categories were summarized in Table 4.6). One modification of the scoring system was the addition of a category labeled process concerns, which were hypothesized to account for reasoning about the task rules. Process concerns refer to a focus on work and learning activities and not on persons or social interactions. Another modification stemmed from one of the goals of the research, which was to determine whether understandings of conventional rules would be associated with concepts of social organization. Therefore, the analyses of justification codings were grouped in four categories: (1) welfare and fairness (combining the others' welfare, appeal to fairness, and obligation categories), (2) social structure (combining custom or tradition, authority, and social coordination), (3) process, and (4) others (including prudence and personal choice).

The percentage of responses coded in accordance with each of these four groupings, for all of the subjects, and summed across the different questions, are presented in Table 5.5. Note that use of the welfare and fairness categories was infrequent for the conventional or task rules. However, insofar as those categories were used for conventional or task rules, it was usually in response to the question about the elimination of the rule in another class within the school. Also note that reasoning about conventional rules was almost always based on the social structure categories. The primary justification for the conventional rules was in social structure reasoning, but in a specific instance the rule could have moral implications – which is what is meant by the second-order phenomenon label.

The main import of the findings in Table 5.5 is the demonstration of the complementarity of criterion judgments and justification categories. Like the criterion judgments, the justification categories differed sharply (and with statis-

Table 5.5. *Justification category responses for rule types (in percentages)*

Justification category groupings	Moral (1)	Moral (2)	Conven-tional (1)	Conven-tional (2)	Task (1)	Task (2)
Welfare-fairness	*94*	*90*	11	5	6	2
Social structure	4	2	*84*	*94*	31	11
Process	0	0	3	0	*62*	*61*
Others	2	8	3	1	1	26

Source: Derived from Dodsworth-Rugani (1982).

relation does exist between domains and thinking about regulations in institutional contexts. In turn, the findings can be viewed as evidence for the definitional propositions set forth in Chapter 3 – namely, that conventions involve coordinations at the level of social organization and that the individual's concepts of social convention, unlike moral concepts, are closely related to more general concepts of social organization.

Ascertaining that reasoning about conventional (but not moral) rules was subsumed under the categories grouped as social structure allowed for an analysis of possible age-related changes in the organization of reasoning about convention and social structure. The analysis, which was based on reasoning specifically about the purposes and functions of conventional rules in the social organization of the classroom and the school, resulted in the identification of the five levels summarized in Table 5.6. Dodsworth-Rugani found statistically significant differences in levels of reasoning among the age groups (level 1 was associated with grade 2, level 3 with grade 5, and levels 3 and 4 with grade 8).

As is indicated in Table 5.6, the levels identified in the Dodsworth-Rugani study characterize concepts of the integrative functions of rules for the social organization of the school. Age-related changes in concepts of social conventions and social structure were also identified in previous research that did not focus on conceptions of school rules (Turiel, 1978a). Those characterizations of developmental changes, which correspond with the levels described in the Dodsworth-Rugani study, are considered in the next chapter.

The systematic nature of social rule concepts

In light of the research findings, some conclusions can be drawn regarding the concepts of rules held by children and adolescents. The evidence shows that from an early age children form systematic, but non-unitary, concepts of rules. Support was not obtained for the proposition that individuals have a unitary concept

Table 5.6. *Concepts of integrative functions of rules for social structure*

A. Rule functions to maintain social structure by controlling the behavior of individuals and defining their role obligations.

   Level 1. The rule maintains the relationships between the elements of the social structure by controlling the behavior of individuals of various roles and is therefore viewed as necessary and unalterable. The social structure is perceived as an aggregate of individuals performing various role functions and having the same goal (learning). The rule is viewed as *the* controlling force over individual's behavior; without the rule, the individuals would be out of control and do what they want. The effects are discussed in terms of disturbing various roles and preventing them from fulfilling their role obligations.

   Level 2. The rule maintains the relationships between the elements by controlling the behavior of individuals of various roles but the rule is no longer viewed as unalterable. The rule is still viewed as the primary controlling force over individuals' behavior but variations in behavior and the rule indicate that the rule is not always necessary. If the behavior of the individuals allows for all to fulfill role obligations without the rule or with a change in the rule, then that is permissible.

B. The rule is no longer viewed as the sole means of maintaining the social structure: the rule now functions to coordinate the actions of members of a unit. Other aspects of the social structure, authority, and various roles are perceived as controlling elements of the system.

   Level 3. The rule functions as the primary means of coordinating the members of the unit. The structure is no longer viewed as an aggregate of individual roles, but as a unit or system of relationships governed by an authority role and rules. The rules are determined by the authority figures and facilitate the authority role maintaining control of the social unit. Therefore, the rule functions to coordinate the interactions among the unit members in order to maintain the smooth operation of the unit and achieve the members' shared goals.

   Level 4. The rule that functions as one means of coordinating the members of the unit can be altered or dispensed with according to the authority role's judgment as to its necessity. The social structure is maintained and coordinated by the authority relationship and rules; therefore, if other means of providing the necessary coordination are apparent, a particular rule can be altered or discontinued.

C. Rules function to protect the social structure and allow elements of the system to achieve their goals by requiring compliance by all members of the system.

   Level 5. Compliance with the rules by all members (as individuals or as units) is necessary to maintain the social system and provide all members the same opportunities. The social structure is viewed as a complex system of relationships which is maintained by all members agreeing to adhere to the same rules. The rules provide a means of treating all subjects the same, providing all with the same opportunities and preventing the actions of one person or class from disrupting other persons or classes. In the school the rules function to maintain order in the unit and system so that any individual who wants to learn can learn. It protects the individual member (and individual class) so that all have the same opportunities (to learn, or to respond to a question, or to get information when needed). The social structure is dependent upon all elements agreeing to compliance with the rules because if one individual or group is allowed to not follow the rules, other elements may follow.

Source: Dodsworth-Rugani (1982).

of rules, which develops from an earlier belief that rules are fixed, absolute dictates to a later understanding that rules have underlying purposes (and are therefore alterable by general agreement). When the domain of the rule is not taken into account (and questions about rules are posed to children or adolescents in the abstract), it may appear that younger children are more inclined than older children to regard rules as fixed and that older children show a deeper awareness of the underlying functions of rules than younger children. This pattern emerged in the study from responses to general questions like "What is a rule?" and "Should rules always be followed?"

However, a different pattern emerges in an examination of concepts about specific rules when they are identified by their domain. Because individuals do not have a unitary rule concept, it is methodologically inappropriate to present them with general questions about rules. To understand how individuals think about rules, it is necessary rather to specify the type of rule. Children and adolescents hold at least two rule conceptions in a noncontradictory fashion. One conception applies to one category of rules, whereas the other conception applies to a second category.

It is also necessary to separate inquiry about informational knowledge of rules from evaluative judgments. One reason that previous accounts of rule concepts are not consistent with our findings stems from the distinction between informational knowledge and evaluative judgments. In the study reported here, most children and adolescents assumed that rules vary from one context to another. Moreover, there was a tendency for young children to accept the existence of rule variation more readily than adolescents. Those responses should be interpreted as estimations of the state of things in other places, in the informational sense. Such estimations were not necessarily consistent with evaluations of the alterability or relativity of the rules.

Finally, it can be concluded that children's orientation to rules is not solely a matter of obedience or disobedience. Rather, children form conceptions of the functions of rules and of the relation between a rule and its corresponding act. Rules are understood as social facts, and a separation is made between rules as legislated facts specifying behaviors and their underlying justifications. Therefore, as far as people's understanding is concerned, the results of these studies are consistent with Dworkin's position. People do not treat rules as commands to be habitually obeyed, and the authority attributed to rules is not solely determined by the system of rule enactment and enforcement. Rules are both separated from, and associated with, moral considerations. Whereas conventional and game rules are independent of morality, other rules are closely tied to moral considerations. As Dworkin maintained, rules are associated with more general social concepts.

6 The development of concepts of social convention and coordination of domains

The analyses of criterion judgments considered in the two previous chapters served two purposes. First, these analyses make it possible to specify the criteria used by individuals in their categorizations of each domain of social knowledge. Second, the analyses of criterion judgments have provided evidence that the differentiation of the two domains emerges early in life, is maintained through childhood and adolescence, and into adulthood.

The finding of a non–age-related distinction in criterion judgments does not mean that there are no developmental transformations in these two forms of social knowledge. Conceivably, the findings may be taken to mean (1) that because such young children differentiate between morality and social convention, their social knowledge is innately determined, and/or (2) that because the differentiation is not age-related, there is no further development in these forms of social knowledge after an early age. The hypothesis about innate factors stems from the idea that the early appearance of complex judgments is evidence contrary with propositions of learning or development. The hypothesis that no further development occurs after an early age (which may or may not be combined with the innate hypothesis) would be related to the view that young children make complex differentiations in their social judgments approximating the kinds of judgments made by adults. Neither of these interpretations, however, necessarily follows from the data.

In the first place, it should be reiterated that a good deal of mental development occurs during the first four years of life. As was stated earlier, by the age of 4 children have already begun to construct knowledge about logic, number, time, and space. Although no investigations have yet been made of morality and social convention for children younger than 3 or 4 years, some information regarding social development in those early years is available. For instance, it has been suggested by Bower (1977) that infants form implicit knowledge of routines of communication with their mothers. Bower proposed an interesting interpretation to explain the common phenomenon of anxiety on the part of infants when they are separated from the mother. Although the mother–infant interaction and attachment has traditionally been described in terms of emotional attachments and bonding between mother and child, Bower has pointed out that there may be idiosyncratic forms of communication between mother and infant that can account for the anxiety at separation. This interpretation implies that the close relation between mother and infant results in consistently organized (conventional) ways of coordinating their interaction.

It is quite plausible, therefore, that children's moral judgments and concepts of social convention begin to develop before the age of 3 or 4 years and that the data we have obtained reflect changes occurring during very early childhood. In turn, it is certainly not necessarily the case that the development of moral and social-conventional concepts are completed by an early age, even though the differentiation between the two domains is constant until late adolescence and early adulthood. As mentioned in Chapter 4, developmental transformations may occur in the justification categories. This is in keeping with the partial-structure hypothesis: Although the distinction between morality and convention is not age-related (as ascertained by analyses of criterion judgments), age-related changes in the organization of thinking within each domain are to be expected. Preliminary evidence of such changes has already been mentioned in the Davidson, Turiel, and Black finding on the moral justification categories. Furthermore, some of the interviews presented in Chapter 5 illustrate the types of age-related changes that may occur in children's moral judgments. Consider again the responses given by 6-year-old John (p. 85) and 13-year-old Ellen (pp. 86–7). John said that "People don't like it if you steal. It's their things, they need them." He also said that a law prohibiting theft should be followed, "because if somebody steals a dress and they need it for a party, they can't go." An understanding of reciprocity is more apparent in Ellen's responses: "If everyone was stealing, if it wasn't a law, then people would just be getting what they want instead of having to work for it and it wouldn't be fair to other people who wouldn't do it. They wouldn't work for what they want, they would just take it and I don't think that would be right... but I wouldn't be able to do anything about it if it wasn't a law."

The development of moral reasoning is considered in the next chapter. This chapter deals, first, with research on the development of concepts of social convention and, then, with research on the coordinations between domains of social concepts. The findings of domain distinctions also should not be taken to mean that no relations are drawn between domains in the reasoning of individuals. As mentioned in Chapter 4, the proposition is that the domains are structurally separate and that components of more than one domain can be combined in certain situations or events. Research into reasoning about situations involving the combination of domains is considered after discussion of the development of concepts of social convention.

Affirmations and negations: equilibrium and disequilibrium in concepts of social convention

Information regarding the development of concepts of social convention comes from two studies, the first cross-sectional and the other longitudinal. In the cross-sectional aspect of the research, which has previously been reported (see Turiel, 1978a), the youngest subjects were 6 years old and the oldest in their mid-20s. Each subject (total of 109 male and female subjects) was administered a straightforward clinical interview (of the type described in Chapter 2). The aim of the interview was to obtain responses for how subjects reasoned about a series of hypothetical stories, each dealing with one of the following specific forms of conventional usage: forms of address (a boy who wants to call teachers in school by their first names), modes of dress (dressing casually in a business office), sex-role-associated occupations (a boy who wants to become a nurse caring for infants when he grows up), patterns of family living arrangements in different cultures (fathers living apart from the rest of the family), and modes of eating (with hands or knife and fork). Each story was accompanied by a set of standard questions, as well as extensive probing questions.

This research identified seven distinct levels of development; Table 6.1 presents summary descriptions of each level and their approximate ages. These levels represent descriptions of seven different ways of organizing an understanding of social convention. At each level the individual's understanding of convention is closely related to his or her concept of social organization. The successive levels, therefore, reflect changes in children's conceptions of social systems, on the one hand, and in their understanding of the role of conventions in social systems, on the other. As levels of development, they are proposed to form a sequence through which the individual passes step by step. The developmental implications of the observed sequence are informed by statistical analyses of the cross-sectional and longitudinal studies, as well as by a consideration of the types of conceptual advances represented by each level over the previous one.

Because a subject's interview responses were analyzed for level of development on a story-by-story basis, it is possible that the level of a given subject's responses may differ from story to story. In addition, a subject's responses to a story may include reasoning corresponding to more than one level. In most cases where this occurred, only two (adjacent) levels of reasoning were used; usually, one level is predominant over the other. The scoring of responses yielded a reliable assessment, and no systematic differences were found in the level of subjects' responses to the different stories in the interview (documentation is reported in Turiel, 1978b).

The sequential characteristics of the levels were examined by assessing their association with age in the cross-sectional study, as well as by a longitudinal

Table 6.1. *Major changes in social-conventional concepts*

	Approximate ages
1. *Convention as descriptive of social uniformity.* Convention viewed as descriptive of uniformities in behavior. Convention is not conceived as part of structure or function of social interaction. Conventional uniformities are descriptive of what is assumed to exist. Convention maintained to avoid violation of empirical uniformities.	6–7
2. *Negation of convention as descriptive social uniformity.* Empirical uniformity not a sufficient basis for maintaining conventions. Conventional acts regarded as arbitrary. Convention is not conceived as part of structure or function of social interaction.	8–9
3. *Convention as affirmation of rule system; early concrete conception of social system.* Convention seen as arbitrary and changeable. Adherence to convention based on concrete rules and authoritative expectations. Conception of conventional acts not coordinated with conception of rule.	10–11
4. *Negation of convention as part of rule system.* Convention now seen as arbitrary and changeable regardless of rule. Evaluation of rule pertaining to conventional act is coordinated with evaluation of the act. Conventions are "nothing but" social expectations.	12–13
5. *Convention as mediated by social system.* The emergence of systematic concepts of social structure. Convention as normative regulation in system with uniformity, fixed roles and static hierarchical organization.	14–16
6. *Negation of convention as societal standards.* Convention regarded as codified societal standards. Uniformity in convention is not considered to serve the function of maintaining social system. Conventions are "nothing but" societal standards that exist through habitual use.	17–18
7. *Conventions as coordination of social interactions.* Conventions as uniformities that are functional in coordinating social interactions. Shared knowledge, in the form of conventions, among members of social groups facilitate interaction and operation of the system.	18–25

Source: Turiel (1978a).

follow-up interview. The following grades were represented in the original cross-sectional sample: first ($n = 9$), third ($n = 10$), fifth ($n = 14$), seventh ($n = 21$), ninth ($n = 13$), twelfth ($n = 13$), college freshmen ($n = 19$), and post-college ($n = 10$). The correlation of the levels with age was .90, indicating a very strong relationship between level and age (also reported in Turiel, 1978b).

Table 6.2. *Mean scores in longitudinal study*

Group	Mean score, time 1	Mean score, time 2	Difference between time 1 and time 2
All subjects ($n = 60$)	4.92	5.32	.39*
1-year interval ($n = 25$)	5.92	6.13	.21
2-year interval ($n = 24$)	4.10	4.70	.59*
3-year interval ($n = 11$)	4.43	4.82	.39**

*$p < .001$.
**$p < .025$.

Insofar as was possible, subjects in the original sample were reinterviewed at a later time (these results have not yet been reported). It turned out that it was possible to reinterview a little more than half the sample (60 subjects). Twenty-five of these subjects were reinterviewed after a one-year interval (the college students); 24 subjects were reinterviewed after a 2-year interval (10 seventh-graders originally in fifth grade; 7 ninth-graders originally in seventh grade; and 7 eleventh-graders originally in ninth grade); 11 subjects were reinterviewed after a 3-year interval (7 tenth-graders originally in seventh grade; 4 twelfth-graders originally in ninth grade).

In this sample, too, there was a strong correlation of levels with age (.80). The somewhat lower correlation in the longitudinal sample than in the original sample is probably accounted for by the greater variability in levels among the older subjects (first- and third-graders were not represented in the longitudinal sample). A comparison of scores for the two occasions of testing provides data more directly relevant to developmental issues. However, the timing of longitudinal interviews in this study allows above all for an examination of whether the levels represent a sequence through which individuals pass in a progressive direction. The data do not adequately test the question of whether the sequence is one through which individuals pass in a step-by-step fashion. Because subjects were not reinterviewed at close time intervals, it was not possible to trace all the changes that may have been occurring.

Two analyses were performed to determine the directionality of change for individual subjects as they got older. The first made comparisons of the average amount of change from the first to the second testing. One score was obtained for each subject by combining the scores on different stories; this score was used to calculate group averages. Table 6.2 presents the average scores, at each time of testing, and the differences, for subjects grouped according to 1-year, 2-year, or 3-year intervals between the two times of testing. Table 6.2 also presents the same results for the entire sample. As shown in Table 6.2, the entire sample and each of the three groups had higher scores on the second testing than on the first.

Table 6.3. *Frequencies of changes in longitudinal study*

Group	Progressive change	No change	Regressive change
All subjects	31 (52%)	23 (38%)	6 (19%)
1-year interval	7 (28%)	13 (52%)	5 (20%)
2-year interval	16 (67%)	8 (33%)	0
3-year interval	8 (73%)	2 (18%)	1 (9%)

Excepting only the subjects reinterviewed after a 1-year interval, the differences between the two testings were statistically significant.

Another means of analyzing the longitudinal patterns is to ascertain the number of individual subjects that show progressive change, no change, or regressive change. Those results are presented in Table 6.3. Throughout the entire sample almost all subjects either progressed or stayed at the same level. Of the 60 subjects, only 6 (10%) showed regressive change from the first to the second testing. All but one of these subjects were in the college-age group reinterviewed after a 1-year interval. In addition, the amount of progressive change increased with the number of years between the two testings. After a 1-year interval, 7 subjects (28%) showed progressive change, although about half (52%) remained at the same level. After an interval of 2 years, 16 of 24 subjects (67%) progressed and the rest remained at the same level. Finally, after a 3-year interval, 8 of 11 subjects (73%) progressed, 2 subjects (18%) stayed at the same level, and 2 subjects (9%) showed regressive change.

The longitudinal findings do not lend support to what, in some quarters, is the "conventional" wisdom – namely, that individuals differ in degree of conventionality. The pattern of development described by the seven levels casts some doubt on the idea that there are people whose stable personal orientations lead them to believe in and uphold society's conventions to a greater extent than other people. (Similarly, it is thought that degree of conventionality is what distinguishes cultures from each other, whereby some cultures uphold convention more firmly than others.) As can be seen in Table 6.1, the sequence of development is one in which there is successive acceptance and rejection, or what may be termed *affirmation* and *negation*, of conventions.[1] A change from one way of thinking about convention and social organization (e.g., level 1) to another (e.g., level 3) occurs through a rejection (e.g., level 2) of the first way of thinking. Affirmation leads to negation, which in turn leads to affirmation; the bases for the affirma-

[1] Piaget has also used the terms affirmation and negation in his recent analyses of contradiction (1980) and equilibration (1977). The concepts of affirmation and negation as characteristic of levels of social-conventional thinking were derived independently of Piaget's work on contradiction and have a somewhat different meaning. As ways of describing levels of development, affirmations and negations should not be taken to be synonymous with Piaget's concepts.

tions or negations differ from level to level. The negation levels are not, however, defined merely by the rejection of specific conventions. It is a reevaluation of concepts of social organization, as well as the conceived role of convention in social organization, that defines a negation phase. Without entailing negation, specific conventions may be rejected by a child in the absence of a more general reevaluation of his or her understanding of the social system. Furthermore, the negation phases do not necessarily involve a complete rejection of conventions; conventions may be adhered to for pragmatic or prudential reasons (e.g., to avoid punishment). The longitudinal findings provide direct evidence that the affirmations and negations reflect different phases in the same individuals. It was found that some subjects who had been at affirmation levels during the first testing were at negation levels during the second testing; similarly, some subjects originally at negation levels shifted to affirmation levels.

The patterns of affirmation and negation are consistent with an equilibration process of development. The affirmation levels characterize the child's conceptions of the social system and its conventions, whereas the negation levels characterize the child's perceptions of inadequacies in that (previously held) way of thinking. In other words, changes in thinking arise from the conflicts, inconsistencies, and inadequacies in an existing way of thinking, a process referred to as *disequilibrium*. The levels have been described more extensively elsewhere (Turiel, 1978b), together with a presentation of fuller examples of subjects' responses. Some brief descriptions and selected statements of subjects' responses are considered here mainly to illustrate the relation of affirmations and negations to the equilibration process. These descriptions show: (1) how the successive shifts from affirmation to negation are part of the construction and reconstruction of concepts of social convention (each affirmation level represents a conception of social organization that at the same time contains the elements that produce its negation at the next level; in turn, the negation entails a reorganization of thought that prepares the way for the construction of a new form of conceptualization); (2) that there are common threads of conceived arbitrariness and social coordination in those concepts; and (3) that each level represents a more comprehensive conception of social coordination than the previous one.

Levels 1 and 2: affirmation and negation of convention as descriptive of uniformity

At the earliest level thus far identified the view of conventions is straightforward and restricted. Insofar as these subjects are aware of, or assume the existence of, social uniformities, those behaviors are regarded as requiring maintenance just because they exist. Subjects at this level have not yet formed systematic notions of social organization. They are aware of differences in power and status (such as those between teachers and students or doctors and nurses), but these differences are not part of a conception of a systematized social organization. In the conventional realm it is thought that persons in positions of authority (e.g., a school principal) can set policy and tell others what to do. John, a 6-year-old, said that the student should not refer to his teacher by a first name, "because what the teacher tells you, you have to obey and it is being nice to call someone what they want to be called. . . . Because he or she is pretty important."

However, in this context, importance attributed to persons by these subjects is related to the task in which they are engaged. Another 6-year-old also stated that titles should be used, "because that is a grown-up and the grown-up is more important – they know more things than the child." Further probing by the interviewer ("How come grown-ups are more important than kids?") showed the specificity of this evaluation in that the subject responded as follows: "I didn't mean to say that. They can teach you a little more and they can teach the children to grow up to be better."

At this level uniformities are not understood to coordinate interactions within social systems. The necessity for conventions is based on their existence; it is their presumed existence that makes uniformities binding. A 6-year-old girl, for instance, stated that a woman could be a doctor because she had seen "lady doctors," even though most women are not doctors. A man, however, should not be a nurse because such people do not exist: "I have seen a lot of lady doctors and you wouldn't really see a man a nurse." Thus, the world is ordered into classes of people and activities that determine how they function. As another child affirmed, in justification of the judgment that a man should not be a nurse, "That is the way it is. . . that is the way they made it."

The judgments of level 1 subjects are not solely based on factual or informational knowledge regarding uniformities in social behavior. The existence of uniformities is also the justification for the judgment that certain behaviors are binding. The reasoning is inconsistent in that if the behavior is binding because of its social uniformity, then a digression would do away with the uniformity and, by implication, its necessity. At level 1 it is not recognized that a digression would eliminate the justification for the bindingness of the behavior. Furthermore, by attributing jurisdiction to persons in authority for the alterability of conventions, level 1 subjects allow for deviations from those uniformities that they otherwise regard as binding.

Instability stemming from inconsistencies in level 1 thinking leads to the level 2 negation of convention. At level 2 there is a recognition that if people were to engage in acts that do not comply with the existing uniformity (such as a boy becoming a nurse), then there would be no uniformity. The justification for affirming convention is thus no longer accepted. Susan, an 8-year-old, stated that the boy could become a nurse "because it doesn't matter. There are men nurses in the hospitals." She also took a critical approach to those who may affirm its necessity: "His father might be old-fashioned and he would think that men could not take care of babies."

At level 2 the possibility of variation is used as evidence for the non-necessity of customary associations of acts to types of persons. It is reasoned that one form of variation implies the non-necessity of the conventional usage ("All the other teachers call teachers by their names, like Patty and Dave, and I think if the teachers can do that why can't the kids. There is really no reason, if they can do it, the kids can do it.").

Levels 3 and 4: affirmation and negation of convention as related to rule and authority system

At level 1 the focus of conventional thinking is on the existence of uniformities and on the personalistic or individual authority of specific adults. The rejection of uniformity as a basis for convention and individual power as a basis for authoritative dictates means that level 2 subjects no longer have a conceptual context for convention. This leads to a new affirmation that rests on an emerging conception of institutionalized forms of convention. Level 3 is characterized by the emergence of a concrete conception of social structure, in which an integral role is attributed to rules and authorities. Social-conventional acts, in themselves viewed as nonobligatory, are evaluated through their relation to rules and the expectations of authorities within bounded social systems.

Bruce (11 years, 5 months): (DO YOU THINK PETER WAS RIGHT OR WRONG TO CONTINUE CALLING HIS TEACHERS BY THEIR FIRST NAMES?) Wrong, because the principal told him not to. Because it was a rule. It was one of the rules of the school. (AND WHY DOES THAT MAKE IT WRONG TO CALL A TEACHER BY HIS FIRST NAME?) Because you should follow the rules. (DO YOU THINK IF THERE WASN'T A RULE, THAT IT WOULD BE WRONG – OR WOULD IT BE RIGHT TO CALL TEACHERS BY THEIR FIRST NAMES?) Right. Because if there wasn't a rule, it wouldn't matter. . . . It wouldn't matter what they called her if there wasn't a rule.

Robert (11 years): I think he was wrong because those were the rules of the school and they were different rules than at his house. (DO YOU THINK THAT RULE WAS FAIR?) Yes, because it was just another rule that they have to call the teachers by Mr. or Mrs. (DO YOU THINK IT MATTERS WHAT PEOPLE ARE CALLED? WHETHER THEY ARE CALLED BY THEIR TITLES OR THEIR FIRST NAMES?) No, because as long as someone is understanding you and they know what you are talking about, I don't think it is wrong. (WHY DO YOU THINK PETER SHOULD FOLLOW THAT RULE IF HE DOES NOT THINK IT IS WRONG EITHER?) Well, that is the rule in the school.

Unlike level 2 thinking, conventions are associated with elements of social systems. Insofar as they are part of a rule system or expected by a person in authority, conventions require compliance. Consequently, the reasoning of these subjects is not circular in the sense of level 1 thinking. At level 3 social relations are seen as governed by a system, a system that provides a basis for uniformity in conventions independent of their existence in practice. At level 3, however, conventions are regarded as nonarbitrary insofar as a rule or authority expectation exists, without a coordination of the functions of rule or authority in relation to the conventional uniformity.[2] On the one hand, the understanding has broadened to include explicit connections of convention to social systems. On the other hand, social units are conceptualized concretely through an affirmation of rules and authority and not as systems that coordinate interactions for specified functions. This lack of coordination is followed by a new phase of negation.

At level 4 the shift is to a focus on the acts and their relation to rules and authoritative expectations. Insofar as rules and expectations pertain to arbitrary acts, there is a negation of the necessity of adherence. As can be seen in responses characteristic of this level, there is an element of affirmation associated with the negations: If the acts do not have a basis in functions served by the rule, then the individual's choice is affirmed. For example, with regard to the use of titles one 12-year-old stated: "I think it is up to him what he calls them because a name is just like a symbol or something and it doesn't really matter, just as long as the teacher knows or everybody else knows who you are talking about." Another 12-year-old put it a little differently:

Robert (12 years, 11 months): Well, all the teachers were strict, right and felt that he should call them sir, or mister. Well if I were a teacher, I don't think it should bother a teacher that he be called by his first name and if I had anything to say about it, I would call a teacher by his first name, but the way it is now, you really can't. But Peter actually should not have done it, because he could get himself into trouble, but I guess he could because that was the way he had been brought up and that was the way he thought it should be done.

The change from the third to the fourth level in the conception of rules pertaining to conventional acts results in the view that conventions are *nothing but* the expectations of others. However, level 4 subjects are not unaware of the aims of situations involving social interactions, such as communication within a classroom or the tasks of a business firm. At level 4 there is greater awareness than at level 3 of the general aims of social systems and of the inadequacy for achieving those aims of the belief in adherence to rules for their own sake. Thus, level 4 subjects accept systems of social interactions and their aims, but they have no means for coordinating those interactions.

---

[2] In level 3 thinking the idea that adherence to social acts is contingent upon rules is applied to conventional acts and not to moral ones. The emphasis given by level 3 subjects to the existence or nonexistence of rules pertaining to the act does not occur in their judgments about acts in the moral domain. Although this would be expected from the findings discussed in the previous chapters, a direct check was made of this question. During the course of the social-convention interview, the subjects were asked whether theft would be right or wrong, given a social system in which it was generally accepted and no rule prohibited it. The majority of subjects at level 3, as well as at the other levels, stated that stealing would be wrong regardless of the rule.

*Levels 5 and 6: affirmation and negation of convention as mediated
by societal standards*

At level 5 there is the emergence of an understanding of social interactions as
forming an organization, in which the individual is considered part of a general
collective and cultural system. The social system is now defined not mainly by
the impositions of rules and authority, but as a system of organization that
controls or guides the social interactions of its members. Social systems are
regarded as hierarchically organized, with individuals described in terms of their
roles and status within the hierarchy. Conventions are affirmed as shared behaviors, regulated and institutionalized by the broader system (often referred to by
level 5 subjects as "society"), so that social acts are judged in relation to a group
or social system to which the individual is subordinate. It is assumed that the
conventional uniformities of a group, particularly at the societal level, are necessary for its maintenance. Although participation in a given group may be determined by individual choice, adherence to conventions is a necessary accommodation
to groups in which one participates. Deviation from the uniformity would result
in exclusion of the individual from the group or, if of a sufficient degree, can
imply a breakdown of the social unit.

Richard (17 years, 1 month): (DO YOU THINK PETER WAS RIGHT OR WRONG TO CONTINUE
CALLING HIS TEACHERS BY THEIR FIRST NAMES?) I think he was wrong, because you have to
realize that you should have respect for your elders and that respect is shown by addressing them by their last names. (WHY DO YOU THINK THAT SHOWS RESPECT?) Informally, you
just call any of your friends by their first names, but you really don't have that relation
with a teacher. Whereas with parents too, you call them Mom and Dad and it's a different
relation than the other two. (WHAT IF PETER THOUGHT IT DIDN'T MAKE ANY DIFFERENCE
WHAT YOU CALLED PEOPLE, THAT YOU COULD STILL RESPECT THEM NO MATTER WHAT YOU
CALLED THEM?) I think he'd have to realize that you have to go along with the ways of
other people in your society. . . .

George (16 years): Yeah, it makes you aware of what the person is. If he is above you,
older, smarter. (IS THAT IMPORTANT TO KNOW?) Yeah, you've got to respect that. . . . They
have had a lot more experience and they know a lot more than you do. (WHY IS CALLING A
TEACHER BY HIS TITLE A SIGN OF RESPECT OR ACKNOWLEDGMENT OF THAT FACT?) Well, he
is smarter than you if he is teaching and you should be somewhat thankful and call him
what he wants to be called by. (BUT THE FACT THAT YOU CALL HIM A DOCTOR, WHY IS THAT
A SIGN OF RESPECT?) Just Mr. or Dr. you recognize that he is a doctor and got his doctorate
in something.

As indicated by these examples, conventions are affirmed to be binding through
the individual's participation in the social system. Moreover, the organization of
the social system establishes different types of relations among its members,
based on their place in the hierarchy. Relations between those of the same status
differ from those of dissimilar status. Again, conventions symbolically affirm the
hierarchically defined relations. As an example, the relation between student and

teacher is determined by the social context of the school. Within the school context, the use of titles represents a uniform means for signifying the relation.

Level 5 subjects affirm conventions by treating them as codified standards in social systems but fail to coordinate this with their functional view of convention. Specific conventions are regarded as functional to social tasks, such as the role of titles in the school process or of modes of dress in the professionalism of a law firm. At the same time, conventions are viewed as standards or uniformities related to the maintenance and definition of the social system. At level 6 conventions are regarded as codified standards of social systems, but there is now a negation of the necessity of such standards for the functions they are presumed to serve in given social tasks. One 17-year-old said: "Just the fact that teachers in schools have to be called Mr. and Mrs. is no valid reason for that. And also they simply refuse to acknowledge the fact that he's used to calling people by their first names. . . . There is no good reason for it, the reason is to give the teacher in the classroom respect and give him a feeling of power and authority over the kids in class."

Whereas the previous form of negation (level 4) included the assertion that conventions are "nothing but" the expectations of other people, at level 6 conventions are regarded as "nothing but" the expectations of "society." Uniformity, per se, is no longer regarded as a necessary condition for the adequate functioning of social systems. It is assumed that conventions exist not to serve societal functions but because they have become habitual and are perpetuated by tradition. At this level tradition means the existence of conventions that have become unquestioned standard procedures.

Level 7: functional view of conventions

At level 7 there is a rejection of conventions as societal codes or as uniformities associated with the defining features of social systems. Instead, conventions are judged to have the functions of coordinating social interactions and integrating elements of the social system. Conventions are thought to be stable and habitual uniformities because they serve to coordinate the interactions of people in ongoing organizational systems. In addition, conventions are not viewed as merely the means by which those with higher status impose their authority upon subordinates. Conventions are shared and agreed-upon modes of behavior that provide the means for mutual knowledge. The purpose of coordinating interactions is to facilitate the operation of the social system. One example illustrates the types of level 7 affirmations that do not rely on codified standards.

Tom (19 years): I can see why she would only be offended by the student calling her by her first name if she connected that with the students possibly thinking of her as a peer instead of someone with authority and a higher status. (WOULD THAT BE WRONG?) Would it be wrong for the student to think of the teacher as a peer? It wouldn't be wrong. It would only be inconvenient if the student thought he was just as authoritative on anything that comes up between the teacher and the student. Because in that case he would argue with the teacher who in the vast majority of the cases is bound to be right or would show better judgment because she is experienced a lot more. So it would be all right for the student to consider the teacher a peer as long as – the thing is it entails a definition of considering a peer, if you feel you have just as much authority when you say something as the other person. You can't, it isn't true. It would be wrong if the student considered himself just as authoritative as the teacher. . . . Conventions make things move along smoothly and also – are most consistently understandable communication. If something involved in the communication of two people involves a certain way, if you communicate with somebody about something, you probably have some conventional way of talking about the thing you want to communicate and the person you are trying to communicate to is familiar with the general way of communicating this convention. Therefore, he is able to follow you more quickly because he automatically is familiar with the way you start to do something, if it is the conventional way of doing something. So he doesn't have to stop and think how is that working, how is this thing said, because he has already been familiar with it. It shortens the process in many cases.

According to subjects at level 7, the primary function of conventions is to facilitate social interactions, thus affirming the necessity of coordination and efficiency. At this level, the premise is, then, that conventions are based on general knowledge (shared norms) within the social system. Each participant assumes a common understanding based on past experiences in similar situations. It is assumed that individuals adhere to convention because of the expectation that others will do so.

Affirmation-negation and developmental transformations

The changes in the individual's understanding of social convention are related to an increasingly complex and abstract conceptualization of social organization that is associated with increasing age. The negation levels of the developmental progression, in that they reflect an attitude of criticalness toward one's own way of thinking, are examples of a feature of social judgment that has received little attention in psychological explanation. This type of criticalness has been given little emphasis in the study of nonsocial, as well as social, judgments (for exceptions, see Langer, 1969, in press; Turiel, 1974, 1977). It is apparent, however, that a critical orientation is more than a minor aspect of social judgments. Pervasive in judgments within social realms are, as examples, criticalness of the behavior of others, of competing ideologies, and of the social policies of governments (one's own and others).

Criticalness in social judgments is not solely reflective of disagreements between people or peoples. The negation levels of social-conventional concepts show that criticalness also takes a form that is associated with changes in the individual's thinking. Although input from others may be a source of change

(Kuhn, 1972; Langer, 1969; Strauss, 1972; Turiel, 1966), the process of change is internally regulated, so that criticalness of one's own thinking is an essential element in developmental transformations. The observed negation levels were interpreted as reflective of reorganizations of thought, in which the rejection of one form of thinking prepares the way for the construction of the subsequent form.

This interpretation of the mechanisms of change has implications for explanations of the status of developmentally prior states. Whether or not earlier developmental phases remain alongside later phases has been a long-time concern of students of development (Freud, 1930/1961; Piaget, 1936/1963; Werner, 1957; Werner & Kaplan, 1963). Often, it is assumed that with developmental progress the earlier state is maintained alongside the new, though in subordinate status. Freud (1930/1961, pp. 18–19), for instance, argued that, unlike bodily development, in mental development the old is preserved alongside the new.

We will turn instead to what is after all a more closely related object of comparison – the body of an animal or human being. But here, too, we find the same thing. The earlier phases of development are in no sense still preserved; they have been absorbed into the later phases for which they have supplied the material. The embryo cannot be discovered in the adult. The thymus gland of childhood is replaced after puberty by connective tissue, but is no longer present itself; in the marrowbones of the grown man I can, it is true, trace the outline of the child's bone, but it itself has disappeared, having lengthened and thickened until it has attained its definitive form. The fact remains that only in the mind is such a preservation of all the earlier stages alongside of the final form possible, and that we are not in a position to represent this phenomenon in pictorial terms.

Perhaps we are going too far in this. Perhaps we ought to content ourselves with asserting that what is past in mental life *may* be preserved and is not *necessarily* destroyed. It is always possible that even in the mind some of what is old is effaced or absorbed – whether in the normal course of things or as an exception – to such an extent that it cannot be restored or revivified by any means; or that preservation in general is dependent on certain favorable conditions. It is possible, but we know nothing about it. We can only hold fast to the fact that it is rather the rule than the exception for the past to be preserved in mental life.

Freud's model of development was neither structural nor transformational. That is, in Freudian theory changes constitute additions of new material to what already exists. In additive models of development it is maintained that new levels of functioning are acquired alongside previous levels; the most advanced level attained subordinates the earlier ones. Although the new may functionally substitute for the old, the old is nevertheless preserved – particularly if it becomes part of the timeless (not subject to forgetting) unconscious. Given the premise of retention of earlier levels, it is also maintained that, under certain conditions (e.g., stress, pathological states, dream states), there may be a reversion or regression to those earlier levels.

As discussed in Chapter 2, in structural-transformational explanations of development, it is maintained that each new level represents a structural reorganization of the previous level. The process of structural reorganization is one in which the previous level becomes part of the new level so that it takes a qualitatively different form. Consequently, an explanation of developmental change as entailing such a transformational process implies that earlier levels are *not* preserved alongside later ones. The transformational model does not preclude the possibility of "regressive" behavior under certain conditions. However, regression would entail disorganization of thought, rather than reversion to the form of an earlier state of functioning (see Turiel, 1974, 1977, for further discussion of these issues).

The developmental sequence of concepts of social convention provides an example of how earlier levels are not retained in their original form with changes to subsequent levels. A change from one level of thinking to another does not solely involve the acquisition of new concepts. Change also involves the negation or rejection of the previous level based on inconsistencies and inadequacies. Each negation level represents a replacement of the previous affirmation that prepares for a new form of affirmation. Therefore, an analogy with Freud's statement that "the embryo cannot be discovered in the adult" may be drawn with mental development. It may be asked, for instance, whether level 1 social-conventional thinking can be discovered in the adult. The course of development of social-conventional thinking suggests that level 1 thought cannot be discovered in the adult. Social-conventional thinking goes through several reorganizations between the form it takes at level 1 and level 7.

Domain combinations

The research just described was designed to obtain information relevant to a characterization of the organization of thinking about convention. The studies were based on responses to events within the conventional domain and not to situations including components from more than one domain. Additional analyses have been done to investigate the coordination of concepts in situations that do include the combination of domains. It will be recalled that three types of domain combinations were listed in Chapter 4: those that are ambiguously multi-dimensional; the mixture of events corresponding to each domain and requiring moral and conventional concepts to be coordinated; and second-order phenomena, in which issues primarily judged as conventional take on a secondary moral significance insofar as others take offense at their violation. Preliminary research into the last two types of domain combinations is discussed shortly and the first type is considered in Chapter 9.

First, however, some clarification can be made of the nature of the domain combinations to be considered. There are situations that include more than one domain in only a minimal sense and are not cases of true mixture. A good example of minimal conventionality in a moral and/or prudential situation is uniformity in driving an automobile on a designated side of the road. Whether people drive on the left *or* right side of the road is legislated within a social system and generally accepted by consensus. In that sense it is conventional. It is only minimally conventional, however, because the decision that everyone drive on one side of the road is not arbitrary from both a moral and a prudential viewpoint. The reason, of course, that everyone drives on the same side of the road is that cars would otherwise collide with each other, thereby causing material damage and great physical harm to persons. It happens that, unlike many other moral situations, either of two alternatives can be chosen as the uniformity that serves exactly the same end. Note that the moral and prudential aims necessitate that everyone drive on only one side of the road. This is different only in a superficial way from the uniformity required by the moral prescription, for instance, that one should not kill innocent children.

In other situations components from more than one domain can, indeed, be combined in nonsuperficial ways. Substantive aspects of two domains may be implicated in a decision, such as where social organizational ends of coordination or efficiency conflict with moral ends of justice or rights. If it is the case that the two domains constitute distinct conceptual categories, then an understanding of how individuals deal with such situations is best accomplished through analyses of the coordination of the two conceptual systems. Conflicting demands from each domain may be sufficiently strong so that the moral considerations are not always regarded as prevailing over conventional ones. Mixed-domain events differ from second-order phenomena where, with regard to a primarily conventional situation, one may consider it unjustified to violate the conventions of another person or group insofar as it causes offense.

Domain mixture

The interview on social conventions contained stories highlighting conventional issues (e.g., forms of address, modes of dress). Each story in that interview was designed to include only a minor conflict whose purpose was to stimulate the subject's responses. For example, in the story pertaining to forms of address a teacher directed the child to use titles in the school setting. As another example, in the story on modes of dress a business partner maintained that formal dress was required in a business setting. A subsample of the same subjects who were administered the social convention interview also responded to one hypothetical story specifically designed to combine moral and conventional considerations. One major component in the story was sex-role conventions regarding expectations about which spouse works and provides financial support for the family.

The second major component pertained to considerations of reciprocity and equality insofar as both the wife and husband desire to work. The focus of the story, which follows, was on potential conflicts between sex-role conventions and the moral considerations:

> Mr. and Mrs. Davidson both had Ph.D.'s and were looking for jobs teaching in a university. An offer came through for Mr. Davidson for a good position in the state of Wisconsin, but there was no position at this time for Mrs. Davidson. They weren't sure what to do but then they decided to go to Wisconsin. They felt they should take advantage of this opportunity for Mr. Davidson to do interesting work. As it turned out, Mrs. Davidson was unable to find a teaching position in Wisconsin. Several years later, Mrs. Davidson was offered a good position in another state. She felt that it was now her turn to pursue her interests. Mr. Davidson agrees but, at the same time, he is very reluctant to leave a good job. She does want to go, but he's not sure what to do.

In addition to the issue of equality in the pursuit of career opportunities for the man and woman, the issue of reciprocity is raised in the story because the woman had previously accepted nonemployment so as to enable the man to pursue his career. With regard to the conventional issue, the context was that at the time of the administration of the interview (the early 1970s), sex-role conventions regarding work and career opportunities were undergoing public discussion and shifts in many quarters. The intention was to provide subjects with a realistic conflict over shifting conventions with which they were likely to be familiar. The youngest subjects in this study were about 14 years of age, since the content of these issues was unlikely to be familiar to younger children. The interview was administered to a total of 58 subjects from the following school grades: ninth ($n = 10$), eleventh ($n = 7$), college freshmen ($n = 19$), college sophomores ($n = 14$), and post-college ($n = 8$).

The analysis of subjects' responses had the specific and delimited purposes of determining whether and how the moral and conventional considerations in the situation depicted in the story were taken into account. The analyses indicated that, in general, subjects were aware of, and gave credence to, shifting conventions regarding the association of sex roles and occupational pursuits. In many cases, this awareness was explicitly expressed. Perhaps more important, it was reflected in the ways subjects reasoned about the decisions facing the husband and wife. With few exceptions, subjects did consider both the moral and conventional components in the situation. The following four broad categories characterized the reasoning of the subjects responding to this one story: (A) predominance of conventional roles and expectations (7% of the subjects); (B) predominance of the moral considerations of reciprocity, equal rights, and mutuality, with rejection of the conventional expectations (31%); (C) uncoordinated relation of moral and conventional components (24%); and (D) coordinated relation of moral and conventional components (38%).

Table 6.4. *Domain mixture: percentage of subjects by category*

Grade	Categories			
	A	B	C	D
9th (*n* = 10)	20	30	50	0
11th (*n* = 7)	29	0	43	29
Freshmen (*n* = 19)	0	37	21	42
Sophomores (*n* = 14)	0	36	14	50
Post-college (*n* = 8)	0	38	0	63
All subjects (*n* = 58)	7	31	24	38

Table 6.4 presents the percentage of subjects in each age group whose responses were classified in accordance with each of the categories. Table 6.4 shows some correspondences between the categories and age. Only a few subjects focused predominantly on the conventional roles and expectations (category A) of males and females in their judgments regarding which of the partners should work. These subjects were the younger ones in the sample (two ninth-graders and two eleventh-graders). Table 6.4 also shows a trend in the direction of older subjects displaying greater coordinated relations of moral and conventional components, whereas younger subjects were more likely to relate the two components in a conflictful or uncoordinated way. For at least three reasons, however, the results should not be interpreted to mean that the categories reflect a developmental progression. First, the interview was not aimed at in-depth analyses of possible age-related changes in reasoning about the relations of the moral and conventional components. Second, some of the age groups contained a relatively small number of subjects. Third, the results are based on subjects' responses to only one story.

The four subjects falling into category A relied on conventional roles and expectations in making their judgments regarding which spouse should work and support the family. These judgments about sex-role conventions corresponded to level 5 thinking (as described earlier and in Table 6.1). For instance, the ninth-graders whose reasoning was at category A considered that male and female roles constituted part of the system of societal organization. Conventional uniformities pertaining to the positions and status of men and women were regarded as binding on members of the social system.

Tony (15 years, 6 months): I think they should stay in Wisconsin. (WHY?) As a woman you take on the responsibility of a family and it is usually the thing for the man to earn the money in the family, or the man to have a job and the woman to take care of the house. (DO YOU THINK IT IS RIGHT OR WRONG FOR MRS. DAVIDSON TO EXPECT HER HUSBAND TO

LEAVE HIS JOB?) I think it's wrong. He has a good paying job and they have to go to another place where everything is new. (BUT IT IS PRIMARILY BECAUSE HE SHOULD BE THE ONE TO SUPPORT THEM?) Yah. (WHY DO YOU THINK THAT HAS TO BE THE WAY IT IS?) I don't think that has to be the way it is, but I think it is usually the way it is. A man is more capable of taking care of the home, working, providing, if he is providing for the family, then he is taking care of the family, and he is working. It's because the society views it that way and it's because it is what they do the best. (IS IT SOME NATURAL DIFFERENCE BETWEEN MEN AND WOMEN THAT MEN ARE BETTER SUITED TO WORK AND EARN A LIVING AND WOMEN ARE BETTER SUITED TO TAKE CARE OF THE FAMILY OR IS IT JUST BECAUSE THINGS ARE DONE THAT WAY?) Women are brought up more to do things around the house than they are to go out and earn a living. And when they are brought up, they do things around a house more than a man would. They are more experienced in the field of learning a family and doing things around the house than they would be at earning a living, going out and earning a living.

David (13 years, 6 months): I think the husband should check out first to see if he could get any work around there and if he could, they could go, otherwise they could probably stay. (WHY DO YOU THINK THEY SHOULD STAY?) Because he already has a job. (WHAT IF THEY ARE GOING TO MOVE TO A PLACE WHERE SHE IS GOING TO GET A JOB THAT IS JUST AS GOOD AS HIS, GET AS MUCH MONEY?) If it is going to be the same things, then why move? Why go through the ordeal of moving? (DO YOU THINK ONE MEMBER OF THE FAMILY HAS MORE OF A RIGHT TO WORK THAN THE OTHER MEMBER?) In that family no, but in a lot of families it does. (WHAT IS THE DIFFERENCE BETWEEN THAT FAMILY AND A LOT OF OTHER FAMILIES?) The wife lots of times stays home with the kids and she just does her job all the time, she picks up the house. (WHY DO YOU THINK IT IS THAT WAY?) Because the wife has to, and that was the way it was at the beginning of time, back with the cave men, so if the wife had children, she probably had to stay with them. (IS THAT STILL THE RIGHT THING TO DO?) I don't think it is now, because now there is no problem in starving to death as was the problem there. That is far fetched. The only problem is dying, getting enough food, and so now it is like getting a job, so I think it doesn't really matter. (YOU MEAN IT DOES NOT MATTER WHICH ONE WORKS TO SUPPORT THE FAMILY?) If I had a wife, I would probably want her to stay home. (WHY?) Because it's just tradition. (WHY WOULD THAT MAKE YOU DECIDE TO DO THINGS A CERTAIN WAY? WHAT DIFFERENCE DOES THAT MAKE?) I guess approval of other people. (YOU THINK THEY WOULD DISAPPROVE IF YOUR WIFE WORKED?) Like a lot of people are really upset, what the neighbors would think and like everything is social to them. (EVERYTHING IS SOCIAL?) Like the idea, I was reading this article yesterday that said this country club in this suburb of Boston, if you don't belong to it, you are really out, and so everyone wants to get into it, it is really important. (SO IT WOULD BE A SIMILAR KIND OF THING?) Yes. (IS THAT A GOOD WAY OF DECIDING ON WHO SHOULD WORK, DEPENDING ON WHAT PEOPLE WOULD THINK AND SOCIAL REASONS?) Yah, because you have to have friends and if that stops you from having friends, you probably should not.

For several of the other ninth- and eleventh-grade subjects (a total of six), neither the moral nor conventional components served as the initial basis for the decision. Those subjects stated first that the decision would be best determined by financial considerations. That is, the couple should simply go where the higher-paying position was available. It was possible, however, to probe further such responses and obtain information regarding their thinking about the moral and conventional components by asking what the couple should do in the event the two positions were equal in financial remuneration. Under that contingency two of the subjects stated that they had no basis for deciding between the two alternatives except insofar as children were involved. (Of the other four subjects initially basing their decisions on amount of pay, one shifted to a predominance of moral considerations and the other three were conflicted.) Those two subjects were also classified in category A (for the total of four) because they affirmed conventional sex roles in child-rearing as the determining factor and did not consider issues of reciprocity or equal rights.

Although the four category A subjects had attained level 5 scores on the straightforward social-convention interview, not all subjects at level 5 dealt with the mixed-domain situation in a category A way. The reasoning in the mixed-domain situation of other subjects at level 5 was distributed across the other three categories; similarly, subjects at levels 6 and 7 were represented in each of the three categories. Thus, the mixed-domain categories of reasoning were not completely determined by level of social conventional thinking.

In contrast with category A thinking, category B reflects a rejection of the validity of sex-role conventions in that situation and a corresponding affirmation of moral considerations. Category B subjects focused on the requirements of reciprocity (i.e., taking turns at each person's opportunity), equal rights, and mutuality in the relationship. In some cases, the conventional expectations regarding sex roles were considered invalid. In other cases, the conventional expectations were considered of subordinate importance to reciprocity and equal rights. The following examples illustrate category B thinking, in which the requirements of reciprocity in the husband-and-wife relationship and/or equality are judged to determine what the Davidsons should do.

Andy (14 years, 7 months): Let's see, I think it is sort of right that she pursue what she wants to do. He had his time but his time is sort of up. It is her right, she has a right to leave, to go, because it is her turn to, so I think she should. (WAS IT RIGHT FOR THE WIFE TO EXPECT THE HUSBAND TO FORSAKE HIS CAREER?) Yah, they both had their career, it is not just her, they both had it. (IS ONE CAREER MORE IMPORTANT?) In that situation – well, it usually is, it is usually the man who goes out and does the work and the woman stays home, but in this thing it's different. If both of them wanted to work and most likely they had that set agreement, when she got another job, they might leave. But I think she had her right, if she is interested and everything, I think she should go, they should. (WHICH MEMBER SHOULD WORK TO SUPPORT THE FAMILY?) The husband is supposed to. Well, not supposed to, it is traditional for the husband to do it. (DO YOU THINK IT SHOULD BE DONE THAT WAY?) No, I don't think so in this position. Because they are both professors.

Ann (18 years, 5 months): I think they should make some kind of compromise between them. I think it would only be fair to Mrs. Davidson to move to where her job was. (WHY IS THAT FAIR?) Because Mr. Davidson had worked in his area, and did what he wanted, because he had the opportunity, and I think he should be willing to make the sacrifice of giving up that position in order for her, his wife to fulfill some kind of need or desire to go to work and fill some kind of teaching position. (WHY SHOULD HE BE WILLING TO MAKE THAT SACRIFICE?) To respect her rights as an individual, as she respected his rights. Now just because at the time that Mrs. What's her name? (DAVIDSON.) Mrs. Davidson didn't, there wasn't an opportunity for her. I'm sure if there was, she would have sacrificed for him, believing that later on in life, he would have sacrificed for her. It's a give and take sort of situation, where Mr. Davidson should be, shouldn't expect his wife to sacrifice, and sacrifice all for him and not return some kind of sacrifice for her.

John (19 years, 6 months): I think they should move to the other state and let her have a job now as a teacher. (WHY?) Because they moved for the man, it seems like they moved for him, it was decided that it might be detrimental to her finding a job, but they had one for him, and now it is the other way around, and now they should move for her. He would have an easier time finding a job because he has been working. (ON WHAT BASIS DO YOU MAKE THAT DECISION, THAT THEY SHOULD MOVE?) I would make it on the basis that if a marriage is an equal partnership, an equal relationship, to move for the man and not for the woman, it seems that it would be bad to me, that is not good. There are some slight differences, like he has been working for 5 years, like that, but I think maybe it comes down to the fact that she is a wife and a woman, and she should be a housewife type thing, and when it comes down to that, she should definitely move. . . . (WOULD IT BE RIGHT FOR THE HUSBAND TO EXPECT HIS WIFE TO FORSAKE HER CAREER INTERESTS?) No, definitely wrong, I know that is wrong for me. A woman has every right to a career as a man. The only real reason it would be if she is a woman, that she would forsake her career to be a housewife and that is wrong.

Kay (18 years, 7 months): She definitely wants to go and he's not sure if he wants to go or not, so like he'd be equally willing one way or the other which would turn the balance in her favor, so they should go. (ON WHAT BASIS ARE YOU DECIDING WHAT THEY SHOULD DECIDE?) Well, like the one partner can't really make up his mind, so he's not really strong on it one way or the other. The other partner is really strong on it in one direction. Well, it should be an agreement between the two people which will make them both happiest. And if they stay, the woman will be unhappy and the husband will be uhh. And if they go, the woman will be happy, and the husband will be uhh. (WHY IS IT A MATTER OF AGREEMENT BETWEEN THE TWO PEOPLE? WHY SHOULDN'T ONE OF THEM DECIDE?) Well, when they got married, they joined their lives together into a partnership so for the rest of their lives, they should try to share decisions that are going to affect both of them. (WHY SHARE? WHY SHOULDN'T ONE OF THEM BE THE DECISION MAKER?) Well, then the marriage wouldn't really be a partnership. And I think that marriage is a partnership.

As can be seen in these examples, the demands of the concepts of equality and reciprocity necessitate that the husband consider the wife's career goals to be as important as his own. For these subjects the conventional aspects were either deemed irrelevant or were critically appraised. Especially for those subjects (i.e., Ann, John, and Kay) who viewed the marital relationship as one of mutuality and cooperation between equals, the conventionality of the situation posed no conflict. However, subjects classified in category C did respond in ways indicative of conflict or vacillation between the two components. Two types of responses reflected an uncoordinated relation of the moral and conventional considerations. In one type, the subject first asserted that the wife had an equal right to employment and a career but then shifted to an assertion of sex-role conventional expectations as the basis for deciding which partner should work in the event that they have children. As the following example shows, the latter assertion is uncoordinated with the concern for equality in that the principle of equal rights is not recognized to have potential relevance to the activity of raising children.

Alex (18 years, 6 months): Well, the woman now has a position and a job and has been there for a few years, either way, I don't know, it has to go one way or the other. If Mr. Davidson goes with Mrs. Davidson to another state, that's definitely all right. Now if she has her job and if they stay there, he has his job, so it would be nice and it would be an ideal setup if they both had jobs, but I guess if they are going to have to go one way or the other. But either way it is all right, as long as they both agree. (WHAT IF MR. DAVIDSON FELT THAT IF YOU HAD A CHOICE, THE MAN SHOULD BE THE ONE WHO SHOULD KEEP THE JOB; DO YOU THINK HE WOULD BE RIGHT OR WRONG IN MAKING HER STAY WITH HIM AT HIS JOB?) I don't think it would be right. It is a woman's lib question, since they both have Ph.D.'s and they are both human and right now there aren't any children, apparently, by this thing. There is nobody, they are both equal in their professions, it could go either way. I believe Mr. Davidson believes in our culture right now that the man has to be the breadwinner, and Mrs. Davidson does not see it that way because she has her career, too. So he should be realistic about the whole thing, even though there are no children now. I think if there were children, I think it should change and she should stay with the children. I think that Mr. Davidson should either be in complete agreement to go with her or in agreement to stay there, they would have to. . . .(SHOULD SHE EXPECT THIS?) I think she should. She made a sacrifice and now I guess it is his turn to make a sacrifice, whether a job is more important than their relationship, that is up to them. I think the relationship is more important than any job. (DO YOU THINK IT MAKES A DIFFERENCE WHICH MEMBER OF THE FAMILY WORKS TO SUPPORT THE FAMILY?) Not in the case of this circumstance. If there are children, I guess the mother has more effect on the children at an earlier stage than a man, so I think the man in that case should be the breadwinner. But in the other case, I don't think it makes any difference. As long as the man does not feel that he is being inadequate when he is not doing anything.

Other subjects (also classified in category C) who did not coordinate the moral and conventional aspects vacillated in a somewhat different manner from that seen in the example just presented. These other subjects, on the one hand, took into account the importance of reciprocity and equality. On the other hand, at the same time they affirmed the societal conventions and judged it necessary to adhere to sex-role uniformities. Consequently, the subjects' responses manifested conflict and inconsistency:

Andrew (14 years, 1 month): If he agrees with her, then they can just go. If he is for it, then they can go. But if he is against it, then they should get a divorce. (DO YOU THINK HE SHOULD BE FOR IT?) If he wants to be, he can find a job there. (SAY HE IS NOT REALLY SURE HE CAN GET A JOB BUT THERE IS A GOOD CHANCE HE CAN.) He has been supporting her, and now she can support him. (DO YOU THINK IT MAKES A DIFFERENCE WHICH MEMBER WORKS TO SUPPORT THE FAMILY?) It all depends on the guy, if the guy thinks that he should support it, and is totally against his wife supporting, then he would not let her. (DO YOU THINK HE WOULD HAVE THE RIGHT TO DO THAT?) Well, he doesn't really have the right to after she has worked for this Ph.D. but they are married and I guess he would sort of have a right to say what he thinks. (DO YOU THINK HE WOULD HAVE A RIGHT TO KEEP HER IN WISCONSIN WITH HIM BECAUSE SHE WAS MARRIED TO HIM?) Well, it would kind of be caging her up, which is what this women's lib thing is all about. (WHAT DO YOU MEAN?) Well, women's lib says that they don't want to be whatever they are and in the house all the time and they want to get out. It said in the story that he was reluctant to leave his job but he was going to anyway. He would probably find work. . . . I would say if he wanted to go then he can, his wife has a point, they have lived here for a year and she is rusty and she wants to get a job and she has been offered a good job, so she could do it. (DOES HE HAVE MORE RIGHT TO WORK THAN SHE DOES?) No, not really. They are both Ph.D.'s and just because he is a man and is supposed to work, if they are both doctors, they both work. I guess one does not have more of a right than the other. They both have a right, but in the family he probably thinks he does and they go by that. (WHAT DO YOU MEAN?) Well, he probably thinks he is the main breadwinner and everything. (DO YOU THINK THAT IS THE WAY IT SHOULD BE?) Well, I don't know, she does have a Ph.D. and everything, so it should not be in that vein. (MR. DAVIDSON WANTED TO GIVE HIS WIFE THE OPPORTUNITY TO TAKE THE JOB BUT HE FELT HE WOULD NOT BE A GOOD HUSBAND IF HIS WIFE SUPPORTED THEM. DO YOU THINK IT IS RIGHT FOR HIM TO THINK THIS WAY?) Yah. (WHY?) Because when you get married you don't want to have to have your wife work, it is a sign of like weakness. (WHY IS IT A SIGN OF WEAKNESS TO LET THE WIFE WORK?) Because he thinks he can support them himself and he is doing good enough for himself. (WHY SHOULD THE HUSBAND FEEL THAT WAY ABOUT THE WIFE, WHY DOESN'T THE WIFE FEEL THAT WAY ABOUT THE HUSBAND?) The wife should not be deprived of working and the man has the obligation to work, he really should. (WHY DOES THE MAN HAVE THE OBLIGATION TO WORK?) Because he's a man and you know the man is supposed to be the main breadwinner. . . . (WHAT IF ONLY ONE COULD WORK, AS IN THE DAVIDSONS' SITUATION? WHAT WOULD YOU DO?) I think the man should work. (WHY?) Because if it comes down to which one should work, he should because he is the man and she should stay home and you know, say they move, and she's working and they have kids, and she is going to work and the guy stays home with the kids, that's not right. (WHY IS THAT NOT RIGHT?) They tried it in Sweden, didn't you ever see that commercial? I think it is totally wrong, period, for a guy to stay home with the kids. (WHY DO YOU THINK THAT IS TRUE?) I don't know, it's just wrong, it is stupid to do that. . . . A guy can't change diapers, and mother knows best and all this stuff.

Paul (19 years, 4 months): I think they ought to stay in Wisconsin. (WHY?) Because he has a job there. I am going to sound like a male chauvinist pig, but he's got the job there, and he is probably supporting his family, if they have a family, but he is probably supporting his wife and he's got the job and I think he should be the one if there has to be a decision made. If one of them has to work, and since he has a job there, I think maybe they should stay there. I don't want to say because he is a guy, because he is a man, but because he had the job first, they should stay there. (DO YOU THINK IT HAS ANYTHING TO DO WITH THE FACT THAT HE IS A MAN?) Yah, I think it does. (WHY?) I don't know, it is changing now, it is unbalanced, as it is thought of now, the man should be the one who supports the family and makes the money. This is a really touchy subject. The other is more definite, and society now is changing. I don't know, I think it is leaning that way, it is leaning still towards the man being the one to support the family, it is still pretty strong. (WHY DO YOU THINK THE MAN SHOULD BE THE ONE TO SUPPORT THE FAMILY?) I didn't say that. I don't think it matters. (WHY NOT?) Because I don't see the difference. It would have to be a mutual agreement on the part of the husband and wife, if the husband did not want to work and the wife wanted to work, fine. . . . (WOULD YOU PREFER YOUR WIFE TO WORK?) No. (WHY NOT?) I don't know, I just wouldn't feel – I would feel like a bum because I guess in this society at least, a man is the one who works and I guess beyond this I would want to conform to the rules of the society more or less and I would want to be the one who works.

The ambivalences, conflicts, and inconsistencies in these examples were not evident in the responses of subjects classified in category D. Category D, it will be recalled, represents a coordination of the moral and conventional considerations. In addition to assuming reciprocity and equality between husband and wife, those subjects made the assumption that the marriage is itself a social unit with common aims on the part of the two participants and requiring conventions to coordinate their interests. The conventional aspect is seen not necessarily as societal expectations or sex-role uniformities, but as a means for arranging a system of interactions between the two partners. For these subjects, alternative ways of forming the social unit, as determined by its members, can be juxtaposed with the moral requirements.

Whereas in category C thinking the two components are taken into account and applied inconsistently, in category D thinking there is an attempt to reconcile them. Two somewhat different modes of coordination were observed. In one, the societal conventions were given legitimacy insofar as *both* partners agreed to establish the relationship in that way and thereby make compromises on equality so as to attain shared goals. As examples, consider the following responses from two subjects, one an 11th-grader and the other a college freshman:

Irwin (16 years): Well, I don't know what the comparative salaries are and what difference that makes. (IT WOULD BE THE SAME.) Then I suppose if he had this job, I suppose it meant that his wife went without work during that period, or what she considered suitable work during that period and I think that it would be considerate of him or fair of him to say okay, let's move to that other city and you have an interesting teaching opportunity there and I will try to find another job. (DO YOU THINK IT MAKES A DIFFERENCE WHICH MEMBER WORKS TO SUPPORT THE FAMILY?) No. (EVEN THOUGH THERE ARE CONVENTIONS IN OUR SOCIETY THAT SAY MEN HAVE TRADITIONALLY BEEN BREADWINNERS, AND WOMEN SIT HOME AND TAKE CARE OF CHILDREN: DOES THAT MAKE A DIFFERENCE?) No, not unless they happen to believe it themselves. If the husband and wife feel that yes, the husband should do it, then let the husband do it. I don't think that it is any more right just because they happen to agree with it, but if that is what they want to do, that is what they can do, but to me it doesn't make a difference. (DO YOU THINK THERE IS A REASON WHY THESE CONVENTIONS EXIST IN OUR SOCIETY?) I think they came from a long time ago, where admittedly there are physiological differences between men and women pound for pound of body weight, men have a larger percentage of muscle than women do. I have no idea what the comparable IQs or mentality rates are, measured by our standards. But I think if the woman in the family can support the family just as well as the husband and the husband does not mind doing the cooking and whatever, then that's fine. The question would come when both – if both want to work, that's fine, too, but then there would be problems about raising a family and wanting to have children. Somehow they would have to take care of the kids, somebody would have to take care of the kids. But if they didn't want to have children, then there would be no problem. (WHAT IF THEY DID HAVE CHILDREN, WHO DO YOU THINK SHOULD TAKE CARE OF THE KIDS?) Well, I guess it would be a combination of the two when they are back from work or the day care center while they are at work. (YOU DON'T THINK ONE OF THEM...) I don't think that – well, for a while, for plainly biological reasons I would say that the mother should take care of the kid for a – every once in a while at least. For the first few months, I am not sure. But after that I don't see that there is any advantage to having the mother take care of the kid as opposed to the father.

Charles (18 years, 8 months): Probably in that case I would hope that the Davidsons could reach some reasonable solution, hopefully that maybe they could go where the wife would have a job. I say that mainly because the husband has had a chance to do his interests for a while, where the wife had sacrificed something and possibly some equality could be reached while the wife reached some interesting occupation and the husband tried to find something. And I can see many problems coming in between there. First of all, I don't think it would be wrong if the man didn't want to leave, mainly because when I say what is right and wrong, I mean specifically for him and for him, it is not wrong – it is not right necessarily to compromise, then I can see it being right for him not to compromise. Do you understand what I mean? In other words, if his values are not like mine, I believe that maybe you should try and compromise, but say that he did not feel that way, then when it came time for them to leave, he wouldn't want to compromise his position. That really would not be wrong in his individual context. Whereas I really do think it would be nice if they went with the wife and let the wife have a chance.... (DO YOU THINK IT MAKES A DIFFERENCE WHICH MEMBER WORKS TO SUPPORT THE FAMILY?) No, I don't, that is speaking very idealistically. Right now I do think it makes a difference, especially in America, and many of the European countries of the world, and in fact, possibly even in some of the Far Eastern countries. I am not sure about their customs, but it might be very important that the man works there, too. In America I think it is and I think it is changing slowly, which is a good thing; but I think it has always been, since the man has generally been the protector of the family, his role has generally been to protect and supervise for the family and it's going to take a while for something that has just become part of men to, I imagine, to become slowly not part of men. It is part of their ego now. Whereas it is also part of the women's outlook I imagine to fit into certain parts of life, and they are slowly coming out of theirs, and I imagine it takes time. I think it takes time before that would be really good, both husband and wife to be able to hold a job, and then be equal in providing for the family.

These subjects assumed it would be more just to provide the wife the opportunity to pursue her career, basing this on reciprocity in their relationship. At the same time, they accounted for the functions served by the conventions in existing systems of social organization. Charles, for instance, accepted the possibility of shared expectations in sex-role differentiations. However, a priority was given to the establishment of equality when it was stated that social changes toward greater equality and reciprocity are positive and desirable.

The second mode of coordinating morality and convention is illustrated in the following responses:

Ed (19 years, 4 months): Okay, well I guess this whole thing comes down to sort of the male-chauvinist type argument. I don't know, I would tend to believe that they should probably migrate off to where the other state is, and give Mrs. Davidson a chance to do what she wants to do for a while. (DO YOU THINK IT WOULD BE RIGHT FOR MR. DAVIDSON TO EXPECT MRS. DAVIDSON TO FORSAKE HER CAREER INTERESTS?) No more than it would be right for Mrs. Davidson to expect Mr. Davidson to forsake his. (WELL, DOES IT MAKE ANY DIFFERENCE WHICH MEMBER WORKS TO SUPPORT THE FAMILY?) Well, there's an argument there, you know, that the woman is biologically suited to bring up the family, or something like that. You know, I'm not really sure whether I agree. I think it's probably never been tried out the other way and if it hasn't ever been tried out, we'd better try it out, just to see. I don't think it's been proven that having the male, you know, cook and wash the dishes and clean the house and raise the kids is particularly bad. I don't think anybody's every proved that, mainly because there hasn't been any test cases.... The fact of having men or women work, and men or women raising – you know – being the housekeeper or whatever, seems to me to be really unimportant to anybody else in society, except the members of that particular family. In other words, if my family was to be based on the fact that I would work, and my wife would do the cooking and cleaning and everything like that, sort of the standard society we have now, whereas your family, you did the work and your husband did the, let's say the duties that my wife did, it wouldn't affect me at all to have your family in that position. Nor would it affect your family to have my family in the traditional way.

Bruce (23 years, 3 months): Probably not stay together. (WHY NOT STAY TOGETHER?) Well, I'm not saying they shouldn't. It just seems to be a likely solution. The basic problem with marriage is a situation like this. It really depends on – obviously this is the ultimate trite statement, but it depends on whether they value being together more than having a job. If they value being together more, they probably ought to flip a coin or something to decide where they want to go. (FLIP A COIN?) Unless there are arguments one way or the other; between them they make a whole lot more money in one of the two places – but let's just say there's nothing like that – and that they value staying together more. Flip a coin to decide where they're going to be. . . . (MR. DAVIDSON WANTED TO GIVE HER AN OPPORTU-NITY TO TAKE THIS JOB, BUT HE FELT HE WOULDN'T BE A GOOD HUSBAND IF HIS WIFE SUP-PORTED THEM. DO YOU THINK IT'S RIGHT FOR HIM TO THINK THIS WAY?) Well, let's amplify this a bit more. What you're talking about is one having to support the other. I have troubles with one supporting the other. The tradition is that the man of the family is the one who supports the family, and maybe the wife helps out, but it's always in terms of helping out. And I don't hold that particularly. (WHY NOT?) It just doesn't seem right at all in a sense. I don't think I would be happy being supported by someone else; consequently, I would have trouble understanding someone who wanted to be supported. I mean, I would love to be supported anonymously; that would be very fine. But knowing that this person was supporting me – of course, maybe I'm doing something like bringing up the kids. But there are no kids in this case so we won't complicate it. So he's right in feeling bad about it, not because she's supporting him necessarily but they ought to each support themselves and if they want to live together, they can live together.

These subjects drew a restricted definition of the boundaries of the social unit constituting the family. Within those restricted boundaries, it is thought that the marriage can and should be established in ways acceptable to each person. Consequently, potentially different forms of conventional arrangements are pro-posed – arrangements that are regarded to be consistent with the requirements of equality and reciprocity.

Second-order phenomena

Whereas certain societal practices may be regarded by individuals as primarily serving social organizational functions of a conventional nature, their violation can also have moral implications if they are responded to by others' taking offense. Insofar as one group of people object to transgressions of their conven-tions, this is another type of situation involving the combination of domains. One can imagine a number of examples that would represent such potentially second-order moral concerns in the context of what are primarily conventional issues.

Persons who judge an activity to be arbitrary may also choose not to engage in that activity on the grounds that it would be seen as undesirable by those adhering to the conventions (e.g., when visiting another culture with different conventions). The example used for research purposes pertained to public nudity at the beach and possible reactions of others who object to public nudity. The issue was put to subjects through the following hypothetical story:

> In California, there was a group of students who considered it more natural and enjoyable to swim and sunbathe in the nude rather than in bathing suits. So they went to a beach where there were men and women of various ages, and selected a relatively isolated part of the beach for themselves. A man who happened to notice them came over and objected strongly to their behavior – he felt that it was wrong to walk around undressed and he told them they should put their bathing suits on, or leave the beach immediately. The students listened to his complaints, but felt they still had the right to swim in the nude, if that's what they wanted to do.

Again, the interview story was not administered to younger subjects. It was administered to 61 subjects from the following grades: 11th ($n = 4$), 12th ($n = 18$), college freshmen ($n = 19$), college sophomores ($n = 11$), and post-college ($n = 9$). The purposes of this inquiry were to determine, first, how subjects evaluated public nudity and, second, how they judged its practice in the face of objections from others. Nudity was chosen as a conventional issue that no longer was negatively evaluated by segments of the population from which the subjects were derived (which is the same as in the domain-mixture investigation), but which was also negatively evaluated by other segments of the population.

The results were supportive of the proposition that primary conventional judgments can take on secondary moral implications. The results also show that an understanding of judgments about the types of social interactions reflected in the story regarding nudity requires analyses of both the primary domain of reasoning and the possible domain implications of a secondary source. It was found, first of all, that none of the subjects in the study regarded public nudity as, in itself, inherently wrong. Almost all subjects judged public nudity as arbitrary in the sense that individual or group preferences for either non-nudity or nudity were acceptable (a few subjects did express a distinct preference for the positive benefits of the "natural" state of nudity). The usual justification for its classification as arbitrary was that nudity does not infringe on the rights of others or cause harm.

In the context of the story, however, one group of subjects, comprising a majority (66%), did also consider the offense that nudity might have on others who object to it because of their societal standards or individual preferences. A second group (33% of the subjects) rejected the secondary moral implications; they did not accept the legitimacy of taking offense to nudity. Each of the two types of responses were about equally distributed across the age groups.

Given the similarities of judgments made by subjects within each response type, just a few examples should suffice to illustrate the two orientations. First consider examples from subjects of differing ages who did treat nudity as having second-order moral implications.

Mike (16 years, 3 months): On a private beach or public? (PUBLIC.) I would say they were wrong. Because it is illegal, and two, because they are offending other people that are on the beach. If they wanted to do it on their own, that would be all right, and then they were not affecting anyone else. But it is a public beach that concerns other people, so I think they should take that into consideration. (WHY DO YOU THINK THEY SHOULD GIVE IN TO THE OTHER PEOPLE RATHER THAN THE OTHER PEOPLE GIVING IN TO THEM?) Because not only for that reason, but the reason that it is illegal. But also because the beach is for the enjoyment of everyone, not just for that select group. And you are not going to be enjoying it if you are going to be offended by somebody else. People have to consider the other guy and make sacrifices, for the other guy. And I don't think that there is enough of that done. I think they should sacrifice and find a place where they can do it on their own, where they won't affect anybody else. (IF A SOCIETY CONSIDERED IT ACCEPTABLE TO SUNBATHE IN THE NUDE, WOULD IT BE ACCEPTABLE TO DO THEN?) I think it would, yes, because I don't think it would be illegal then and I don't think that people would be offended by it, they would be very comfortable with it. Here people don't feel very comfortable about it. (SUPPOSE THAT HERE IT WAS NOT ILLEGAL, BUT PEOPLE WERE NOT COMFORTABLE ABOUT IT, WHAT WOULD YOU THINK ABOUT IT THEN?) I would still believe that they should not do it, because people felt offended, uncomfortable, and the beach is for the enjoyment of everyone else. And if they were offended and felt uncomfortable, I don't think they should be doing it. . . . (WHY DO YOU THINK SOMEONE WOULD OBJECT TO NUDE SUNBATHING?) I think they would object to it if they felt uncomfortable about it, and in this country nudity is something that is not commonplace, that you see every day. And lots of people would feel uncomfortable to see someone standing around in the nude.

Brian (17 years, 8 months): I think it was wrong for them to sunbathe in the nude because it was a public place. It would not be wrong if they went to some secluded beach where no one would see them, but like by being in a public place where the majority of people go to swim, we can assume that the majority of people feel that it was wrong. Then probably it was wrong. (WHY?) When you go to the beach, is it a public beach? (BUT THEY WENT TO A LITTLE CORNER, A RELATIVELY ISOLATED PART OF THE BEACH, BUT PEOPLE STILL OBJECTED.) Could people see them openly? (NO, NOT UNLESS THEY CAME THAT WAY.) No, then I will take that back, I don't think it was wrong if they made an effort to seclude themselves and made an effort to be inoffensive. (WHY?) Because in that case they would not be offending anybody else. Had they chosen to plant themselves in the middle of a beach that was overflowing on a Sunday afternoon, then they would have – I better make this clear. I don't think that sunbathing in the nude, or going swimming or whatever, is wrong, but it is something that inside it would be difficult to do, because you have social pressures working against you. And the social pressure I guess is to conform to what other people will think of you. And I would say that it was not wrong. Although they might have to be pretty brave to do it. Right or wrong is hard to apply there. (IT IS GENERALLY ACCEPTED IN SOME COUNTRIES, WHERE THE PEOPLE DESIRE IT TO SWIM AND SUNBATHE IN THE NUDE, DO YOU CONSIDER IT THE SAME WAY THERE EVEN IN A SOCIETY WHERE IT IS CONSIDERED ALL RIGHT TO DO?) No, I guess there when society accepts it, if they are not doing anything abnormal by swimming in the nude on a public beach, where in the United States, that would be considered abnormal, they would be breaking some custom, but it would not be wrong.

Tom (19 years, 2 months): Well, I probably – I would have to know a little more about the situation, if they were off on a very isolated part of the beach, where very few people, like one or two people saw them, then yes, it is okay. I don't see anything wrong with it, they are not hurting many people. (SUPPOSE THAT THE MAJORITY OF THE PEOPLE WHO LIVED IN THE AREA DISAPPROVED OF THE USE OF THE BEACH FOR THAT PURPOSE?) Then they don't have a right because there are plenty of beaches where they could go and they could do this and not be bothered, that is one thing and they are doing something that is bothering other people, they are not – other people have to take action to notify it – in other words, it is bothering enough other people so they have to get up and take action, do something about it, and so I don't think they have a right to do that.

George (24 years, 2 months): Do I think it was right or wrong? Well, it depends. If there were a lot of people and what they were doing was effectively keeping the other people from enjoying themselves, then it might be wrong. If you really think the other people are really wrong, what they think, and it is really inconveniencing them and depriving them of their own value structure or whatever, or punishing them because of their value structure or whatever, then it is not right. And the fact that the people object so strongly would be an indication that it is really strong to these people and the students might be wrong. However, if the students really think that this might be a general shock to these people, to see that their values are not really right, then maybe it would change them; that this display would be a good way of changing people's minds, without coercing them, then it would be okay. This situation sounds like people have a right to not have bathing suits on, because somebody had to come over to tell them in this isolated spot on the beach and these other people could go somewhere else, if it is not too inconvenient for them. Bathing in the nude has nothing to do with it, if you wanted to.

As can be seen in these examples, it is thought that the presence of a convention or tradition among a group of people can be the source of being offended by transgressions. The same action is legitimate among people who do not adhere to the convention. These subjects asserted both that the action is arbitrary and that the source of negative reaction was the societal convention. For other subjects, however, the assessment that nudity is not inherently wrong and that it is related to conventionality produced an opposite conclusion regarding the validity of the students' desire to be nude on a public beach. They maintained that because the action is arbitrary people should not be offended by it. That is, those subjects' criticalness of the offense taken by others to nudity led them to discount the potential second-order moral implications of the situation. Some examples follow.

John (17 years, 2 months): It is right. They are not affecting or infringing on anybody else, they are not going to goof someone up psychologically or physically, so it is a situation if they see a person walking naked on the beach they will probably arrest him. But if a kid or someone breaks a bottle on the beach and puts glass all over the place and everyone steps on it, and cuts their foot, that kid won't be arrested. But if a lady or girl walks naked on the beach, they will probably get arrested, so that is the values that are kind of screwed up. (SUPPOSE THE MAJORITY OF PEOPLE WHO LIVED THERE DISAPPROVED OF USE OF BEACH FOR THAT PURPOSE, SHOULD THEY STILL DO IT?) If the majority of people disapproved, they would probably send the cops down there, so they wouldn't be able to continue to do it. But if they don't infringe on anybody, if they are not doing it on someone's private beach, or littering the place, and stuff like that, they should continue to do it. (SO YOU DON'T THINK IT MAKES A DIFFERENCE THAT THERE IS A LAW AGAINST IT?) Again, they are not infringing anybody else's rights, people don't have to look. And even if they look, it is not affecting them, so they can continue to do it, even if there is a law against it. If they get arrested, they won't be able to continue, so I think they should be able to continue. (WHY DO YOU THINK SOMEONE WOULD OBJECT TO NUDE SUNBATHING?) Some people, if they see a naked person, it is a goofy thing, they don't want them on the beach, it gives the beach a bad name or something like that. It is one of those taboo things I guess. (DO YOU THINK OTHER PEOPLE SHOULD RESPECT PEOPLE'S FEELINGS ABOUT THAT?) They should respect them, but again, they are not really – they should respect their feelings, but they know they are not really infringing on them. They might feel it is not okay, but they know they are not really infringing on their rights. So they should respect them, and maybe move to a more secluded place, but if they want to continue there, they know they are not affecting the people.

Susan (18 years, 11 months): I think it was right. (WHY?) Well, it's really your own choice and you're not hurting anyone really by just being out. (WHY SHOULD SOMETHING LIKE THAT BE YOUR OWN CHOICE?) Because it's your body; and it just doesn't hurt anyone else. I mean they can accept it. (WHAT ABOUT THE MAN WHO'S OFFENDED BY IT?) Well, then he can just go to the other side of the beach. (WHY SHOULD HE BE THE ONE TO SORT OF GIVE IN AND LEAVE?) Well, they seemed like they were being isolated. Even if they weren't really, he could just turn his back and ignore it. I mean I don't think it's that major; I don't see anyone being offended by it. (WHY NOT? WHY CAN'T YOU?) I don't know. It's just that that really doesn't matter.

At this point no explanation can be offered for why subjects differ in their orientations to second-order moral implications – just as no explanation could be offered for the different categories of domain mixture. In the domain-mixture analysis, as stated earlier, the subjects' level of social-conventional thinking did not discriminate between the two different mixed-domain categories. Only one type of relation between social-conventional level and orientation to the second-order phenomenon was apparent: Of the subjects who discounted the validity of taking offense to nudity, the majority (64%) were predominantly at level 6 (22% were predominantly at level 5 and 16% predominantly at level 7). This is consistent with the negation of convention characteristic of level 6. Yet, this is not the entire story, because a number of level 6 subjects did consider the second-order moral implications. Of the subjects in that group, 33% were predominantly at level 6, 45% at level 5, and 21% at level 7.

Although no explanation can be offered of the different orientations, it is apparent that some situations include a combination of domains entailing the coordination of different types of judgments. The earlier analyses of reasoning within each domain provided the prerequisite information for the analyses of domain combinations. In turn, these analyses of domain combinations inform the analyses, in Chapter 9, of the coordination of judgment and action.

7 The development of moral judgments

There is an extensive body of research on the development of moral judgment and behavior conducted by researchers who take a structural approach, as well as by those who take nonstructural approaches (e.g., social learning, psychoanalytic, and sociobiological theories). Researchers guided by a structural theoretical approach have investigated the development of judgments in the attempt to describe age-related transformations in the organization of moral thought (e.g., Kohlberg, 1969; Piaget, 1932). However, the research findings discussed in Chapters 3 and 4 have led to somewhat different, though related, interpretations from those previous formulations. As we have seen, the criteria of obligatoriness, generalizability, and impersonality apply to the judgments of children as young as three or four years of age, as well as to older children and adolescents. Most previous research has not accounted for the ways in which young children's moral judgments are distinct from their nonmoral social judgments. In those descriptions of transformations in the organization of moral thought, it was proposed that young children do not differentiate morality from rules or authority or prudence or convention.

In the present chapter, therefore, those structural explanations of moral development are examined in light of the findings discussed in the earlier chapters. In subsequent chapters the nonstructural approaches are examined, again, in light of those findings. Furthermore, in evaluating theory and research from the perspective of a definition of morality consistent with the findings, it is necessary to consider the validity of the types of social events and issues that have been presented to subjects in empirical investigations. Children classify some social issues as outside the domain of morality, although they classify other social issues within the domain of morality. Therefore, in any given study the validity of analyses of children's judgments or behavior is related to the domain-appropriateness of the events and issues presented to subjects. The first task, then, is to briefly outline the types of events used in research (structural and nonstructural) that has yielded findings that have provided the data base for the theoretical explanations.

130

Classification of events and issues used as stimuli

In conducting research on moral development, one must decide which events to use in eliciting the subject's behaviors or which issues to present for discussion in analyses of the subject's judgments. The appropriateness to the domain under investigation of the events or issues chosen from the research is central to whether or not adequate results will be obtained. An obvious example of a clearly inappropriate choice of a stimulus would be to use a mathematical task in the study of children's moral judgments. It is not very likely that a researcher would use an issue as conceptually distant as a mathematical task to study morality. Moreover, it is likely that the results of such a study would be self-correcting in that subjects' responses would be so apparently discrepant with the aim of the research.

A more ambiguous situation exists, however, in assessing the appropriateness of the actual choices that have been made of events and issues for moral development research. An array of events and issues have been used, which in most cases are social in nature. Consequently, those events that may be inappropriate for research on moral development are conceptually closer to the moral domain and pose a less clear-cut assessment problem. Nevertheless, in principle, an assessment of the appropriateness of a mathematical task for moral development research is similar to an assessment of a social task. It is necessary to have criteria for the moral domain by which the task can be evaluated.

A fairly diverse set of events have been used as stimuli in moral development research. As discussed elsewhere (Turiel, 1978a), diverse criteria exist for classifying stimuli, and the events actually found in research vary (as can be seen in Table 7.1, which is reproduced from Turiel, 1978a). The range is from events dealing with harm to persons and distributive justice, to prohibitions against touching toys, to rules in games. These choices of events in the design of research have often been based on either explicit or implicit definitions of morality that are at a very general level. Some examples include the general definitions of morality as (1) evaluations of good and bad, right and wrong (Mischel & Mischel, 1976), (2) the rules or norms or values held by social systems to provide for their survival and optimal functioning (Maccoby, 1980; Stein, 1967), and (3) social rules and restrictions that conflict with individual needs and desires (Aronfreed, 1969; Hoffman, 1977; Parke, 1967). Definitions at this level of generality do not allow for discriminations among different social domains, as was discussed in Chapters 3 and 4. Even those researchers working with less general definitions (e.g., morality as justice) have sometimes made assumptions about young children's general and undifferentiated orientation to morality that have resulted in the use of events like game rules and damage to material objects (e.g., Piaget, 1932).

Table 7.1. *Social stimulus events used in research*

Reference	Event used to elicit response	Type of response	Classification
Hartshorne & May (1928)	Academic tests in classroom situations, with possibility of cheating	Behavior in classroom-experimental situation	Testing situation
	Academic tests done at home, with possibility of cheating	Behavior in home-experimental situation	Testing situation
	Athletic contests, with possibility of cheating	Behavior in school-experimental situation	Testing situation
	Party games, with possibility of cheating	Behavior in party-experimental situation	Game
	Party game, with possibility of stealing money	Behavior in party-experimental situation	Moral
	Classroom situations, with possibility of stealing money	Behavior in classroom-experimental situation	Moral
	Questionnaire about previous classroom cheating, with possibility of lying on questionnaire	Questionnaire responses	Moral
	General questionnaire about conduct, with possibility of lying	Questionnaire responses	Moral
Allinsmith (1960)	Imagined aggression (wishing someone else's death)	Reactions to transgression in story: projective story completion (guilt)	Moral
	Theft (stealing a baseball glove)	Reactions to transgression in story: projective story completion (guilt)	Moral
	Disobedience of parental instructions (not to take boxes down from closet)	Reactions to transgression in story: projective story completion (guilt)	Social convention
Aronfreed (1960)	Verbal aggression resulting in other's death	Reactions to transgression in story: projective story completion (guilt)	Unclassified
	Negligence resulting in other's death	Reactions to transgression in story: projective story completion (guilt)	Moral
	Causing loss of someone else's money	Reactions to transgression in story: projective story completion (guilt)	Moral
	Cheating in a race	Reactions to transgression in story: projective story completion (guilt)	Moral
	Withholding important information as form of retaliation	Reactions to transgression in story: projective story completion (guilt)	Moral

132

	in conjunction with	Reactions to own presumed transgressions in experimental situation / Behavior in experimental situation	
Aronfreed (1963)	Material damage: machine breaks in course of experimental manipulation	Reactions to own presumed transgressions in experimental situation (guilt)	Material damage
Aronfreed, Cutick, & Fagen (1963)	Material damage: doll breaks in course of experimental manipulation	Reactions to own presumed transgression in experimental situation (self-criticism, reparation)	Material damage
	Material damage: doll breaks in course of experimental manipulation	Reactions to own presumed transgression in experimental situation (self-criticism, reparation)	Material damage
Aronfreed & Reber (1965)	Prohibition against touching desirable toy	Behavior in experimental situation	Quasi-convention within experimental situation
Burton, Maccoby, & Allinsmith (1961)	Bean-bag game, with possibility of cheating	Behavior in experimental situation	Game
Burton, Allinsmith, & Maccoby (1966)	Bean-bag game, with possibility of cheating	Behavior in experimental situation	Game
Cheyne (1971)	Prohibition against touching desirable toy	Behavior in experimental situation	Quasi-convention within experimental situation
Cheyne & Walters (1969)	Prohibition against touching desirable toy	Behavior in experimental situation	Quasi-convention within experimental situation
Cheyne, Goyeche, & Walters (1969)	Prohibition against touching desirable toy	Behavior in experimental situation	Quasi-convention within experimental situation
Grinder (1961, 1962)	Ray-gun game, with possibility of cheating	Behavior in experimental situation	Game
La Voie (1974)	Prohibition against touching desirable toy	Behavior in experimental situation	Quasi-convention within experimental situation
Parke (1967)	Prohibition against touching desirable toy	Behavior in experimental situation	Quasi-convention within experimental situation
Parke & Walters (1967)	Prohibition against touching desirable toy	Behavior in experimental situation	Quasi-convention within experimental situation
Sears, Rau, & Alpert (1965)	Prohibition against touching desirable toy	Behavior in experimental situation	Quasi-convention within experimental situation
	Ring-toss game, with possibility of cheating	Behavior in experimental situation	Game
	Rule of bowling game—violations imposed by situation	Behavior in experimental situation	Game

Table 7.1. (cont.)

Reference	Event used to elicit response	Type of response	Classification
	Live hamster disappears when subject leaves caretaking to play with toys	Behavior in experimental situation	Unclassified
	Prohibition against taking someone else's candy	Behavior in experimental situation	Moral
Slaby and Parke (1971)	Prohibition against touching desirable toy	Behavior in experimental situation	Quasi-convention within experimental situation
Stein (1967)	Prohibition against momentarily leaving assigned task to look at an attractive movie	Behavior in experimental situation	Social convention
Stouwie (1971)	Prohibition against touching desirable toy	Behavior in experimental situation	Quasi-convention within experimental situation
Walters, Parke, & Cane (1965)	Prohibition against touching desirable toy	Behavior in experimental situation	Quasi-convention within experimental situation
Wolf (1973)	Prohibition against touching desirable toy	Behavior in experimental situation	Quasi-convention within experimental situation
Piaget (1932)	Rules of marble game	Observations of naturalistic behavior/judgments about naturalistic behavior	Game
	Material damage: breaking cups; soiling tablecloth; cutting hole in dress	Judgments about hypothetical situation presented in story form	Material damage
	Lying	Judgments about hypothetical situation presented in story form	Moral
	Stealing	Judgments about hypothetical situation presented in story form	Moral
	Retributive justice: Child ignores father's request to buy bread	Judgments about hypothetical situation presented in story form	Social convention
	Lying	Judgments about hypothetical situation presented in story form	Moral
	Ignores request not to play ball and breaks window in process	Judgments about hypothetical situation presented in story form	Material damage
	Breaks brother's toy	Judgments about hypothetical situation presented in story form	Material damage

134

Study	Situation	Method	Domain
	Breaks pot of flowers while playing ball	Judgments about hypothetical situation presented in story form	Material damage
	Spots picture book	Judgments about hypothetical situation presented in story form	Material damage
	Betrays fellow criminal	Judgments about hypothetical situation presented in story form	Moral
Kohlberg (1958, 1969)	Saving another person's life	Judgments about hypothetical situation presented in story form	Moral
	Stealing	Judgments about hypothetical situation presented in story form	Moral
	Mercy-killing	Judgments about hypothetical situation presented in story form	Moral
	Breaking promise	Judgments about hypothetical situation presented in story form	Moral
	Reporting person who escaped from prison	Judgments about hypothetical situation presented in story form	Moral
Gilligan, Kohlberg, Lerner & Belenky (1971)	Sexuality	Judgments about hypothetical situation presented in story form	Social convention
Stein (1973)	Sexuality	Judgments about hypothetical situation presented in story form	Social convention
Damon (1973)	Sharing of goods	Judgments about hypothetical situation presented in story form	Moral
DeMersseman (1976)	Sharing of goods	Judgments about hypothetical situation presented in story form/behavior in experimental situation/judgments about behavior in experimental situation	Moral
Irwin & Moore (1971)	Material damage	Choices about hypothetical situations presented in story form	Material damage
	Stealing	Choices about hypothetical situations presented in story form	Moral
Freud (1923/1960, 1930/1961)	Aggression	Clinical observations/historical reports	Moral
	Sexuality	Clinical observations	Social convention

Source: Turiel (1978a).

One basis for evaluating research findings, therefore, is the appropriateness of the stimulus event to the domain under investigation. This will be taken into account in considering the adequacy of explanations of moral development and their research findings. For any given study, it must be asked, is it the case that, from the perspective of the subject, moral judgments and/or behaviors are being measured?

Analyses of the development of moral judgments

A series of studies reported by Piaget in 1932 were the first extensive analyses of children's moral judgments. At that time morality was one of several topics examined by Piaget in his early attempts to formulate a theory of mental development. The proposed explanation of moral judgment was closely tied to his explanations of nonsocial cognitive development. Piaget and his colleagues have continued to research a variety of topics in nonsocial cognitive development, through which substantial revisions were made in the theory. No additional moral development research was undertaken by Piaget, nor did he revise the original formulation to account for the changes in his general theory. As a consequence, Piaget's explanation of the development of moral judgments is based on what is, by his own standard, an outdated and less valid theory of structural development. After 1932 there was no extensive research on moral judgments until the work begun by Kohlberg (1958, 1963, 1969) in the late 1950s. To a large extent, Kohlberg's formulation combines elements from the earlier and the more recent theories of Piaget.

Piaget's explanation of moral development revolved around the idea that morality can take two qualitatively different forms, one based on constraint and the other on cooperation. In addition, he associated constraint with custom or convention and cooperation with morality (Piaget, 1932, p. 350):

It shows finally that if. . .we wish to distinguish between opinion and reason, between the observance of custom and that of moral norms we must at the same time make a vigorous distinction between a social process such as constraint, which simply consecrates the existing order of things, and a social process such as cooperation, which essentially imposes a method and thus allows for the emancipation of what ought to be from what is.

In distinguishing between is and ought, Piaget on the one hand grouped opinion, custom, and constraint, and on the other hand grouped reason, moral norms, and cooperation. Note that Piaget proposes that the social process of cooperation *allows for the emancipation* of what ought to be from what is. In other words, morality (ought) can be indistinguishable from custom (what is), and the process of cooperation, rather than constraint, serves to produce the distinction of morality from custom. In Piaget's analysis these two types of morality form a developmental sequence. Children progress through two levels of moral judgment (following an early premoral phase), the first entailing a *heteronomous* orientation (generally corresponding to ages 3 to 8 years) and the second entailing an *autonomous* orientation.

The child's heteronomous orientation is a form of judgment that has its basis in a nonmutual, unilateral respect for adults (regarded as authority), who are seen as the sources of rules and prohibitions. The origins of morality, a sense of duty or obligation as reflected in a heteronomous orientation, are in the respect the young child has for individuals perceived to be superior ("the child in the presence of his parents has the spontaneous feeling of something greater than and superior to the self," p. 379). Unilateral respect for adults results in a morality of obedience, of adherence to externally determined and fixed rules. Heteronomy leads to the developmentally more advanced autonomous orientation, characterized by reason, morality (i.e., justice), and cooperation. At the autonomous level unilateral relations are largely replaced by relations of mutual respect. Relations of mutual respect are part of the emerging norms of reciprocity and justice.

Piaget's interpretation of the process of moral development, as reflected in the proposed sequence of the two types of morality, heteronomy and autonomy, was that it entails a differentiation of justice from custom, convention, and tradition. The obedience and constraint of the heteronomous level, which was equated with custom and convention, precedes and is displaced by concepts of justice. The general propositions that children are unable to distinguish morality from custom and that development entails their differentiation are inconsistent with the findings of the several studies discussed in previous chapters. However, Piaget's explanation cannot be evaluated solely on the basis of these general propositions. Two levels of analysis must be considered. In addition to the general characterization of a differentiation process in development, Piaget delineated specific elements of each of the two levels that provide the details of the proposed explanation of how moral judgments are made.

Elements of the heteronomous orientation

Two factors were central to Piaget's explanation of moral development. One was the child's general mental or cognitive state and the other was the nature of social relations during childhood. On the basis of previous research Piaget had proposed that the thought of young children, as reflected in several domains, is first egocentric and then progresses to a perspectivistic state. Egocentrism refers to a centering by the child on the self that stems from the inability to clearly differentiate subjective from objective experience. Thus, the young child confuses the internal with the external, the self with the nonself, and mental or psychological phenomena with physical events. A consequence of egocentrism is the reification and externalization of internal states, so that they are imbued with objective and real status.

As a proposed general feature of thought, egocentrism was presumed to be manifested in various realms. Dreams, for instance, are regarded by young children as an aspect of objective reality rather than as internal mental events (Piaget, 1929). Young children believe that the dream experiences are actual events occurring while one sleeps. More generally, for the child, thought is not solely internal mental activity, but has material quality undissociated from the external world (Piaget, 1929). In the realm of language children confuse objects and words, so that names are regarded as intrinsic, nonarbitrary aspects of objects (Piaget, 1923; see also Werner, 1957). Furthermore, the young child does not differentiate physical events from social phenomena, so that there is a confusion between physical laws and social regularities (Piaget, 1929). Another manifestation of egocentrism, and one directly associated with social relations and judgments, is that the child is unable to take the perspective of others. The perspective of the self is assumed to be the same as that of others. For example, Piaget (1923) maintained that in communicating with others the child cannot take into account the requirements of the listener.

It is abundantly clear from this listing that in his early theoretical formulations Piaget considered egocentrism to be a general feature of the child's thought applied to various realms. It was also Piaget's contention that, in conjunction with the period of egocentrism, the child's social experiences predominantly entail *constraint* (as opposed to cooperation). Social constraint refers to relations in which an individual exerts authority over another; constraint can be contrasted with relations of cooperation, in which there are interchanges between individuals on an equal basis.

Relations of constraint result from the way adults relate to children, the developmental status of children, and the way children interpret the status of adults. Parents generally provide young children with directions, instructions, and commands. To a greater or lesser extent, young children are not allowed the freedom to do as they wish or to make independent decisions. Many decisions are made by parents and imposed upon children, often in ways that invoke one form of coercion or another. However, relations of constraint are not solely a result of the methods used by adults to control children who are dependent physically. Constraint comes about through the interaction of those methods and the child's egocentric state. In the first place, the adult exerts constraint and coercion because of the child's relative cognitive immaturity. The child's level of egocentric thought renders it more likely that adults will impose external rules and exert their authority. In turn, the child reifies those external rules and commands. Furthermore, egocentrism leads to intense feelings of respect by the child for individuals in authority (unilateral respect), given the differences in size, power, and status between children and adults. In Piaget's formulation, egocentrism and constraint are interactive processes; constraint strengthens egocentrism, and egocentrism leads to the acceptance of constraint on the child's part as well as to a greater likelihood of its use by the adult.

These two factors – level of general cognitive development and types of social relations experienced – are the organizing principles that tie together the specific elements of each level of moral judgment into structured systems. Developmental change in the child's moral judgments is also explained by the two factors. Shifts in the child's cognitive level, from egocentrism to perspectivism, along with changed social relations, from constraint to cooperation, form the basis for the explanation of the transition from heteronomous to autonomous moral judgments. With the shift to perspectivism, the child is able to differentiate the subjective from the objective, to take the perspective of others, and to distinguish between the physical and the social. On the side of social experience, a better context for cooperative relations is provided, according to Piaget, by the increased emphasis in late childhood and early adolescence on relations with others close to one's own age, status, and power. The lack of constraint and the equality of status in peer relations allows for the emergence of an autonomous morality based on reciprocity, equality, and a rational sense of justice.

The general cognitive orientation of egocentrism was not, in Piaget's explanation, meant to be all-inclusive of the young child's moral judgments. Moral judgments were seen rather as one type of specific branching from the general cognitive orientation. Indeed, it is the conjunction of egocentrism with social constraint that was hypothesized to produce heteronomous judgments specific to the moral domain, characterized by what Piaget referred to as "moral realism." Young children's judgments in other domains have a quality of realism that parallels moral realism. However, the elements of moral realism are unique to that domain. Moral realism was defined by Piaget (1932, pp. 106–107) as:

the tendency which the child has to regard duty and the value attaching to it as self-subsistent and independent of the mind, as imposing itself regardless of the circumstances in which the individual may find himself.

Moral realism thus possesses at least three features. In the first place, duty, as viewed by moral realism, is essentially heteronomous. An act that shows obedience to a rule or even to an adult, regardless of what he may command, is good; any act that does not conform to rules is bad. A rule is therefore not in any way something elaborated, or even judged and interpreted by the mind; it is given as such, ready made and external to the mind. It is also conceived of as revealed by the adult and imposed by him. The good, therefore, is rigidly defined by obedience.

In the second place, moral realism demands that the letter rather than the spirit of the law shall be observed. This feature derives from the first. Yet it would be possible to imagine an ethic of heteronomy based on the spirit of the rules and not on their most hard and fast contents. Such an attitude would already have ceased to be realist; it would tend towards rationality and inwardness. . . .

In the third place, moral realism induces an objective conception of responsibility. We can even use this as a criterion of realism, for such an attitude towards responsibility is easier to detect than the two that precede it. For since he takes rules literally and thinks of good only in terms of obedience, the child will at first evaluate acts not in accordance with the motive that has prompted them but in terms of their exact conformity with established rules.

The theoretical and empirical analyses of the young child's heteronomous orientation revolved around the three issues mentioned by Piaget in defining moral realism (obedience to authority, rules, and objective responsibility), as well as the additional issues of relations between retributive and distributive justice and notions of fairness. As further discussion of the analyses of each issue shows, Piaget delineated several specific elements of the young child's heteronomous judgments, which were contrasted with the corresponding elements of the developmentally more advanced autonomous judgments.

1. *Obedience or conformity to adult authority.* According to Piaget, unilateral respect is the source of moral obligation and duty for the young child. Consequently, commands and rules coming from adults in authority are automatically accepted as right. Conformity with the dictates of those in authority is considered right and disobedience wrong. At the autonomous level, by contrast, obedience is not the criterion for the right or good. The child's notions of the just and unjust may be in contradiction with the commands of authorities.

2. *Rules as external, fixed, and absolute.* Many of the commands and expectations transmitted by adults to children take the form of rules of behavior. And most of the rules young children learn are taught to them by adults. The source of rules, therefore, is an authority for whom there is unilateral respect. Consequently, rules are external entities that are thought to be immutable. The feeling of respect for adults is generalized to the rules; thus, strict adherence is required and even alterations in rules are, in the child's mind, equivalent to transgressions. In reifying rules the young child focuses on their existence as fixed entities, without an understanding of the rationale behind the rule. Rules, therefore, are not regarded as social constructions nor as being determined by consensus.

According to Piaget, adherence to social rules is not clearly distinguished from physical regularity, as would be expected from the proposition that the young child is unable to differentiate the mental from the physical. Social and physical regularities are similar phenomena, each seen as fixed and purposeful: "This idea of a law that is both physical and moral is the very core of the child's conception of the world; for under the effect of adult constraint the child cannot conceive the laws of the physical universe except in the guise of a certain obedience rendered by things to rules" (p. 340). Moreover, legitimacy in rule differences among people is not acknowledged. The child's belief is that the same rules are held by everyone; insofar as others do not adhere to the same rules, they are judged to engage in moral transgressions. This nonrelativistic position follows from the young child's egocentric inability to take the perspective of others into account.

The shift to the autonomous level includes a transformation in the child's orientation to rules. The basis for understanding and evaluating rules becomes the moral concept guiding specific rules (and underlying a system of rules, in general). This change is signified by the emergence of concepts of justice and a new understanding of the origins, functions, and aims of rules. Whereas rules were previously viewed as externally derived and laid down by persons in authority, they are now seen as emerging from rational discussion among cooperating members of a social system. Whereas rules were previously thought to be fixed, they are now thought to be alterable by consensus. And whereas it was previously expected that rules should be the same for everyone, it is now expected that rules will vary in accordance with different circumstances and collective decisions.

If children at the heteronomous level do not conceptualize the reasons underlying rules, it follows that they would believe rules must be obeyed in the specific way they are stated. That is, the possibility would not be there for deviation from or modification of a specific rule in a given context in order to maintain its underlying purpose. It is with this sense in mind that Piaget stated that moral realism demands that the letter rather than the spirit of the law shall be observed. Correspondingly, in the child's mind all rules, regardless of their content, are the same. For instance, Piaget (pp. 188–189) maintained that:

most parents burden their children with a number of duties of which the reason must long remain incomprehensible, such as not to tell lies of any kind, etc. Even in the most modern education, the child is forced to adopt a whole set of habits relative to food and cleanliness of which he cannot immediately grasp the why and the wherefore. All these rules are naturally placed by the child on the same plane as actual physical phenomena. One must eat after going for a walk, go to bed at night, have a bath before going to bed, etc., exactly as the sun shines by day and the moon by night, or as pebbles sink while boats remain afloat. All these things are and must be so; they are as the World-Order decrees that they should be, and there must be a reason for it all. But none of it is felt from within as an impulse of sympathy or of pity is felt.

The actual research reported by Piaget, forming the basis for his generalizations on children's conceptions of rules, dealt with the rules of marble games. Children were posed with three groups of questions about rules, pertaining to their alterability (Can rules be changed?), historicity (Have the rules always been the same as today?), and origins (How did the rules begin?). The decision to use game rules as the stimulus for research on rule conceptions was based on two factors. First, games have clearly stated rules with which children have some familiarity. Second, it was assumed that it does not matter what type was used because children fail to distinguish between different rules.

3. *An objective conception of responsibility.* As Piaget stated in the passage quoted earlier, the child's moral realism produces judgments that place great emphasis on external and tangible factors. The child judges by outward conse-

quences, amount of damage, and degree of observable deviation. This is what Piaget meant by an objective (as opposed to subjective) conception of responsibility. An objective conception of responsibility is traceable to the heteronomous child's literal interpretation of rules and definition of the good as obedience. Because rules imposed by adults are regarded as categorical obligations, the intentions of an actor are not taken into account in evaluating transgressions. Regardless of an individual's intentions, the rule or the command must be obeyed. Therefore, the benevolence of motives does not alter the judgment of malevolence, insofar as the act constitutes a deviation from a rule or command.

In addition to ignoring motives, the heteronomous child's evaluations of the relative wrongness of acts would be based on physicalistic dimensions. In part, the child's orientation to physicalistic dimensions stems from the inability to differentiate the social and the physical. Thus, the child judges by material results, by the amount of physical consequences. Similarly, the child evaluates actions by the degree to which an act is at variance with the rule. The contrasting conception of subjective responsibility at the autonomous level is not based on external consequences or deviations from fixed rules. The differentiation of internal psychological processes from external events allows for a comprehension and evaluation of the actor's motives and intentions. At that level the evaluation of the intention, on moral grounds, takes precedence over the result of the action.

Children's conceptions of objective and subjective responsibility were studied through interviews designed to assess the relative importance attributed to intentions and consequences in situations involving stealing, lying, or clumsiness that results in property damage. In each case, children were presented with story-pairs presumed to establish a conflict between consequences and intentions. In the stories on clumsiness a fortuitous or well-intentioned act resulting in greater material damage was contrasted with a negatively intended act resulting in lesser material damage. For instance, in one story a child who is called to dinner accidentally causes 15 cups to break upon opening a door, and in the other story a child, in his parent's absence, causes one cup to break while attempting to take jam from a high cupboard. (For additional examples of this sort see Piaget, 1932, p. 118.) In the stories about stealing, an altruistically motivated theft of a bigger or more expensive item was contrasted with a selfishly motivated theft of a smaller item (e.g., a child steals bread for poor and hungry friends vs. a child steals a ribbon for her dress; additional examples on p. 119). The stories on lying paired a lie told without bad intentions that includes a glaring departure from fact with a lie that had plausible content and was told with the intention to deceive (e.g., a child frightened by a dog tells his mother he has seen a dog as big as a cow vs. a child tells his mother he has received good grades in school, when he had received no grades; additional examples on pp. 144–146).

On each of these issues, according to Piaget, young children evaluate the actions on the basis of the consequences (objective responsibility) and older children evaluate the actions on the basis of intentions (subjective responsibility). Children at the heteronomous level judge greater material damage to be worse than lesser damage that is negatively intended; they judge altruistic theft of a greater amount to be worse than selfishly motivated theft of a smaller amount; and they judge the more implausible lie to be worse than a lie intended to deceive with plausible content. According to Piaget, however, the items dealing with theft and deception produced more clear-cut age trends than the clumsiness items.

4. *Retributive and distributive justice.* Although the morality of heteronomy is oriented to rules and obedience, the morality of autonomy is oriented to justice. The notion of justice, in Piaget's view, is a product of cooperation and develops out of mutual respect and solidarity among children. It is the emergence of concepts of justice that distinguishes the type of moral product that arises from relations among children on an equal plane from the type of moral product seen in the heteronomous attitude toward rules and authority that results from the unequal, unilateral relations of child and adult. Two kinds of justice were studied by Piaget: retributive and distributive. Retributive justice refers to the relation between acts and rewards or punishments. Distributive justice refers to the equality or inequality of the division of resources.

Piaget's interpretation of the heteronomous child's view of retributive justice corresponds to his interpretation of the child's view of rules and authority. The violation of rules and disobedience is associated with sanctions meted out by authorities whose rules and commands are not being obeyed. At the heteronomous level punishment itself is accepted as just and necessary, without distinctions in type or goal of retribution. There is no connection drawn between the content of the transgression and the nature of the punishment. Punishment is, in Piaget's term, expiative, that is, transgressions require punishments. The purpose of punishment is to inflict pain that will lead to a realization of the seriousness of the misdeed and thus ensure future obedience. Therefore, severe punishments are often judged to be appropriate.

Children were given several stories depicting transgressions, presented with a series of possible punishments for each transgression, and then asked which punishment would be the fairest. One example will suffice to illustrate the nature of this procedure. In this story a boy had broken a toy belonging to his little brother. The three potential punishments are that he (1) give one of his own toys to the brother, (2) pay for having it fixed, or (3) not be allowed to play with any of his own toys for one week.

Whereas the younger children's judgments were expiative (e.g., not be allowed to play with his toys for a week), the older children judged punishment by reciprocity. In these children's judgments punishments should be in proportion to the act and reciprocal, thus serving to inform the transgressor about the consequences of the act. An example of a reciprocal punishment would be depriving the actor of what has been deprived of others through the misdeed. At the autonomous level punishments are viewed as restitutive; that is, as a way of restoring the situation to the state existing prior to the transgression (e.g., paying for or replacing a broken or stolen object).

Judgments of two specific types of punishment – collective punishment and "immanent justice" – were investigated by Piaget. Three examples of collective punishment were presented to children. In the first, an adult punishes an entire group for a transgression committed by one or two members, without attempting to identify the culprits. Children of all ages considered such punishment unjust. In the second case, the punished group had refused to identify the transgressor. At each level collective punishment was accepted by some children and rejected by others. It was only the third case of collective punishment that distinguished the different age groups. In that situation the adult attempted to identify and punish the transgressor, but no one was aware of his identity. Thus, the adult punishes the entire group. Children at the heteronomous level accept such punishment because it is a necessary reaction to transgressions. Children at the autonomous level regard such punishment as unjust.

Children's belief in immanent justice reflects their inability to differentiate the social and the physical. Natural events resulting in harm to a person who had committed a transgression are regarded as a form of punishment. Children believe that transgressions can result in punishments through natural events. For instance, in one story a boy who had stolen something runs across a bridge that collapses and he falls into the water. A child with a conception of immanent justice believes that falling into the water was a direct and purposeful consequence of the transgression.

The idea of retribution in the heteronomous child's moral thinking supersedes any idea of equality of *distributive* justice. In heteronomous thinking justice is subordinated to adult authority; just or equal distribution is not distinguished from obedience or retribution. For the autonomous child the idea of equality as constituting justice overrides the justice of obedience to rules and authority. The heteronomous child accepts that the distribution of resources and rewards may be determined by the relative degree of obedience to adult authority displayed by children. A parent may legitimately give more resources to a child who has been obedient than to one who has been disobedient. The autonomous child regards equality as a more just basis for the distribution of resources.

Similarly, insofar as conflicts exist between authority and equality, the heteronomous child chooses authority and the autonomous child chooses equality. Acts on the part of an authority entailing inequalities (e.g., unequal treatment of children by parents) are viewed as fair by the heteronomous child. The specific situations used by Piaget to assess such judgments were ones in which parents assign some children more tasks to perform than other children in the family. The younger children accepted unequal task assignments as fair because they are commands from authority, thus showing a failure to distinguish fairness from conformity to rules and commands. Older children judged the fairness of the situation, first by strict equality, and then by equity (i.e., defining equality in relation to needs, competencies, and extenuating circumstances).

The autonomous-level child's view of justice as equality also manifests itself in an acceptance of the legitimacy of punishment or retaliation by reciprocity between children. It is thought that a child should be able to retaliate against another child who has transgressed against him. The heteronomous child's view is that punishment ought to be left to adult authority.

Does heteronomy precede autonomy?

As stated earlier, the formulation of the two levels of moral judgment was related to the change from egocentrism to perspectivism, which at the time Piaget assumed to be an aspect of the child's general mental development. At least in part, therefore, the moral judgment explanation is dependent on the validity of (a) egocentrism and perspectivism as a developmental dimension, and (b) the proposition that moral judgments are closely related to nonsocial cognition. A reconsideration and reinterpretation of these two theoretical propositions is very relevant to the topics of the next volume and would take us too far afield from the present concerns. For now, the specific elements in Piaget's characterization of the heteronomous level are considered in relation to the evidence of young children's moral and conventional judgments.

First, Piaget's definitional criteria for morality at each level can be compared with the criteria for morality and convention used in our research that was outlined in Chapter 3. Insofar as Piaget did touch upon children's conceptions of convention, it was through inferences derived from the investigations of moral judgments. On that basis, he maintained that the heteronomous child's thinking is oriented to custom or convention. Indeed, Piaget's formulation of heteronomy as a failure to differentiate the moral from the nonmoral can be said to combine some of our criteria for morality and convention. According to Piaget, morality for the child at the heteronomous level is obligatory and applied in a generalizable or universalistic way in that the good or right is assumed to be the same for everyone. Moreover, rules are neither determined nor alterable by consensus or general agreement. Although these specific features, in themselves, are consistent with our definitional criteria of the moral, in Piaget's view they are actually determined by an inadequate understanding of morality on the part of the young child. Obligatoriness and universality are not based on a conception of intrinsic features of right and wrong or the just and unjust. Instead, heteronomous morality is contingent on extrinsic factors, including adult commands (so that morality is not distinguished from authority), fixed rules (so that moral and nonmoral rules are undifferentiated), and existing practices (so that commands and rules are valued in themselves without comprehension of moral or social organizational justifications for them).

By contrast, at the autonomous level rules are viewed as owing to mutual agreement or consensus and, thereby, as changeable and relative to the social context. However, a distinction is made at the autonomous level between rules and their underlying justifications. It is at this level that intrinsic moral judgments are made. The criteria of obligatoriness and universality, in their moral senses, apply to autonomous-level thinking in that concepts of mutual respect, equality, and justice are viewed as binding and are applied in a generalizable fashion.

The proposition that young children are heteronomous in their moral orientation – that their morality is based on conformity and their conceptions are dominated by confusions of moral and nonmoral forms of evaluation – is not supported by the research findings reviewed in earlier chapters (as well as other recent research). In contrast with the research reported by Piaget, those studies were based on an explicit, analytic separation of morality and convention and, thereby, children's conceptions of convention were directly investigated. The studies on moral and conventional concepts are especially relevant to an evaluation of the heteronomous elements of obedience to authority and an orientation to rules and sanctions. Other research, not designed to examine conventionality, is relevant to the hypothesis that the young child has an objective conception of responsibility.

Two studies discussed in Chapter 4 bear on the issue of whether or not young children view *obedience to authority* as right, regardless of the content of their commands. Both the Weston and Turiel (1980) and Davidson, Turiel, and Black (in press) studies demonstrated that young children do not always view conformity to those in authority as right and that evaluations of the practices or commands of those in authority are related to the content of those practices and commands. In the Weston and Turiel study it was found that young children critically evaluated the practices of authority that contradicted their own judgments about an act. Moreover, the same children accepted the legitimacy of authoritative jurisdiction in the realm of convention, even when the practices were in contradiction to their own (nonmoral) evaluation of the act. A similar pattern was found in the Davidson et al. study. Directives from persons in authority to violate rules pertaining to moral issues were considered wrong, whereas such directives to violate rules pertaining to conventional issues were not considered wrong.

Therefore, the evidence from these studies is inconsistent with the proposition that children's moral judgments are contingent upon the commands of those in authority, as well as with the corresponding proposition that adherence to the commands of authority is viewed as morally right. Piaget also maintained that social rules, transmitted by adult authority, are reified by the child (i.e., treated as external, sacred, immutable, and absolute) because of unilateral respect for the source of the rule and because of conceptual confusions of the social with the physical. The contention that young children treat all rules alike and fail to understand their underlying rationale led Piaget to use game rules as stimuli in the attempted study of children's moral-rule conceptions. The use of game rules represents an example of an inappropriate stimulus in the study of moral judgment. Piaget, however, was not unaware that game rules are nonmoral stimuli. The choice of game rules was based on the presumption that children would treat game rules, as well as all other rules, in the same way as moral rules. He explicitly stated (p. 2), "It is of no moment whether these game rules strike us as moral or not in their contents. As psychologists we must ourselves adopt the point of view, not of the adult conscience, but of child morality. Now, the rules of the game of marbles are handed down just like so-called moral realities, from one generation to another, and are preserved solely by the respect that is felt for them by individuals."

This claim that game rules could legitimately be used with young children in order to study their moral-rule conceptions depends on the validity of the hypothesis that they do not distinguish moral from nonmoral rules. In Piaget's work the claim is best viewed as hypothesis, because no studies had been conducted comparing children's judgments of game rules with rules pertaining to moral issues. It is clear from the findings reported earlier that the hypothesis does not hold up and that the game rule is an inappropriate stimulus for the study of moral-rule conceptions. Game rules are not part of child morality. As we have seen, children conceptualize game rules differently from rules pertaining to acts in the moral domain. Game rules are regarded as definitional to the nature of the game and changeable by general agreement.

Piaget's own data, in fact, do not seem to support his hypothesis. The interpretation made by Piaget of interview responses was that children regard game rules as unchangeable and that any modification of the rules, even if based on consensus, would be regarded as wrong. It appears, however, that this interpretation of judgments regarding the changeability and relativity of game rules was based not on what children said about changeability but on what they said about the origins of rules – which constitutes information about game rules. The children interviewed did state that game rules could be changed (see pp. 46–52); it was also the case that the children were unable to provide any specific explanations of how the rules originated. Vague attributions of the origins of rules to persons in authority and to past generations led Piaget to assume that the child views rules as sacred and immutable. However, this interpretation of evaluative judgments does not follow from responses that pertain to informational features of rules – as shown by the pattern of results from the study reported in Chapter 5.

It is perhaps in the realm of rule conceptions that the results of studies comparing morality and convention are most strikingly discrepant with the proposition that the young child's orientation is heteronomous. In the studies reviewed earlier (Davidson et al., in press; Much & Shweder, 1978; Smetana, 1981a; Weston & Turiel, 1980), it was found that all rules are not treated alike by young children (three years of age or older). In children's thinking, the evaluation of some acts is rule contingent; some rules are regarded as changeable by consensus, others are not; some rules are judged relative to the context, others are not.

Rules are regarded as external entities by the child, but not in the reified sense assumed by Piaget. Rules are regarded as external entities in the sense that they are seen as proscriptions or prohibitions that are put into effect and enforced by persons in authority. However, the systematic discriminations made between different rules indicates that children understand and interpret them from the perspective of reasoning about their domain. Some rules are evaluated and understood on the basis of moral criteria, whereas other rules are understood on the basis of criteria for conventionality. Insofar as rules are viewed as unalterable, it is because the acts are judged always to be wrong and not because of heteronomous reification of the rule, of authority, or of a confusion of social regularity with physical law. The same children, when dealing with the conventional domain, understand rules to be alterable by consensus and to be potentially different from context to context in what they consider legitimate ways.

Therefore, a separation of moral and conventional rules shows that there is no connection, assumed to exist by Piaget, between (a) an orientation to authority or tradition as the justification for rules, and (b) the view that the rule is unalterable and absolute. In a sense, it is the reverse. It is just those rules whose existence children justify by authority and existing practice that are regarded as contingent, alterable, and relativistic. It is those rules whose justification is based on intrinsic reasons, such as fairness, welfare, and avoidance of harm (see especially the Davidson et al. and Nucci studies) that children regard as noncontingent, unalterable, and not determined by general agreement.

Accordingly, child morality is not adequately characterized as oriented to rules, and the child's orientation to rules is not adequately characterized as based solely on conformity to external entities. Children's concepts within the moral and conventional domains constitute some understanding on their part of the rationales underlying rules. Young children do make moral judgments that go well beyond heteronomous obedience to authority and rules.

If young children's moral judgments are not adequately characterized as heteronomous obedience to rules and authority, then it may be that they do not have a global undifferentiated view of punishment. Piaget maintained that in the child's heteronomous orientation no connections are made between the content of transgressions and the type or severity of associated punishments. Children's conceptions of punishment in relation to the morality-convention dimension have not been extensively studied. At present, no evidence is available regarding morality and convention in relation to immanent justice, collective punishment, or reciprocal punishments. However, the available evidence does not support the idea that the young child has a global view of punishment, with a belief in the necessity of severity of punishments.

In the study by Smetana (1981a), children between 2½ and 4½ years of age did make connections between severity of punishment and types of transgressions. They stated that moral transgressions should be given more severe punishments than conventional transgressions. Similar findings were obtained by Davidson et al. with 6-year-old children. Three measures used in that study are relevant. A question stated in general terms regarding possible consequences to a transgression was put to them: "What should happen to _____?" With regard to moral transgressions the majority of the children responded to this question by suggesting that punishments be administered. By contrast, punishment was not suggested by the majority of children with regard to transgressions of conventions. However, when children were asked whether the transgressor (moral or conventional) should be punished, most children responded in the affirmative. Nevertheless, they specified punishments of greater severity for moral transgressions than for social-conventional ones. Another indication from the Davidson et al. study that children make conceptual connections between punishments and the content of transgressions was evident in responses to the question of whether it would be all right to violate a rule in the absence of punishment by authority. Moral-rule violations were judged to be wrong even if they were not associated with punishment. Conventional-rule violations were considered acceptable in the absence of punishment.

Young children's understandings of sanctions involve greater discriminations than is implied by heteronomy. In addition to the discriminations made in relation to social and conventional transgressions, it has been shown that they distinguish between deserved and undeserved retributions and restrict punishment to the social domains. In a study by Irwin and Moore (1971), children from 3 to 5 years of age were presented stories in which punishments were administered by authority to persons who were guilty or innocent of moral transgressions. In measures of preference the children consistently chose the depictions of punishment of guilty persons over punishment of innocent persons. That children believe punishment should be restricted to the social domain was demonstrated in a study by D. Weston and this author. Children from 5 to 7 years of age were presented stories depicting children who had engaged in social transgressions, as well as that of a child who had made an arithmetical error (i.e., the child maintained that one plus one equals three). They were then asked whether the parent should and would punish the child in the story. Many of the children stated that punishment should and would be administered for the social transgressions, but virtually all the children stated that the child making the arithmetical error should not be punished.

The final element to be considered in Piaget's characterization is the child's conception of objective responsibility. Several dimensions are involved in the proposed formulation of an objective conception of responsibility, including (1) that evaluations of transgressions are based on outward consequences, (2) that intentions or motives are not taken into account, and (3) that the degree of material damage to objects is part of moral judgment. The last dimension again stems from Piaget's assumption that what are nonmoral stimulus events from the perspective of the adult will be treated as moral ones by the child (1932, p. 130): "Most parents draw a distinction which the children precisely neglect to make: they scold, that is, according to the extent of the material damage caused by the clumsy act, but they do not regard the act exactly as a moral fault. The child on the contrary seems...not to differentiate the legal, or as it were, the purely police aspect from the moral aspect of the question."

As would be expected from the findings reviewed until now, recent research shows that young children judge situations involving physical harm to persons in a different way from those producing damage to material objects. In three studies (Elkind & Dabek, 1977; İmamoglu, 1975; Keasey et al., as reported in Keasey, 1979) that used methods adopted from Piaget's procedures, children evaluated transgressions that cause harm to persons to be worse than actions that lead to property damage. In the Imamoglu study, it was found that 5-year-old children judged items involving harm to a person on the basis of intentions, whereas material-damage items were judged on the basis of consequences. In still another study (Berg-Cross, 1975), young children evaluated acts resulting in harm to persons, whether the degree of harm was high or low, to be worse than acts resulting in material damage, whether the degree of damage was high or low.

Some additional evidence that children judge moral consequences differently from material consequences comes from a study by Lickona (1971). First-grade children were interviewed on both stories dealing with material damage and stories that varied the intentionality and plausibility of deceptions. These children judged situations involving lies on the basis of intention and material-damage items on the basis of consequences. Furthermore, it should be recalled that Piaget reported more clear-cut age trends from his studies of theft and deception than from the studies of clumsiness and material damage.

If children do distinguish moral consequences from material damage, then the use of the material-damage items to study moral judgments is methodologically inappropriate. The question of whether their moral judgments (e.g., regarding theft or lying) are based on consequences rather than intentions still remains. Many recent studies (extensively reviewed in Keasey, 1979) were designed to deal with this issue. Several studies replicated Piaget's methods and obtained similar findings. In a number of other studies variations were made in the experimental paradigm, such as in mode and order of presentation of the items. Results from these studies are inconsistent and cannot be said to produce a systematic explanation of children's use of intentions and consequences (see Keasey, 1979). One reason for the inconclusiveness of research on this issue may stem from inconsistencies in the original propositions put forth by Piaget. First, it must be noted that by objective responsibility Piaget did not mean that children have no understanding of intentionality. Piaget assumed an understanding of intentionality, per se, on the part of the heteronomous child. Indeed, this assumption has been supported by a number of recent studies (see Keasey, 1979, for a review). Objective responsibility was meant to refer specifically to the use of consequences and intentions in children's moral judgments. It seems, however, that Piaget was actually offering the following two propositions in explanation of objective responsibility: (1) The child judges by consequences because consequences are used to assess the degree of deviation from conformity to external rules and commands, and (2) the child is unable to coordinate concepts of moral intentions and motives with concepts of consequences.

It has already been seen that children's judgments are not based on conformity to rules and authority. It would not follow that consequences are used as a way of assessing deviation from rules and commands. It is more likely that the child's focus on consequences rather than intentions reflects an inability to coordinate the two in making moral judgments. The Davidson et al. study provides some informative results in this regard. It will be recalled that in that study children at all the ages evaluated moral transgressions *negatively* (95% of the 6-year-olds, 95% of the 8-year-olds, and 100% of the 10-year-olds). Unlike evaluations of conventional transgressions, the evaluations of moral transgressions were based on justifications dealing with harm, welfare, and justice.

Thus, the 6-year-olds, as well as the older children, made moral judgments about certain acts that were not solely based on rule violations or other extrinsic factors. Those children were also provided with descriptions of the same outward acts, but were told of the good intentions of the actors. Evaluations of the well-intentioned acts did yield age differences. Although 90% of the 10-year-olds now evaluated the act *positively*, 60% of the 6-year-olds still evaluated it *negatively* (it was evaluated positively by 67% of the 8-year-olds). These results are consistent with the expectation from Piaget's concept of objective responsi-

Table 7.2. *Responses of 6-year-olds regarding act evaluation and punishment in well-intentioned condition (%)*

| | | Stimulus event | |
| | | Familiar moral | Familiar conventional |
Question	Response		
Is act wrong (when	Yes	60	50
well-intentioned)?	No	40	50
Should (well-intentioned)	Yes	46	10
actor be punished?	No	54	90

Source: Davidson, Turiel, and Black (in press).

bility in that more of the younger than of the older children failed to judge on the basis of the actor's intentions. However, the findings were not entirely consistent with Piaget's expectations in that it was also his assumption that objective responsibility is associated with a rule-and-authority orientation. In the Davidson et al. study the 6-year-olds who did not take intentions into account had judged rules and transgressions on the basis of intrinsic factors. Furthermore, it was found that those 6-year-olds, as well as the older children, considered a bad-intentioned act worse than a well-intentioned one.

A comparison of responses to questions regarding possible punishment to the actor for moral transgressions and for conventional transgressions provides evidence that the young children were not coordinating intentionality with their judgments of moral actions. With regard to acts in the moral domain, children's views of whether punishment should be administered corresponded to their evaluation of the well-intentioned act: 54% of the 6-year-olds stated that the (well-intentioned) actor should be punished, whereas 75% of the 8-year-olds and 91% of the 10-year-olds said the actor should not be punished. As in the moral act, more of the younger than of the older children had negatively evaluated well-intentioned transgressions of conventional rules (there were no age differences in evaluations of bad-intentioned conventional transgressions). In this case, however, the large majority of 6-year-olds (90%) stated that the well-intentioned actor *should not* be punished (the majority had said that the bad-intentioned transgressor should be punished). These patterns of results are summarized in Table 7.2.

The difference between children's views of punishment for well-intentioned moral and well-intentioned conventional acts indicates that a failure to take intentions into account is specific to moral issues. Young children's negative evaluations of acts in the moral domain are not attenuated by what they know of the intentions of the actor. The act itself is seen as intrinsically wrong and the intention of the actor is not a relevant dimension to such an evaluation (thus the actor should be punished, regardless of intent). By contrast, acts in the conventional domain do not have the same "impersonal" status as in the moral domain and the actor's intentions are relevant. Children's evaluations of those acts are attenuated by what they know of intentions, so that they believe that a well-intentioned actor should not be punished. Older children do consider intentions when evaluating moral acts. They coordinate an evaluation of the act with the actor's intent and on that basis make a moral evaluation. In sum, the young child's failure to account for intentions represents a predominant focus on the nature of the act itself.

Modifications in analyses of heteronomy

Piaget's early view of development as entailing a set of general differentiations (e.g., between the objective and subjective, the physical and social) was modified through his subsequent research on nonsocial cognitive development. Revisions were, in turn, made in the theory of structure and development, as discussed in Chapter 2. The most extensive research on moral judgments following that of Piaget was conducted by Kohlberg (1958, 1963) and had its basis in both Piaget's early work on moral judgments and his later theoretical formulations. In one part of his formulation Kohlberg drew some general relations between the proposed sequence of the development of moral judgments and the sequence of nonsocial cognitive development, as formulated by Piaget. Revisions of the Piaget formulation of moral development are included in the developmental sequence proposed by Kohlberg, which can also be examined from the perspective of the body of data on morality and convention.

Kohlberg studied the ways in which children, adolescents, and young adults make moral decisions by giving them an interview revolving around a series of hypothetical stories dealing with moral conflicts. In keeping with the aims and methods of the structural approach, each of these stories presented conflicting claims in order to elicit the respondent's reasoning about moral considerations. On the basis of his analyses of responses to the stories, Kohlberg formulated a sequence of six stages of moral judgment. Whereas Piaget maintained that there are two kinds of morality – a heteronomous morality of obedience and a morality of justice and cooperation – Kohlberg has, to state it generally and simply, maintained that there are three kinds of morality that form a developmental order: first, a morality of restraint; second, a morality of rules, authority, and convention; and third, a morality of justice and principle. These three kinds of morality are represented by three levels into which the six stages are grouped.

The stage descriptions formulated by Kohlberg represent a comprehensively elaborated system that attempts to draw together relations among a variety of components thought to be centrally relevant to the structure of moral judgments (those components are: law, conscience and decision, affectional relations, authority and civic order roles, civil rights, contract-promise-trust, punishment, life, property rights and rules, truth, and sexual roles). The stage descriptions constitute an impressive and scholarly enterprise involving careful analytical formulations of empirical data. However, the primary source for the description of the stages is a scoring manual that serves as the method for assessing interview responses. Given that the scoring manual is unpublished, the details of the complexity of the stage descriptions are not likely to be known to those familiar only with the published summaries. Pointing out that the scoring manual is unpublished is not, by any means, meant to be a criticism. Indeed, the scoring manual has been made readily available, as attested to by its widespread use by researchers. This observation is meant rather to point out that the scoring manual is both a methodological tool and a detailed description of the stages. This discussion does take into account the stage descriptions presented in the scoring manual, as is necessary for a fair and accurate assessment of Kohlberg's formulations. However, the full extent of the stage definitions is not considered at this time. Kohlberg's approach to morality, as delineated in the stage descriptions, encompasses personal, familial, societal, and psychological concepts. The general developmental framework is not the concern here. The present discussion concerns the origins of moral judgment and the relations between morality and convention.

Kohlberg's explanation of the origins of moral development shares some of the features of Piaget's explanation in that his earliest stages are also ones in which the child's morality is based on extrinsic features wherein the child is characterized as failing to differentiate the moral and nonmoral. At the earliest stages of the sequence proposed by Kohlberg, moral judgments are determined by obedience to authority and a strict adherence to rules, and they are contingent on sanctions. It was Kohlberg's contention, however, that Piaget had overinterpreted young children's moral orientations in attributing to them a sense of respect for authority and feelings of sacredness for social rules. According to Kohlberg, young children's moral judgments are instrumental in that the right is associated with power, punishment, and physical consequences. Although young children do equate right with obedience to adult authority, such obedience is based, not on respect for authority, but on a pragmatic orientation to the rewards and punishments administered by them. Thus, the child's obedience is based on what is perceived as superior power on the part of authority. Similarly, the child's belief in strict adherence to rules is based not on a sense of sacredness, but on fear and prudence. In the child's mind, rules and laws are associated with power and serve as guides to the avoidance of punishment.

The first level of the sequence proposed by Kohlberg (approximately 6 to 11 years of age) includes two stages and is labeled preconventional (stage 1: punishment and obedience orientation; stage 2: instrumental purpose and exchange). Kohlberg's position regarding punishment and sanctions in the child's morality is, therefore, stronger than that of Piaget. The association of morality and sanctions was interpreted by Piaget to be an outgrowth of the deep respect felt by the child for adult authority. In Kohlberg's formulation the association of morality and sanctions is primary in that the child does not differentiate morality from punishment or prudence. At the first stage, morality is contingent on sanctions, which form the rationale for right and wrong in the child's mind. To put it another way, Piaget, like Kohlberg, maintained that the child does not differentiate what he referred to as the "purely police" aspect from the moral aspect. For Piaget the orientation to the police aspect stems from respect, whereas for Kohlberg it stems from fear and prudence. Moral obligation is both external and coercive. Fairness is not differentiated from the power structure.

In Kohlberg's scheme it is not until early adolescence that something akin to (but with some differences) Piaget's heteronomous morality emerges. The second level (approximate ages 12 to 17 years) includes the third and fourth stages and is labeled conventional morality (stage 3: mutual interpersonal expectations, relationships, and interpersonal conformity; stage 4: social system and conscience). The third stage is characterized by the emergence of a concept of morally good persons, stereotypical images of good persons, and an orientation toward social approval. The right is defined as conformity to the expectations of others and adherence to stereotypic role relations (e.g., son, brother, friend). At the fourth stage the orientation toward the social order and the right is defined as doing one's duty, conforming to and maintaining the rules of society, and respecting authority.

In moral judgments at the second level, and particularly at the fourth stage, there is a failure to clearly distinguish between fairness or justice and the demands of the social system. Morality is contingent on what exists in the social order, on law, and authority. Somewhat as in the case of Piaget's description of heteronomous morality, at stage 4 laws are regarded as sacred and there is respect for those in authority. Rules and laws are viewed as part of a fixed system and generally require adherence so as to maintain social order. Respect for authority is viewed as morally necessary, because it symbolizes respect for the social system. Consequently, adolescent moral thinking is characterized by a more abstract concept of law, authority, and the social system than is the case in Piaget's characterization of heteronomy. Nevertheless, in Kohlberg's formulation, as well, development progresses through a stage in which morality is undifferentiated from authority and constraint. In referring to the level of conventional morality, Kohlberg (1976, p. 33) stated: "The term 'conventional' means conforming to and upholding the rules and expectations and conventions of society or authority just because they are society's rules, expectations or conventions."

The sequence proposed by Kohlberg also parallels the Piagetian sequence in that it is the differentiation of morality from social order, of what ought to be from what is, that leads to an autonomous morality of concepts of justice. Moral judgments that are distinct from prudence (level 1) or social order (level 2) do not emerge until late adolescence or early adulthood. The third level encompasses the last two stages and is labeled postconventional or principled morality (stage 5: social contract or utility and individual rights; stage 6: universal ethical principles). At stage 5 there is an understanding of the functions of mutual agreement and social contract. The right is defined in terms of rules and laws that are based on consensus and that serve to maximize social welfare. At stage 6, moral decisions are based on what are regarded as principles that ought to be applied universally; contractual agreements and legitimate laws rest upon such principles. As in the autonomous level described by Piaget, in Kohlberg's third level the conventional rules and expectations of the social order are subordinated to the newly constructed concepts of mutual respect, justice, and rights. On that basis, there is a differentiation of socially defined authority from moral authority or the authority stemming from moral precepts. At this level, as well, laws are interpreted through an understanding of their underlying purposes.

In sum, according to Kohlberg the emergence of autonomous and differentiated concepts of justice occurs even later than had been supposed by Piaget. The two major modifications of Piaget's formulation made by Kohlberg are (1) that at the earliest levels moral judgments are based not on respect for authority and rules, but on an orientation to power and punishment, and (2) that the preconventional level is followed in adolescence by the conventional level so that autonomous morality is seen as developing during late adolescence or early adulthood. A structural assumption in the sequence proposed by Kohlberg is that in ontogenesis morality is initially conceptualized through simple, concrete notions of punishment, prudence, and obedience – manifested in a global orientation to social relations and regulations. Morality takes the form of prudential but inflexible concepts of what is dictated by authority and associated with sanctions. The entry into a nonprudential and noninstrumental conception of morality is in early adolescence and stems from emerging conceptions of systems of social relations. At first those conceptions are linked to direct and immediate social relationships (stage 3) – especially familial ones. This is followed by an impersonal conception of morality based on the broader social system, with rules, legal codes, and authority relations understood as independent of sanctions. The existing system of social arrangements determines what is right or just.

The research reviewed in earlier chapters has shown that the entry into noninstrumental moral conceptions comes earlier than adolescence and is not by way of social system conceptions. We have seen that young children's moral conceptions are not solely instrumental or oriented to punishment in that they make differential associations of severity of punishment to types of transgressions (Smetana, 1981a) and that they judge moral transgressions independently of existing sanctions (Davidson et al., in press). Noninstrumental moral conceptions are evident in early childhood and are based on inferences about interpersonal relations, especially those pertaining to harm and unequal treatment.

In some respects both the Piaget and Kohlberg formulations have tapped significant aspects of young children's judgments. A concern with consequences and obligatoriness are elements of their moral judgments. The concern with consequences, however, is not solely instrumental. It is a concern with harm to others and self that forms a basis for early moral inferences. Early moral judgments include concepts of obligatory and unalterable ways of relating to others. Moreover, the concern with harm is not undifferentiated. A recent study by Tisak and Turiel (1982) found that children distinguish between the relevance of consequences in rules pertaining specifically to interpersonal relations (e.g., "Do not hit another person") and self-related prudential rules involving harm (e.g., "Do not ride a bicycle when the ground is wet and slippery").

The research also shows that emerging conceptions of social systems exist in early childhood. Young children do not equate the right with existing authority expectations or sanctions. In adolescence the construction of an abstract conception of hierarchically organized social systems (level 5 of the sequence described in Chapter 6) brings with it an increased commitment to conventionality. The commitment to the social system is based on concepts of coordinations and efficiency and does not constitute a definition of morality as adherence to existing societal arrangements. Moral authority, as we have seen, is distinguished from nonmoral social authority much earlier than adolescence or than the proposed emergence of stage 4 in the Kohlberg sequence.

Age-related changes in moral judgments

The conception of morality offered by Piaget and Kohlberg is, in its general terms, consistent with the definition used here and is supported by the findings of studies comparing morality and social convention. In those formulations, however, distinctive moral understandings are said not to exist in young children and the claim is made that the development of distinctive moral understanding involves a gradual process of separating nonmoral from moral concepts. The evidence that very young children do make moral judgments that are distinct from rules, authority, prudence, instrumentality, and convention suggests that a developmental analysis requires specification of the origins of the domain of moral judgments and qualitative changes within the domain. That young children, as well as older children and adolescents, make distinctively moral judgments does not imply that no developmental changes occur in the moral domain.

It implies that the precursors of developmentally advanced concepts have their origins within the domain.

Investigations of age-related changes within narrowly defined aspects of morality would provide information about developmental transformations. One such study by Damon (1977) dealt specifically with conceptions of distributive justice. Children from 4 to 10 years of age were interviewed using hypothetical stories that dealt with conflicts over how to distribute or share goods among a group of people. The interview was designed to elicit responses regarding the reasons for sharing, the conditions under which sharing could occur, and the procedures to be used to achieve fair distributions. As an example, one story depicts a classroom of children who make paintings and crayon drawings to be sold at a school fair. The sale brings in a good deal of money and the class now has to decide how to divide the money. In the course of the interview, additional information is provided about children in the class that is relevant to the distribution of the money: Some children made more paintings and drawings than others; some made better ones; some children were lazy; some children came from poorer families than others.

The findings from Damon's research illustrate the types of changes that occur during childhood in the organization of thinking about justice. Children's responses to questions about distribution led to the formulation of a sequence of six levels characterizing development from approximately 4 to 10 years of age. For the present purposes it is not necessary to consider the first two levels (level O-A: "Positive justice choices derive from subject's wish that an act occur"; level O-B: "Choices still reflect subject's desires but are justified on the basis of external, observable realities," Damon, 1977, p. 75) because they essentially represent negative characterizations in that the young child is described as lacking a concept of distributive justice. It may, indeed, be the case that children as young as 4 or 5 years of age have not yet formed concepts of distributive justice. It may also be the case that the difficulties inherent in using interviews with children under 5 years of age may be the source of the negative characterizations. Using alternative methods, research by Nucci and Turiel (1978) and Smetana (1981a) has shown that 3- and 4-year-old children make distinctively moral judgments. Whether the negative characterization reflected in Damon's description of level O-A and O-B is accurate remains to be seen.

By about the ages of 6 or 7 years children have formed concepts of equality related to prescriptive judgments of moral necessity. At level 1-A "the operating justice principle is one of equal action; that is, everyone should get the same treatment under any circumstances" (Damon, 1977, p. 75). The overriding theme at this level is equal treatment. Fairness means equality and equality functions to prevent conflicts among people. Equality is the criterion for fair distribution of resources. Regardless of the contributions made to an endeavor, resources should be shared in such a way that everyone receives the same amount.

At level 1-A, it is recognized that a means is required to distribute available resources and, thereby, resolve conflicts stemming from competing claims. Strict equality accomplishes these aims. However, in their application of the notion of equality these children do not account for other factors, such as varying contributions of members of the class. It is not that differences are treated as nonmorally relevant; differences are not accounted for in any way. At the next level such differences are accounted for through the notion of merit as a criterion for fair distribution. At level 1-B reciprocity enters into the decision in the form of compensation for merit and in the form of "fair exchange." It is considered necessary to take merit into account in deciding the validity of different people's competing claims. Justice entails rewarding people for their good work or for their differential contributions. The reciprocity of fair exchange means, for these children, that there is the obligation to return favors and rewards.

The basic change at the next level is to a focus on persons rather than on the person's acts. In determining how to distribute resources, children at level 2-A consider the different claims and attempt a systematic solution to the problem. The nature of their solution, however, is not a plan of action but a set of compromises. By means of such compromises everyone's merit and needs are given consideration. The focus on persons at level 2-A involves a concern with the equality of persons; compensation for differences among people are aimed at achieving an equality of their respective conditions. As a consequence, there is now a concern with *need*. Rewarding need is seen as necessary to maintain the equality of persons. Therefore, inequality in actions (e.g., giving more to one person than to another) compensates for existing inequalities.

The next level (2-B) is also characterized by a concern with all the participants in a situation that requires a system of distribution. However, those children seek a systematic basis for arriving at the most just solution for the situation under consideration. Consequently, they draw connections between the way rewards are allocated and the functions of the rewards in the specified context. Children at level 2-B consider the nature of the situation in which people interact, their contribution, and the goals of the activity. Rewards are based on the functions they serve in accomplishing the stated aim. Moreover, there is a rudimentary understanding of contractual obligations in social interactions.

The age-related changes observed in concepts of distributive justice complement the findings of non–age-relatedness in the distinction between morality and convention. Whereas concepts within the two domains are distinguished across ages, developmental changes occur within each domain. As described in Chapter 6, developmental changes in concepts of social convention and social organization have been documented in individuals from the age of 6 to the early 20s. The levels of concepts of distributive justice provide evidence for developmental changes in a significant aspect of moral judgment. It is still necessary to extend the analysis to other aspects of children's moral judgments, including their concepts of the value of life, human rights, trust, and contractual obligations.

8 Noncognitive approaches to moral development: internalization and biological determinism

One feature common to all the structural approaches compared in the previous chapter is their emphasis on analyses of judgments in the study of moral development. In contrast with a structural approach, there exist several social scientific accounts that deemphasize the individual's judgmental processes in the area of morality. Indeed, one of the major controversies has been and continues to be about the role of thought in moral functioning and development. It is often assumed by psychologists that nonrational or irrational processes determine behavior in the social domains. Some psychologists, such as the strict behaviorists (e.g., Skinner, 1971; Watson, 1924), have asserted that thought is not relevant to explanations of any form of human behavior, which, of course, includes morality. Others who may accept the relevance of thought processes to explanations of certain realms, such as mathematics or physics, nevertheless reject its applicability in social realms. The view that social behavior is nonrational is apparent in the explanations considered in the present chapter: Freud's psychoanalytic theory and the behavioristic tradition (from strict behaviorism, to neobehaviorism, to contemporary social-learning-behavioristic analyses). Nonrationality is also part of a perspective – labeled sociobiology – that is only briefly considered here.

Although the wide array of events used in research on moral development (see Table 7.1) is partially owing to choices that are made without clear-cut criteria for the domain, it also reflects the differences in how researchers have defined morality. In contrast with the structural view of social development as the construction of conceptual categories through individual–environment interactions, psychoanalytic and behavioristic theories explain development as causally determined by the environmental content to which the child is exposed and/or by biologically built-in characteristics (traits, instincts, capacities). The behavioristic and Freudian approaches, each in its own way, regard moral behavior as the product of an internalization of external standards. In the Freudian explanation, however, a complex set of relations between innate and environmental factors is seen as producing a morality that represents the imposition, to a greater or lesser extent, of the social environment upon the individual. In behavioristic explanations, it is assumed that moral development is a straightforward process of learning socially acceptable behaviors and incorporating transmitted standards and values. Biological traits or capacities form a backdrop that may facilitate or impede the rate and strength of the child's incorporation of environmental content.

The explanations of the individual's morality as causally determined by social-environmental content are based on a functional view, which represents another contrast with the structural analyses of morality as involving systems of thought about social interactions. In each theory the individual's moral behavior is regarded as a functional adaptation to social contingencies, rather than the structuring of knowledge. Morality represents an ontogenetic adaptation of the initially unsocialized, impulsive, self-interested child to the demands of other persons and the general social system in the environment. An extensive and comprehensive analysis of social adaptation has been provided by Freud, who attempted to detail the various components of such a model. Freud's model, which was primarily based on data from clinical reports and psychohistory, includes some general and complex concepts that are difficult to evaluate empirically. In contrast, behavioristic-internalization explanations, which have borrowed heavily from the Freudian model, are largely restricted to the study of mechanisms of learning or acquisition, with only vaguely stated assumptions regarding the initial unsocialized state of the individual or the societal need for modification of the child's behavior. The analyses of acquisition mechanisms are usually experimentally based and thus provide a means for evaluation of methods and data. Together, the Freudian and behavioristic explanations provide concrete examples of the various components of socialization-internalization conceptions of development. On the one hand, Freudian theory, if considered at a general level, explicates the necessary elements of the individual–social-environment relation in the socialization process. On the other hand, behavioristic theories provide both detailed propositions regarding mechanisms of acquisition and concrete empirical demonstrations of the ways individual–social-environment interactions are conceived. In these two approaches the psychological features of the socialization or enculturation processes are explicated.

It should be noted that the purpose of examining nonstructural explanations of morality is, of necessity, somewhat different from the purpose of the previous chapter's comparisons of alternative structural approaches. In the previous chapter the data from research on morality and convention were used in a direct way to evaluate other structural-developmental propositions. It would be another and less legitimate matter to use those data to *directly* evaluate propositions from entirely different theoretical and methodological paradigms. Research in each paradigm is predicated on sufficiently discrepant assumptions and goals from the others that evidence from one is often not comparable to another.

Therefore, evaluations drawing on empirical evidence must proceed cautiously.

One of the aims of considering the nonstructural approaches to moral development is to place the structural approach in the context of the wider body of theory and research on moral development and, thereby, draw explicit contrasts and comparisons. Insofar as research evidence on morality and convention is used in these comparisons, it is in an effort to reinterpret the results of some of the studies done from nonstructural perspectives. Moreover, given that nonstructural approaches have generally asserted that moral thinking is not closely related to behavior, the present chapter provides a context for the subsequent chapter's discussion of the relations between judgment and action.

Before proceeding to the discussion of the Freudian and behavioristic explanations, mention should be made of approaches that emphasize biological traits as the source of moral behavior. Most notably, it has recently been proposed by *sociobiologists* that moral behaviors are primarily genetically and not culturally determined (in this view the social environment may serve to facilitate or impede the emergence of biologically fixed actions). Indeed, in direct contrast with the environmental emphasis of the behavioristic-internalization theorists, sociobiologists explicitly argue that morality is an appropriate topic for biological investigation. The leading proponent of sociobiology, E. O. Wilson (1975, p. 562), has stated, "Scientists and humanists should consider together the possibility that the time has come for ethics to be removed temporarily from the hands of the philosophers and biologicized." Referring to neo-Darwinian evolutionary theory as the Modern Synthesis, Wilson more generally claims (p. 4) that "it may not be too much to say that sociology and the other social sciences, as well as the humanities, are the last branches of biology waiting to be included in the Modern Synthesis. One of the functions of sociobiology, then, is to reformulate the foundations of the social sciences in a way that draws these subjects into the Modern Synthesis."

Sociobiology is predicated on the idea that human behavior is determined by natural selection in ways that are very similar to the influences of natural selection on bodily forms. In addition, it is maintained that evolutionary explanations, used to interpret systematic studies of social behavior and social organization in insects, can be applied to human social behavior. It is proposed that there are universal features of human social behavior and human social organization that are determined by characteristics that evolved by natural selection. "The accumulated evidence for a large hereditary component (of human social behavior) is more detailed and more compelling than most persons, including even geneticists, realize. I will go further: it is already decisive" (Wilson, 1978, p. 19).

A large hereditary component is presumed to exist for human moral behavior (generally defined as altruism). Neo-Darwinian theory holds that all organisms evolve by natural selection. That is, those organisms that are better adapted to their environment survive and reproduce, whereas those less able to adapt tend to die out. For sociobiologists, however, the primary unit of selection is not the species or the group, but the individual. From an evolutionary point of view, the organism's function is to reproduce its genes. The relevant measure of natural selection is the extent to which an individual's genes influence the distribution of copies of the genes in the future. By definition, it follows that the better-adapted organisms (fitness) are those that contribute to gene reproduction. Furthermore, if fitness refers to the ability to reproduce genes, then those genes that are reproduced are the ones that are fit.

The principles of natural selection are applied by sociobiologists to behaviors at a very specific level in that there is an attempt to analyze the genetic advantages of fairly specific acts, such as engaging in acts of helping or altruism. Specific classes of behavior are explained on the basis of natural selection. Moreover, the definition of an act is tied to the biological explanation, as is evident in the sociobiological definition of altruism (Wilson, 1975, p. 117): "When a person (or animal) increases the fitness of another at the expense of his own fitness, he can be said to have performed an act of altruism." Several illustrative examples of animal altruistic behavior fitting this definition have been provided. One of the frequently used examples is that of worker castes in insect societies (ants, bees, wasps). For instance, the stinging behavior of worker bees serves to repel intruders who might take the colony's honey or otherwise pose a danger. However, in performing such an act, the stinging bee's organs are usually torn out and it dies shortly thereafter. Thus, the bee's act of altruism results in its own demise.

Such altruistic acts may appear to contradict the proposition that they evolve by natural selection, insofar as they benefit others to the detriment of the actor. According to sociobiologists, however, altruistic acts of this kind actually increase the chances that the actor's genes will survive and, thus, are consistent with the principle of natural selection. Altruism has evolved through natural selection because an individual's altruistic acts toward a relative, though reducing his or her own fitness, may increase the fitness of the relative. Because the relative has some of the same genes as the actor, he or she may be increasing the chances of reproduction of those genes (it is the ability to reproduce one's genes that defines fitness). Consequently, natural selection favors the evolution of genes for altruism insofar as they increase the chances that the actor's genes will survive. Furthermore, it is maintained that only altruistic acts serving to increase gene reproduction will be selected for. If altruism does not have this effect, then it would be selected out.

The explanation of altruism toward relatives, termed "kin selection," does not account for acts directed toward nonrelatives. In humans, for instance, one person may jump into a river to save a previously unknown person, even at some risk for his or her own safety. It is claimed that this type of human behavior also evolves through natural selection. Saving the drowning person benefits the rescuer if the drowning person (or someone else) reciprocates at a future time (Trivers, 1971). On that basis, natural selection in the long run favors individuals who risk their lives to save each other over those who do not: "A population at large that enters into a series of such moral obligations, that is, reciprocally altruistic acts, will be a population of individuals with generally increased genetic fitness" (Wilson, 1975, p. 120).

Notwithstanding the apparent difference between sociobiology and behaviorism (behaviorism maintains that morality is, in the main, environmentally determined, whereas sociobiology holds that it is, in the main, genetically determined), there is a major and significant similarity in the two approaches. Like behaviorism, the unit of analysis is located in behavior and not in thought. The sociobiological claim is that an individual's morality or altruism is determined by one's inherited genetic makeup, which directly manifests itself in specific behaviors. It is assumed in both approaches that a valid explanation of morality can largely ignore moral judgment. A lack of concern for moral thought takes two forms. First is the lack of concern for the philosophical underpinnings of the concept of morality (Stent, 1978). Second is the lack of inclusion of the individual's processes of moral reasoning in analyses of moral behaviors. Behaviorists short-circuit reasoning processes by directly and causally linking behavior to prior (conditioning) experiences. Sociobiologists short-circuit reasoning processes by directly and causally linking behavior to genetic material. Moreover, it is not apparent that explanations currently exist regarding the relations between behavior and genetic material. The molecular biologist G. S. Stent has stated the problem as follows (1978, p. 18):

But by mid-century, molecular genetics had managed to identify the gene as that element of genetic material, or DNA, in which the amino acid sequence of a particular protein is encoded. It is in this sense, under which the gene is conceptualizeable in absolute rather than differential terms, that nearly all working geneticists now employ the term "gene." And the ensemble of genes, encoding the structural information for thousands of different proteins, is referred to as the genome of an organism. What is less well known, however, is that the nature of the relation between that genome and the physical realization of the actual animal, or its phenome, is an extremely complex, and as yet quite unsolved conceptual problem. That is to say, it is not yet possible to state in just what way any physical and behavioral feature of an animal can be said to be "determined" by its genes. . . . The conceptual obstacle to providing such an account lies mainly in the role played by the enormously complex context in which the genes find themselves in the course of embryonic and post-embryonic development.

Although behaviorists have attempted to study human behavior, there are virtually no such sociobiological investigations. Sociobiological propositions are based essentially on a set of assumptions that are not empirically verified regarding the nature of altruistic behavior in humans, coupled with accounts of how those behaviors can result in genetic fitness. In this regard, the argument is that if a behavior exists, it must have undergone natural selection. An explanation is then proposed to show how the behavior is adaptive and could have evolved through natural selection.

The circularity of this line of reasoning produces a confusion of terms, as was also pointed out by Stent (1978). For instance, the term "altruism" is used by sociobiologists in its usual sense, with moral connotations, to refer to helping others or, more generally, to the regard by one person for the interests of other persons. In turn, the term "selfishness" is used in its usual sense to refer to a person's disregard for the interests of others. However, as already mentioned, the term "altruism" is also used by sociobiologists in reference to behavior that increases the fitness of another at the expense of one's own fitness. Altruism of that sort is, however, not truly at the expense of one's own fitness, because it is presumably an act that actually increases fitness; the act is, therefore, selfish (see especially Dawkins, 1976). Accordingly, morality (altruism) is indistinguishable from any other type of behavior. Because moral (altruistic) acts are supposed to serve the function of gene reproduction, their function is the same as any other behavior that has undergone evolution. If it were the case, for instance, that allowing drowning people to die served to spread one's genes, then such an action would have the same genetic source and would have evolved for the same reason as the altruistic act of saving a drowning person. In other words, within the sociobiological explanation there is no basis by which to distinguish between the function of what are labeled moral acts and the function of their opposites. One of the reasons sociobiologists fail to provide criteria for acts is that they have not made direct studies of human social behavior or patterns of social interaction. In the absence of such investigations, the proposed biological determinants of specific behaviors are speculative (Gould, 1978; Hubbard, 1978). Sociobiological data on other species and explanations of morality still need to be grounded in sound conceptions of the topic, as well as on data on human behavior (if not judgment).

Superego formation

Freud's explanation of moral development, like most internalization views, has as its starting point a proposed dichotomy between the individual, in an unsocialized state, and the social system, which in turn implies a dichotomy between the individual in an unsocialized state and in a socialized state. The dichotomy of individual and social system usually refers to a variety of dimensions, including the self and others, the individual and the group, self-interests or selfishness and altruism, personal needs and social obligations. The corresponding dichotomy refers to two states of the self, with the first, apparent in the earliest years of life, characterized by impulsiveness, self-interest, and lack of self-control, and the second by self-control and consideration of the interests of others.

According to the Freudian interpretation, the proposed dichotomy between the individual and the group stems largely from a sharp distinction between the individual's instinctual makeup and the character and aims of the social system. The nature and functions of the social system, however, are directly associated with and largely determined by the nature of individuals. Culture or civilization, as Freud referred to systems of social organization, serve the twofold purpose of protecting and defending against individuals. Civilization serves to protect persons by ensuring their survival and by providing for some degree of the instinctual satisfaction that is necessary for their well-being. One central function of civilization, therefore, is to guard against the dangers inherent to the individual in the natural or physical world. Civilization must also include means for defending against individuals by restricting the extent of their instinctual satisfaction. The second central function of civilization is a moral one, entailing the protection of individuals from each other. Social regulations maintain a balance in social relations within the family, the state, and society.

It is the instinctual endowments of humans that make a system of social regulation necessary for the perpetuation of civilization. Moral development is, therefore, the process by which the child's original state is transformed through the influences of the social environment: "It is impossible to overlook the extent to which civilization is built up upon a renunciation of instinct, how much it presupposes precisely the non-satisfaction (by suppression, repression or some other means?) of powerful instincts" (Freud, 1930/1961, p. 44). Civilization places restrictions on two kinds of instincts – sexuality and aggressiveness. One reason why civilization requires restraints upon the sexual life of its members, according to Freud, is so that they will channel psychical or mental energies to other activities that contribute to cultural aims. Sexual instincts are sublimated and transformed into activities, such as scientific and artistic ones, that play a role in the formation and development of civilization. Moreover, the restricted nature of sexual attachments constitutes a second reason civilization restrains the sexuality of individuals. Attachments among the members of a social system are of a wider scope than those inherent in sexual relationships.

The other serious impediment to civilization stems from hostile impulses that also exist in all persons (Freud, 1930/1961, p. 58):

Men are not gentle creatures who want to be loved, and who at the most can defend themselves if they are attacked; they are, on the contrary, creatures among whose instinctual endowments is to be reckoned a powerful share of aggressiveness. As a result, their neighbour is for them not only a potential helper or sexual object, but also someone who tempts them to satisfy their aggressiveness on him, to exploit his capacity for work without compensation, to use him sexually without his consent, to seize his possessions, to humiliate him, to cause him pain, to torture and to kill him.

Regulations in social systems arise from the need to impose restrictions on individuals in order to protect them from the consequences of their own biologically determined instinctual forces. Hostility among people is the natural state, in the biological sense. Transformations of that natural state serve the functions of maintaining and perpetuating the social system, given the dangers posed by unrestrained aggressiveness:

> Thus culture must defend against the individual, and its organizations, its institutions and its laws, are all directed to this end; they aim not only at establishing a certain distribution of property, but also at maintaining it; in fact, they must protect against the hostile impulses of mankind everything that contributes to the conquest of nature and the production of wealth. [Freud, 1927/1953, p. 4]

It is apparent that in Freud's view a substantial conflict is inherent to relations between the individual and the social system, and that an accommodation must be reached between the claims of the individual's nature and those of the culture. Antisocial or anticultural tendencies necessitate societal coercion so as to produce instinctual renunciations by the individual. In ontogenesis the restrictions on instinctual impulses are at first maintained through external coercion. To be effective, the process of internalizing restrictions on both sexual and aggressive tendencies must begin in childhood. During childhood there generally comes about the repression and modification of instincts, as well as the replacement of external coercion with an internalized agency of control: "Civilization, therefore, obtains mastery over the individual's desire for aggression by weakening and disarming it and by setting up an agency within him to watch over it, like a garrison in a conquered city" (Freud, 1930/1961, pp. 70–71). The agency within the individual that functions like a garrison in a conquered city is the *superego*. The superego and the *ego* (which refers to rational capacities and defensive functions that develop to cope with external reality) are the two mental agencies constituting the transformed aspects of the *id* (which refers to the instincts).

Freud's explanation of the formation of the superego attempted to describe, in a comprehensive fashion, the various psychological dimensions of moral functioning and development. One component is the source and nature of the initial, unsocialized state of the individual. The Freudian explanation of instincts and the governing principle of homeostasis or constancy serve to explicate the assumption that the individual's earliest states are antisocial, impulsive, and lacking in self-control. A second component is the explanation of types of social experiences that modify or transform the child's initial state. A third component is the psychological mechanisms that account for the transformation of the individual from one state to another. A fourth component is the psychological mechanism regulating moral behavior subsequent to its internalization. One of Freud's primary developmental concerns was with how the individual's complex instinctual functions become transformed. It was proposed that by middle-childhood (6 or 7 years of age), a marked transformation occurs through the development of a superego.

Instincts are characterized by their source, object, impetus, and aim (Freud, 1915/1959). The source of an instinct is physiological and is always directed toward an object. The object is generally another person, though it could also be the self. As will be evident shortly, the possibility of the self as an object of instincts is central to Freud's explanation of self-regulation of moral behavior. The impetus of instincts refers to their energy, which is necessary for all behavior and psychological activity. The impetus for activity originally resides in the instincts, but can be, and often becomes, channeled into other functions. The aim of instincts is satisfaction, which is accomplished through the reduction of stimulation and the attainment of constancy. The need for reduction of instinctual arousal is a fundamental and predominant characteristic of psychological processes. It guides behavior and motivates changes in mental functioning. It is largely this motivating quality of instinctual impulses that produces the need for societal regulation and suppression of the individual.

Freud's proposition that civilization restricts sexuality and aggressiveness was based on his formulation of the two general classes of instincts, the life (Eros) and the death (Thanatos) instincts. However, the dichotomy of life and death instincts, meant to represent the opposition between self-preservation and self-destruction, was for all intents and purposes used as a dichotomy between sexuality and aggression. Although Freud speculated about the idea of a death instinct (Freud, 1920/1970), in his systematic analyses of development he treated it as an instinct of aggression.

During childhood an interaction of these two types of instincts results in a major conflict with the social environment that produces the conditions for the internalization of morality. The maturation of sexuality through stages of psychosexual development in infancy and early childhood (Freud, 1905/1962), provides one of the essential conditions for superego formation. Maturation through the psychosexual stages (oral, anal, phallic) produces the phallic stage, with its dominance of the genital zone and a shift of the object of instinctual energy from the self to another person. Generally, it is a person of the opposite sex close to the child who becomes the potential source of sexual gratification. That is, the child forms a sexual attachment to the opposite-sexed parent.

The assumption that the child forms an intense sexual attachment to the parent had great relevance for Freud's view of moral internalization, because it constituted the basis for a major conflict between the child's instinctual impulses and the demands of the social system. The conflict takes shape within the family unit, in the form of what Freud referred to as the Oedipal conflict, with the parents representing the more general societal restrictions. In addition to the sexual attachment to one parent, the child regards the other parent as a rival and directs aggression (also of an instinctual origin) toward that person. Both types of instinctual impulses must be renounced by the child. A sexual attachment to members of one's family is prohibited by society (the incest taboo), and aggression must be controlled within the social life of the family unit. The consequence of all of this is an intense emotional conflict within the child owing to highly energized instinctual impulses. First, the child's conflicts over the sexual attachment to one parent and hostility toward the other parent stem from a strong fear of retaliation (especially in the imagined form of castration for the boy). The child fears punishment from the same-sexed parent who is a rival for the opposite-sexed parent's affections. The conflict is compounded insofar as the child also has a positive affectional attachment to the same-sexed parent. In such a case, the fear of retaliation is combined with strong feelings of ambivalence toward the parent.

The Oedipal conflict, as just described, constitutes a heightened sense of tension for the child because it evokes strong instinctual impulses and because of the anxiety engendered by the perceived consequences from others. Because the child cannot gratify the sexual or aggressive impulses, some other resolution must be sought. Indeed, it is just such conflicts that, in Freud's model, account for major developmental shifts. That is, the mechanism for developmental shifts is the experience of strong emotional conflicts and the concomitant need for their resolution in order to reduce tension.

In the case of the Oedipal conflict the resolution is accomplished through a marked change in instinctual aims and energies (Freud, 1924/1959). The Oedipal conflicts are resolved through suppression of the sexual desire for one parent and its replacement by an identification with the other parent. At the same time the child also suppresses the aggressive impulses toward the parent. It is through the identification with the parent that the child incorporates as his own the parental moral standards and values. The newly acquired state of internally regulated moral standards was seen by Freud as having two components. One is the incorporation of the parental moral standards, of an ego-ideal. The second component is the conscience, which refers to the means by which adherence to the standards of the ego-ideal is maintained. The conscience is a superego function that maintains internal surveillance over the actions and intentions of the self (ego). It censors and controls the ego's intentions and actions by observing, criticizing, and punishing it. The control exerted by the conscience is experienced as *guilt*.

Freud's explanation of how the child develops the conscience, or a sense of guilt, is related to the suppression of the aggressive instinct with the resolution of the Oedipal conflict. In Freud's scheme, instincts cannot be eliminated, but they can be repressed (i.e., made unconscious) or modified. It is the rechanneling of aggression that explains the origin and functioning of the sense of guilt. The renunciation of aggression toward the parent during the Oedipal phase means that aggression must be directed elsewhere; it is turned on the self. The self becomes the object of these impulses and thus the aggressiveness is internalized in the sense that one part of the self (the superego) punishes or criticizes another part of the self (the ego) through experiences of guilt. The redirection of aggression serves a twofold purpose. It is society's way of controlling the aggression of individuals and it serves as a means of regulating moral behavior (Freud, 1930/1961, pp. 70–71).

Freud's psychological explanation, then, for the commonly applied notion of a sense of guilt is that it is aggression, with all its instinctual impetus, forced by social reality to be directed toward the self. Self-directed aggression is experienced as guilt, which entails self-criticism and self-punishment for the ego's failure to meet the standards of the superego. The formation of internalized guilt and the corresponding introjected moral standards represent the major developmental accomplishments in bridging the initial dualism of the individual and the social, of individual interest and collective or social aims. In the Freudian formulation there must occur a significant modification of the individual's instinct-bound, instinct-controlled state to one of self-control, allowing for the inhibition of instincts. A developmental shift of such major proportions, producing a new mental agency, requires intense energizing or motivating forces. The powerful forces that provide the impetus for the formation of the superego as an internal agency of control include strong fears of physical consequences and the intense instinctually based emotions, sexual and aggressive, revolving around the child's relations with the parents. Insofar as change does occur, the intensity of the conflicts allows for sufficient modification in the individual to produce an increased adjustment to the social environment.

Clearly, there are fundamental differences between the psychoanalytic and the structural-developmental conceptions of social development. Perhaps the most basic divergence from the structural conception is the psychoanalytic proposition that morality enforces restraints on the individual entailed by the social environment. In the psychoanalytic view, morality does not involve judgments about right and wrong, nor is it a set of discriminations between social relations of a prescriptive nature and social relations of a descriptive-conventional nature. Corresponding to this difference in the two conceptions of the nature of morality are differences in the explanations of its development. According to psychoanalytic theory, self-restraint, self-control, and moral standards are initially acquired through one fundamental modification at about 6 or 7 years of age. The nature of this modification is determined by the impositions placed on the child by the parents. The findings presented earlier also show that morality generally has begun to develop at an early age, as was proposed by Freud. However, those findings indicate that there are moral understandings and discriminations at these early ages that go beyond what is predicted by theories of restraint or absolutistic conformity to a set of standards. In contrast with the Freudian interpretation of the young child's morality, the judgments and behavioral responses assessed in the studies discussed in previous chapters indicate that young children are able to evaluate patterns of social interactions in complex and conceptually flexible ways (e.g., make discriminations regarding their alterability, relativity, and rule or authority contingency). The structural interpretation of those findings is that children make inferences based upon social interactions experienced in early life. Moreover, as has been seen, social concepts can be described as undergoing gradual, long-term qualitative transformations beyond early childhood.

From a structural viewpoint, the process of transformation in the form of social concepts includes a criticalness of one's own way of thinking. Self-criticism is an important component of both psychoanalytic and structural theory. However, the form that self-criticism takes and the functions it serves reflect basic differences in the two formulations. In the Freudian view, it is an internalized emotional reaction representing a dynamic interaction of two internal mental agencies. Its function is to provide self-maintenance for those behaviors that have been forced on the self and are in conflict with natural tendencies. In the structural view, criticalness is a conceptual process. It involves the recognition of errors, inconsistencies, and internal contradictions in one's system of thought. Criticalness, in this view, is not a form of punishment, nor does it serve to maintain imposed behavior. Rather, it is a reflective process that produces developmental transformations.

These two conceptualizations of self-criticalness are related to the different ways in which each view has formulated the relation of stimulus and response. As discussed in Chapter 2, the structural view assumes a reciprocal relation between stimulus and response or between the individual and the environment. The reciprocal relation includes the type of feedback from experiences that stimulates self-criticalness and a reorganization in thinking. The Freudian explanation of individual–environment interaction is closely tied to the constancy principle – that the individual strives to reduce stimulation and tension. Responses are aimed at gratifying instinctual impulses and at reducing the tensions or anxieties that the external environment may produce. In Freud's conception of stimulus-response relations, however, instinctual stimulation is not reduced in a straightforward fashion through responses. As we have seen, instincts constitute stable, long-term forms of stimulation that can remain in the unconscious or be transformed into other functions. The formation of a superego is an example of a developmental acquisition stemming from modifications of instincts, and motivated by the need to reduce individual–environment tensions and thus achieve constancy.

Because the formation of the superego is presumed to involve an incorporation of the values and standards of the group, any type of societal restraint on instincts, including those on aggression and sexuality, can have the status of moral restrictions. In the sexual realm, the prohibition on incest was regarded as primary by Freud. Nevertheless, more general prohibitions on sexual activities result from the incest taboo. However, the status of moral and societal functions served by instinctual restrictions is ambiguous in Freud's formulation. It is restrictions on aggressiveness, on the harm that persons would otherwise do to each other, that Freud regarded as the most important. Furthermore, Freud regarded order and cleanliness as requirements of civilization. It is not superego formation that produces order and cleanliness. Activities associated with the anal stage of psychosexual development result in the formation of personality traits of "parsimony, a sense of order and cleanliness" (Freud, 1930/1961, pp. 43–44).

By contrast, the behavioristic-internalization position is unambiguous in that morality is defined as equivalent to convention. Although there are several versions of what is being referred to here as the behavioristic-internalization approach, each is predicated on the assumption, also made by psychoanalytic theory, that social development entails modifications of the initially unsocialized, self-interested child because of the demands of the social environment. As in psychoanalytic theory, moral development is viewed as the acquisition of standards transmitted to the child by others, the replacement of external surveillance over behavior with internal regulation of those same behaviors, and the acquisition of the means for self-control over impulsive tendencies.

Behavioristic-internalization approaches

Despite an acceptance of the general psychoanalytic socialization paradigm, there are considerable differences in the behavioristic-internalization proposals regarding the means by which socialization occurs. In particular, behavioristic-internalization theorists have contended (Bandura & Walters, 1963; Skinner, 1971) that several of Freud's constructs are imbued with mentalistic and dynamic content that should be reduced to simpler behavioral and learning processes. The most extreme form of behaviorism was proposed by Skinner (1971), who, in reducing morality to conditioned responses, rejected any type of internal construct (not only the Freudian ones, but also the notions of judgment and knowledge, as well). In reference to the moral domain, Skinner has stated (1971, pp. 107–108):

This is an area in which it is easy to lose sight of the contingencies. A person drives a car well because of the contingencies of reinforcement which have shaped and which maintain his behavior. The behavior is traditionally explained by saying that he possesses the knowledge or skill needed to drive a car, but the knowledge and skill must then be traced to contingencies that might have been used to explain the behavior in the first place. We do not say that a person does what he "ought to do" in driving a car because of any inner sense of what is right. We are likely to appeal to some such inner virtue, however, to explain why a person behaves well with respect to his fellow men, but he does so not because his fellow men have endowed him with a sense of responsibility or obligation or with loyalty or respect for others but because they have arranged effective social contingencies. The behaviors classified as good or bad and right or wrong are not due to goodness or badness, or a good or bad character, or a knowledge of right and wrong; they are due to contingencies involving a great variety of reinforcers, including the generalized verbal reinforcers of "Good!" "Bad!" "Right!" and "Wrong!"

In the Skinnerian view, therefore, the acquisition and functioning of moral behavior is the same as any other learned behavior (given that all behaviors are learned through the same mechanisms). It is not solely an equation of morality with other social restrictions that is proposed by Skinner. The equation is with any type of behavior, including learning to drive an automobile or having an aversion to some foods. As Skinner (1971, p. 109) put it:

Relevant social contingencies are implied by "You ought not to steal," which could be translated, "If you tend to avoid punishment, avoid stealing," or "Stealing is wrong, and wrong behavior is punished." Such a statement is no more normative than "If coffee keeps you awake when you want to go to sleep, don't drink it."

In less strictly behavioristic analyses than those of Skinner, it is proposed that there is a domain of morality, distinguishable from nonsocial behaviors, that involves not only learned behavioral responses but also the acquisition of standards, values, and evaluative judgments (Aronfreed, 1968; Bandura, 1977; Mischel & Mischel, 1976). Nevertheless, in these behavioristic-internalization analyses it is also maintained that the Freudian constructs have "surplus meaning and...frequently personify the controlling forces" (Bandura & Walters, 1963, p. 162). Most frequently, it is the following Freudian constructs that have been criticized: the superego as an internal mental agency, identification as a global and unitary acquisition mechanism, guilt as part of the superego and as internalized aggression, and both the dynamics of the Oedipal conflict and its status as the setting for the major developmental shift. In their stead, it is maintained that throughout childhood specific behaviors and judgments are acquired that serve to alter the otherwise impulsive, self-interested state.

Although the rejection of the Freudian constructs may obviate some of the more imprecise Freudian notions of mental agencies and dynamic interactions, the result for behavioristic-internalization theorists has been a number of unspecified – or even more vaguely formulated than in Freudian theory – components in their socialization paradigm. In Freud's theory, for instance, assumptions regarding the child's initial state are based on the explanation of instincts, which in turn forms part of the proposition of inherent conflicts between the individual and society. An attempt is made to specify the individual tendencies, as determined by the instinct formulation, that would interfere with societal and cultural aims. By contrast, the behavioristic-internalization assumption that the child's initial state is one of self-interest remains unexplained. It has the status of an assumption rather than a hypothesis or set of propositions. Consequently, research has not been done to provide support for the assumption. Similarly, it is assumed, without extensive elaboration, that the social environment is made up of social norms, standards, and obligations that conflict with the nature of the initial state of the child. It follows, therefore, that Bandura and Walters (1963, p. 165) would assert that "in all cultures there are social demands, customs and taboos that require a member to exhibit self-control." However, specification of the nature and function of social norms is necessary in order to explain the relation of what exists at the cultural level to individual development and behavior. Whether or not social demands, customs, and taboos require self-control depends on what they entail.

Another largely unspecified component of the socialization paradigm is the definition of morality. In theory and research the domain is identified not through a systematic definition of its parameters, but through the hypothesized process of acquisition. Morality is assumed to be those behaviors and standards that parents or other adults impose upon or transmit to children. Therefore, in the behavioristic-internalization scheme morality is arbitrarily determined through those behaviors, standards, or judgments that happen to be transmitted to children (Bandura, 1977). This strategy has generally been used in the choice of stimulus events for research. As discussed shortly, insofar as a definition of morality emerges from the research on internalization, it is that morality is adherence to restrictions established by persons in authority.

As noted earlier, behavioristic research has concentrated mainly on the mechanisms of acquisition. The research provides systematic and detailed explanations of developmental processes within the context of the nonrational view of social development as an accommodation to the social environment. This allows for close examination of the contrasts between accommodation and cognitive interpretation perspectives on individual–environment interactions.

The causal effects of socialization practices in shaping the child's behavior and acquisition of standards have been examined in two types of studies: naturalistic studies of parental child-rearing practices and experimental analyses of the hypothesized mechanisms of acquisition. Beginning with the assumption that in our culture it is the parents who have the primary responsibility for socializing children, the naturalistic studies have examined correlations between measures of (a) parental methods of rearing and discipline, and (b) the degree of moral internalization in the child (Hoffman, 1970, 1977; Hoffman & Saltzstein, 1967; Sears, Maccoby, & Levin, 1957). The assessment of methods of discipline has usually been derived from parental reports regarding how they respond to transgressions on the part of their children. Assessments of the child's moral internalization have included parental reports of the child's behavior, measures of transgressions in experimental situations (usually of cheating in a competitive game), measures of the degree of internalized guilt, and measures of the extent to which the child spontaneously confesses to transgressions (see Hoffman, 1970, 1977, for reviews of this type of research).

A typology has been postulated that includes three forms of parental discipline (Aronfreed, 1968; Bandura & Walters, 1963; Hoffman, 1977). The three types of discipline are labeled *power assertion, love withdrawal,* and *induction.* Power assertion refers to the use of physical power and control of resources as a means of disciplining the child. It includes physical punishment and the deprivation of material objects and privileges. Love withdrawal refers to nonphysical expressions of disapproval in reaction to the child's actions. It involves withdrawal of attention (e.g., ignoring the child, refusing to communicate with the child) and temporarily withdrawing signs of affection or the expression of dislike. Induction refers to the use of explanation in order to persuade the child to behave differently. The method of induction involves reasoning with the child and, in the process, highlighting the effects of the child's actions to himself or herself and to others (e.g., pointing out the harmful consequences of an action for another person). Although induction is typed as a discipline technique, it does not truly constitute discipline in the usual sense of the term. It involves engaging the child in a process of communication regarding the rationale for one's actions and the reasons for prohibitions. One reasons with someone as a means of communicating ideas in an effort to get the other person to comprehend the validity of those ideas and, thereby, change his or her thinking about the issue. Simply because it is a parent who is communicating with a child does not, in itself, render the process a form of discipline. If the process were reversed and the child reasoned with the parents, thereby changing their ideas, it would not be said that the child had disciplined the parents.

It has consistently been found that, of these three, the induction method is the most highly correlated with measures of moral internalization. Power assertion is associated with an external moral orientation, and love withdrawal shows no consistent relation to moral orientation (Hoffman, 1977). It turns out, then, that research about the effects of discipline on the child's moral development has produced results indicating that parent–child interactions involving communications about underlying reasons for norms, standards, and behaviors are the most effective in stimulating moral development. Although induction has been assimilated to the typology of discipline techniques, the results can be interpreted as negative findings in the sense that it was actually found that variations in discipline techniques are not strongly related to indexes of moral development. That is, the findings show that interactions of a nondiscipline nature between parent and child are most closely associated with moral development. It follows that the results can be interpreted as supporting the proposition that judgments are central to moral decisions and that reciprocal interactions regarding communication of justifications contribute to the process of development. Moreover, actual attempts to discipline a child are also likely to include implicit forms of communication. Bearing in mind that children make judgments about their social interactions, it may be that parental uses of physical punishment and love withdrawal provide the child with information about the expectations of others and the rules and conventions of social situations.

Experimental studies on social development following the behavioristic-internalization approach parallel the paradigm of the studies of parent–child relations. The experimental findings are also readily interpretable as reflecting the child's cognitive orientation to adult behaviors directed toward them. In that light, the experimental findings lend support to the proposition that discipline techniques are implicit communications. Three major behavioristic explanations are based on experimental analyses. The first is the learning of secondary drives (Miller & Dollard, 1941), the second is observational learning (Bandura, 1962; Bandura, 1969; Bandura & Walters, 1963), and the third combines three factors: learning through conditioned anxiety, observational learning, and the incorporation of cognitive representations (Aronfreed, 1968, 1976).

Experiments stemming from the secondary drive and observational learning hypotheses have dealt with imitative activities in children. For the most part, those experiments were not explicitly designed to assess the imitation of moral behaviors. However, the explanations of social development are meant to include morality, and certain experiments have dealt with the modeling of moral behavior and judgment (Bandura & McDonald, 1963; Stein, 1967). Miller and Dollard (1941) conducted one of the earliest experimental studies designed to apply principles of instrumental conditioning (Hull, 1934) to the learning of social behaviors in children. It was proposed that a habit of imitation, which acquires the status of a secondary drive, is learned when imitative responses to environmental events or cues are associated with rewards or reinforcements of primary drives. Initially the child's behavior matches the actions of others by chance. Insofar as such matching behaviors result in rewards, the tendency to imitate is strengthened. With sufficient reinforcements, imitation becomes stable, habitual behavior, through which other social responses are acquired. Reinforcement also serves to maintain the learned response. The strength of imitation is diminished if it is repeated without reinforcement, eventually to the point of its extinction.

These propositions regarding the learning and extinction of imitative responses were tested by Miller and Dollard through the following experiment. The setting for the experiment was a room containing two separate stools on which were two small boxes in which candy could be placed. Subjects in the study were told that they would be given an opportunity to find candy in one of the boxes. The subjects were first-grade children who were assigned either to an *imitative* or to a *nonimitative* experimental condition. In each of those conditions other children served as "models" who had been trained to go to one of the two boxes at the experimenter's signal and take out one piece of candy. In the imitative condition two pieces of candy were placed in one box and none in the other. On each trial, the model took the first turn, went to the box containing the candy, and took one piece. If the subject then went to the same box as the model ("imitative" response), he or she too would find a piece of candy (reinforcement). If the subject went to the opposite box ("nonimitative" response), he or she would not obtain a reward. Conversely, in the nonimitative condition one piece of candy was placed in each box so that the subject obtained a reward only when he or she did not make the same response as the model.

In both conditions the initial tendency of the subjects was to make the nonimitative response; the large majority of subjects in both conditions made the nonimitative response on the first trial. After a number of trials all subjects formed consistent imitative or nonimitative responses, depending on which response was reinforced. The findings were interpreted as providing support for an instrumental conditioning explanation of imitative behavior: Both imitativeness and nonimitativeness are response tendencies produced and strengthened by reinforcement. According to this interpretation, the child's (acquired) desire for candy stimulates him or her to go to the same box as the model (imitative response) when he or she sees the model go to that box (cues). Each time candy is obtained (reinforcement), the imitative response is strengthened.

The Miller and Dollard experiment and the secondary-drive interpretation of its findings parallels the naturalistic research on parental discipline. In each case the primary, if not sole, consideration is given to the way the actions of other persons, particularly the rewards and punishments administered, directly condition or shape behavior. In each case little attention is paid to the cognitive variables that may account for the child's responses. As in parent–child interactions, however, the experimental situation can also be viewed as including implicit communications that are cognitively interpreted by the subject and that lead to his or her responses. That is, in experimental situations subjects attempt to determine solutions to the tasks presented. In the Miller and Dollard experiment the task is to determine, on each trial, which box contains candy. The activities of the model and the parameters of the task itself, including the placement and discovery of the reward, serve to provide the subject with information that is helpful in solving the problem.

Therefore, an alternative interpretation of the Miller and Dollard experiment is that subjects use all the available information in order to solve a problem – in this case, where to find the candy. The model's actions and the subject's own actions provide information for this quest. By observing where and when the candy was found on each trial, the subject would have been able to understand the experimenter's strategy. For example, in the imitative condition, subjects would have concluded that two candies were always placed in one box and none in the other (though the location was randomly varied), because candy could be found only in the box from which the leader had obtained candy. A simple arithmetical calculation would lead the subject to the realization that he or she should go to the same box as the model to obtain the candy that is being given away.

The validity of this alternative cognitive interpretation of the Miller and Dollard experiment was demonstrated by a study in which modifications were made of their procedures (Turiel & Guinsburg, 1968). The cognitive interpretation says that subjects use information, obtained from a series of experimental trials, to determine where the candy is placed. Thus, if subjects were provided with the same information verbally, it could be expected that they would know where to obtain the candy in the absence of reinforcement. By contrast, if the response is learned and strengthened by the reward, it is to be expected that subjects would require a number of trials for the rewards to be associated with their responses. The Turiel and Guinsburg study tested these alternative hypotheses by making one modification in the Miller and Dollard procedures. Immediately before beginning the experiment (after the task had been explained in the Miller & Dollard manner), subjects in the imitative condition were told the following: "There are two pieces of candy in one box and none in the other." Subjects in the nonimitative condition were told the following immediately before beginning the experiment: "There is one piece of candy in one box and one piece of candy in the other box." In accordance with the Miller and Dollard procedure, for each condition the subject took his turn after the model had made a response on the experimenter's signal. As was predicted by the cognitive hypothesis, almost all subjects (28 of 30 first-graders) went to the box with the candy on the very first trial.

A further test of the cognitive and secondary drive interpretations of imitation is to measure the persistence of the response over altered conditions. A corollary to the Miller and Dollard proposition that reinforcement strengthens imitative (or nonimitative) responses is that, once acquired, such responses will gradually undergo extinction when their performance goes unrewarded. The implication is that if the response has been learned in the usual Miller and Dollard procedure (presumably strengthened by several rewarded trials), then several unrewarded trials would be required for a weakening of the response. The alternative interpretation is that extinction trials provide the subject with information regarding altered experimental conditions and hence the need for a new solution to the task.

These hypotheses were tested in the Turiel and Guinsburg study through two experimental phases. The first phase involved a direct replication of the Miller and Dollard experiments (no verbal information provided). The experimental trials were continued in imitative and nonimitative conditions until the subject made six rewarded responses successively. For the trial immediately following, the experimental condition was shifted to an extinction procedure. For subjects in the imitative condition, the procedure was changed so that one piece of candy was placed in each box (if the subject made the previously "learned" response on the seventh trial a reward would not be obtained). In addition those subjects were given the following information immediately before the seventh trial: "Now there is one piece of candy in one box and one piece in the other." For subjects in the nonimitative condition, the procedure was changed so that two pieces of candy were placed in one box and none in the other. Those subjects were told: "Now there are two pieces of candy in one box and none in the other." Again, the findings were consistent with the proposition that the experimental conditions provide the subject with information relevant to the task. All ten subjects changed their responses on the first "extinction" trial (i.e., zero-trial extinction).

Both sets of results from the Turiel and Guinsburg study show that secondary-drive learning experiments of imitation actually do include implicit communications that the subject can comprehend and then apply for a correct solution to the task. The immediate performance of the correct response (before its reinforcement) demonstrated that the rewards and verbal information are interchangeable. Similarly, nonrewarded trials in experimental extinction procedures inform subjects that the parameters of the situation have changed, thus calling for a new solution to an altered task. Of course, the consequences of altering the Miller and Dollard experiment by introducing the verbal information to subjects are not, by any means, surprising. Despite their obviousness, the findings highlight the importance of assessing the types of information communicated to children by what are regarded as training techniques by experimenters (e.g., rewards) and discipline methods by parents.

An assessment of the information communicated to subjects in experimental tasks is also relevant to observational-learning explanations of imitation and social development (Bandura, 1962; Bandura & Walters, 1963). It was proposed by Bandura that the child's observations of modeled behavior is a sufficient condition for the acquisition of that behavior. Reinforcement (which may be direct or vicarious) serves to control the reproduction of social behaviors, once they have been acquired through the observation of models. In some typical experiments on observational learning (Bandura & Huston, 1961; Bandura, Ross, & Ross, 1963a) a subject is first exposed to an adult model performing some behavior (such as an aggressive act toward an inflated plastic doll), and then is left alone in a room after having been told he may do anything he wants. It is generally found that when left alone children reproduce the model's behavior.

The apparent imitative activities of subjects in observational learning experiments may also reflect responses to implicit communications from the experimenter. From the subject's point of view, those experiments represent more ambiguous situations than the Miller and Dollard experiment in that no goal or task is established. As a consequence, the subject is left to determine what is expected in the situation. In the absence of any explicit instructions, the experimental procedures (i.e., the behavior of the model) would constitute implicit communications or directions regarding the requirements of the situation; that is, an instruction to do what has been shown by the model.

A study by Kuhn and Langer (1968) supports the interpretation that a model's behavior acts as an instruction to the subject when no explicit instructions are provided. Subjects who had observed the model's performance were then given one of several different instructions, ranging from *explicit* instructions to copy the model, through a *neutral* instruction to do whatever they want (similar to the procedure used in observational learning experiments), to *explicit* instructions *not* to copy the model. It was found that children imitated the model under the neutral condition almost as much as in the explicit instruction-to-copy condition. By contrast, considerably less imitative behavior was displayed by those explicitly instructed not to copy the model's behavior. The study thus demonstrated that in an experimental situation a model's behavior can serve the same function as explicit instructions; thus the model's behavior itself constitutes implicit instructions providing information regarding expected behavior on the task.

In both the Turiel and Guinsburg and Kuhn and Langer studies, it was feasible to use simple experimental manipulations to demonstrate the role of communication and cognitive variables in secondary-drive and observational-learning experiments because the subjects' tasks were also simple (e.g., learning the location of candy in a two-choice situation and punching a plastic doll). Although a more complex set of experimental procedures are used in research explicitly designed to examine moral internalization, cognitive variables and the communicative functions of the experimental manipulations account for the findings of those studies as well (Turiel, 1978a).

The focus of moral-internalization experiments has been on three environmental influences: punishment (or reward), modeling, and the transmittal or reasons (akin to induction in the parental discipline research). As seen in Table 7.1, the major proportion of moral-internalization studies have revolved around one kind of experiment, which may be referred to as the *forbidden-toy paradigm*. In the forbidden-toy experiments the behavior examined is whether or not, or the extent to which, a child learns to adhere to a prohibition against playing with some toys available in the experimental room. An example of the basic outline of the experimental situation is as follows:

A child is brought into an experiment room and told that he or she and the adult (experimenter) will talk about some toys. Then the child is successively presented with pairs of toys – in each pair one toy is more attractive than the other. With each pair presented the child is told (a) to choose one of the two to pick up and talk about, and (b) that some choices are not permitted. During each presentation of the pairs of toys the child is administered a mild punishment (e.g., a verbal reprimand, a high-intensity tone, or deprivation of candy) whenever he or she chooses the more attractive toy. At a certain point, the experimenter says that he must leave the room for a while. Upon leaving, the experimenter says that he will lock the door and that when he returns he will knock on the door so that the child can unlock it (thus assuring the child that there is no surveillance). The experimenter then observes the child's behavior (perhaps through a one-way mirror) and measures the amount of transgression; that is, the extent to which the child touches the attractive toy.

The rationale for this experimental paradigm is that, when left alone, the child is tempted to play with the prohibited toys and that the amount or duration of toy touching is an indication of the extent to which a *moral* response has been internalized. Varying manipulations have been used in these experiments, in accordance with the specific environmental influence under investigation. In studies of punishment the effect of variations in the timing of its administration has been most frequently assessed. Comparisons are made between punishment administered immediately before the child touches the toy (referred to as *early punishment*) and shortly after the child has picked up the toy (referred to as *late punishment*). A consistent finding has been that children receiving early punishment transgress (i.e., touch the prohibited toy) *less* than those receiving late punishment. The interpretation of the different effects of the timing of punishment is that moral behaviors are most strongly internalized through the conditioning that stems from the anxiety produced by the punishment that is associated with the initiation of the prohibited responses (Aronfreed, 1968, 1969; Parke, 1969).

An additional proposition is that, in conjunction with conditioning, children internalize moral behaviors through the incorporation of verbally transmitted statements. In some forbidden-toy experiments variation in the timing of punishment is combined with presentation of an explicit statement of the prohibition and the reasons for it (e.g., so that the toys will not be broken). In these experiments children displayed equal amounts of transgression, regardless of whether they were in the early- or late-punishment condition. Moreover, children in each punishment condition who received the verbal statement transgressed considerably less than children in the early-punishment condition who got no verbal statement.

The behavioristic-internalization interpretation of findings from the two sets of studies (punishment alone and punishment combined with verbal statement) is that moral internalization occurs through both conditioning and the incorporation of cognitive representations. It is maintained that, on the one hand, punishment serves to condition the acquisition of moral responses and that, on the other hand, verbally transmitted statements can serve to facilitate an incorporation of those responses.

As with the secondary-drive and observational-learning experiments, the forbidden-toy experiments, it can be argued, produced results that are accounted for by the subject's understanding of the experimental task, as communicated by the experimental manipulations. However, because the experiments presumably deal with moral behaviors, the cognitive interpretation of the forbidden-toy experiments must differ from the interpretation of the nonmoral behaviors studied in the other types of experiments. Recall that the interpretation of observational-learning experiments was that subjects behaved in accordance with instructions conveyed by the experimenter. In previous chapters, however, it has been maintained that children's moral judgments are not determined by dictates of persons in authoritative positions. Consequently, it would not follow that children simply adhere to the experimenter's instructions in situations involving moral behaviors (as they do in the morally neutral behaviors of the observational learning experiments).

It would follow, however, that children in the forbidden-toy experiments adhere to the experimenter's instructions if the required behaviors are regarded by the child as morally neutral. Indeed, from the point of view of the definition of morality presented earlier, the forbidden-toy experiments assess behaviors that are morally neutral. Moreover, the findings on the types of moral-conventional distinctions made by young children indicate that they would approach the prohibition on playing with certain toys as a nonmoral restriction. In this regard, the most relevant feature of the forbidden-toy experiment is that the event itself is arbitrary. That is, the action required of the child – to refrain from playing with designated toys – is an arbitrary restriction established by the experimenter for the experimental situation. There is no intrinsically prescriptive basis for the restriction, such as avoiding harm, or violating the rights, freedom, or equality of others. The restriction is arbitrary in the sense that the experimenter could require an opposite action without altering the moral status of the act. For instance, instead of prohibiting the child from playing with the more attractive of the pairs of toys, the experimenter could prohibit the child from playing with the less attractive toy or with none of the toys. In fact, several such variations on the restriction have been used in experiments (Parke, 1967; Parke & Walters, 1967).

It has been argued by others that the validity of the forbidden-toy experiments is diminished because the restriction is trivial. This is not the argument being proposed here. Regardless of the significance of the act, a prohibition on playing with toys in an experimental situation is consistent with the theoretical formulation of moral internalization from which the experiments stem. The stated aim of research using the prohibited-toy paradigm is to determine how children learn to behave under a restriction established in the laboratory (which presumably parallels children's learning of restrictions in naturalistic settings). Therefore, in these experimental situations the definition of the moral is adherence to the experimenter's instructions. The children considered to behave in the moral way are the ones who follow the experimenter's instructions, whereas those who do not follow the experimenter's instructions are considered not to have behaved morally. More generally, the definition of the moral is adherence to socially (parents, teacher, "society") designated proscriptions and prohibitions. Therefore, the use of arbitrary acts (such as a restriction upon playing with a designated toy) is consistent with the internalization definition of morality as conformity to external norms. Just as going against the experimenter's designated prohibition is a moral transgression on the part of the child participating in the experiment, going against the group consensus is a moral transgression on the part of a member of the society. In the internalization view, moral behaviors are arbitrary acts that become behaviorally nonarbitrary under certain psychological conditions. The forbidden-toy experiments were designed to study conditions that lead to the child's acquisition of arbitrary acts transmitted by an adult authority.

Given the assumptions that (a) the event in the forbidden-toy paradigm is arbitrary and (b) children, therefore, would not apply moral judgments to the event, the experimental results can be accounted for by the same cognitive and communicative variables that explain the Miller and Dollard (secondary drive) and Bandura (observational learning) findings. The experimenter's behavior, including the punishments administered, provides the subject with information regarding the rules and expectations of a situation that has a seemingly arbitrary restriction and is highly ambiguous. The experimental conditions of variation in timing of punishment demonstrate how this is the case (as detailed in Turiel, 1978a).

The experimental situation is ambiguous because the prohibited toys are not identified for the subject. Consequently, one of the subject's tasks is to discriminate between two types of toys: those that can and cannot be touched. As in the Miller and Dollard experiments, young children are able to make this discrimination readily. Subjects in both punishment conditions generally needed only two or three trials to learn that they should not choose the more attractive toy. When the experimenter leaves the room the subject is presented with another ambiguity in that he or she is not told if the attractive toy should still not be touched. The subject's behavior would then depend, in part, on what has been surmised about the experimenter's expectations and the rules of the situation.

Now consider the specific manipulation in the early- and late-punishment conditions. It will be recalled that in the early-punishment condition the punishment is administered just before the child touches the toy, whereas in the late-punishment condition it is administered after he or she has already picked up and played with the toy. Therefore, a feature differentiating the two conditions is that in one the experimenter actively prevents the child from touching the more attractive toy each time the child is about to reach for it, but in the other the experimenter allows the child to play with the more attractive toy before stopping him or her. The experimental conditions constitute two different communications regarding the experimenter's expectations in the following sense. When the subject in the early-punishment condition is prevented from touching the attractive toys, it is likely that the experimental situation will be perceived as revolving around both the discrimination task during the experimental trials and the general prohibition against touching the attractive toys. By contrast, by allowing the subject to touch the toys in the late-punishment condition, it is likely that the experimental situation will be understood solely as a discrimination task, without a general prohibition.

The greater clarity of the communications in the early-punishment condition regarding a general prohibition produced stronger adherence to instructions than the late-punishment condition. Findings from the studies mentioned earlier in which subjects were provided with an explicit verbal statement explaining the prohibition support this interpretation; the timing of punishment made no difference whatsoever. Consequently, punishment is interchangeable with a verbal communication, demonstrating that the punishment conditions represent different explicit instructions. In addition, when presented with the explicit communication subjects touched the attractive toys considerably less than in the early-punishment condition with no verbal statement. Similarly, the communication of task instructions accounts for the findings of forbidden-toy experiments that combined punishment and modeling (Turiel, 1978a).

Two general points emerge from the analyses of the behavioristic-internalization experiments. One is that a child's responses are partially determined by the nature of the event to which a prohibition pertains. In this regard, it is of interest to note a study allowing for a comparison between the forbidden-toy paradigm and an event most likely to be regarded as nonarbitrary by children (Sears, Rau, & Alpert, 1965). In addition to the forbidden-toy paradigm, Sears, Rau, and Alpert included a situation in which the child was informed by the experimenter that some candies in the experimental room should not be touched because they belonged to someone else; then the child was left alone and the amount of candy taken was measured. The relevant finding from this study, as shown by a recent reanalysis of the data (Turiel, 1978a), is that the children did not respond in the same way to the two "temptations" and transgressed less in the candy situation than in the forbidden-toy situation.

The second point is that in any social setting children make judgments about ongoing events, including the punishments administered by adults. The reinterpretation of the experimental research refers to the interpretation of the parental discipline research discussed earlier, providing support for the proposition that punishments administered by parents are likely to serve as implicit communications. The reinterpretation of the experimental research also has a bearing on explanations of the acquisition of broader cultural content. The transmission of prepackaged units of culture has been proposed as the source of social development. As in experimental situations, however, the transmission of cultural content includes communications that are interpreted and transformed by the receiver. Issues related to the cultural sources of social development are considered further in Chapter 10.

9 Social judgments and actions: coordination of domains

The title of the present chapter refers to social judgments and actions, although the chapter's primary emphasis is on issues pertaining to moral judgment and action. The broader term, social judgments, is used because it will be claimed that an understanding of the relations between moral judgment and action requires analyses of the individual's coordination of different domains of social judgments (including moral judgments, of course) in behavioral situations. Surprisingly little attention has been given to the study of the relations between nonmoral social judgments and action. For instance, it could be asked whether there is a relation between concepts regarding the efficient operation of social groups and the ways individuals actually establish and maintain groups they join. Similarly, issues pertaining to relations between judgments about friendship and behavior towards friends could be posed. These are only two examples among others that could be mentioned to illustrate the kind of judgment–behavior relations in nonmoral domains that are not often studied. Many situations calling for a behavioral decision of a moral nature also include nonmoral social components that impinge on the decision-making process. Behavior in such situations is not based solely on an application (or lack of application) of moral considerations, but would be related to the coordination of different domains of judgment. Therefore, an understanding of how individuals deal with the problem of coordinating domains of social judgment is also important to analyses of judgment–action relations. The present chapter is concerned with both judgment–action relations and judgments involving the coordination of domains.

The paucity of concern with judgment–behavior relations in nonmoral domains is not, by any means, paralleled in the moral domain. There has traditionally been a great deal of concern with the relations between moral judgments and behavior, which is manifested not only in research (see Blasi, 1980 for a comprehensive review), but also in the persisting critical scrutiny of the way behavior is treated in theory and research on morality. Sometimes it is claimed that research on moral judgments is of lesser value than research on moral behavior or that it should always be combined with research on moral behavior.

187

Some of the reasons for the ubiquitous concern with behavior in the moral domain are readily understandable. It is felt that people's actions toward each other are ultimately of the most significance regarding moral issues. It is through one's actions, and not thoughts, that moral good or harm is accomplished. Even genuinely held judgments are not beneficial to others if there is a failure to act in accordance with them. It is often the case, therefore, that applied and political concerns lead to an emphasis on the study of moral behavior; and sometimes they lead to a devaluation of research on moral judgments that is not closely tied to the study of behavior.

Although these applied-moral concerns are clearly of much significance, they cannot be the bases for an assessment of the validity of research efforts to explain moral development. Because explanatory questions of a scientific nature are different from the practical and social interests in behavior, the validity of explanations for the development of moral judgment can be assessed independently of their contributions to applied concerns with behavior. Moreover, however important the issue of behavior may be (and that is certainly not being denied here), it is not necessarily the case that the direct and immediate study of behavior is the fastest route to obtaining the information needed for solution to applied-moral problems. A substantial amount of research must still be done to obtain the type of knowledge about behavior that can be put to effective applied uses. Furthermore, it may very well be that a powerful explanation of moral thought is a prerequisite to the formulation of an adequate explanation of the relations between judgment and action. In such a case, concentration on the study of behavior, in the absence of such explanations of moral judgments, would not be the most efficient means to an understanding of behavior. In fact, an argument could be made that the traditional emphasis on behavior has had a retarding rather than a facilitating effect on the progress of research within this domain. The intractability of the moral judgment–action problem suggests that there is some merit to this argument and that researchers would be justified in taking a long-term perspective on the contributions that they can make to the applied questions.

Research on the relations of moral judgment and action

It is not always the case that a focus on moral behavior is solely based on its perceived practical importance. A concentration on behavioral analyses on the part of a number of researchers is motivated by the assumption that people's actions are not closely related to their moral judgments. In both the psychoanalytic and behavioristic-internalization explanations discussed in the previous chapter, behavior is at least to some extent disassociated from judgment. According to Freudian theory, stable moral responses are acquired through the rechanneling of instinctual tendencies into restrained superego functions and maintained through affective guilt reactions. Therefore, control over behavior is not maintained by rational processes. Moreover, to a substantial extent moral behavior is formed and determined by unconscious forces, which are often discrepant with consciously derived judgments. Consequently, moral judgments are accorded the status of epiphenomena and are viewed as rationalizations (rather than rational activities) that are different from the direct determinants of one's moral orientation expressed through behavior and unconscious symbolization.

Moral judgment is also accorded the status of an epiphenomenon by behavioristic theorists who maintain that behavior is determined by conditioning (see especially Skinner, 1971). A somewhat more complex position on the potential relations between judgment and behavior is taken by the behavioristic-internalization theorists. As discussed in the previous chapter, moral judgments for those theorists are internalized cognitive representations of content transmitted to children by the social environment. Moral judgments or verbalized values, which may differ from learned behaviors, are in conflict with needs and interests. Therefore, the verbal espousal of moral value, in itself, is not sufficient for the realization of those values in actual behavior. The learning of self-control is required to bridge the gap between moral thought and behavior (Aronfreed, 1968, 1976; Grinder, 1964; Mischel & Mischel, 1976). In the absence of strongly internalized mechanisms of self-control, discrepancies will exist between verbally espoused judgments and behavior.

It has been claimed that the evidence shows that behavior and judgment are not closely related. Furthermore, this interpretation of the evidence is taken to mean that judgment and behavior are mediated by the strength of affective mechanisms of self-control. For example, Aronfreed (1968, p. 9) has stated:

Although it is generally assumed that values are the most significant source of control over social conduct, . . . the available evidence usually points to great discrepancies between children's verbal expression of evaluative standards and their actual behavior in a real social context. . . . Knowledge of the standards of conduct to which a child subscribes will often not permit an accurate prediction of its behavior under conditions where the child is not exposed to the surveillance or reactions of external agents of control.

In stating that the available evidence points to great discrepancies between children's verbal expressions and actual behavior, Aronfreed was, at the time, primarily referring to studies using two types of assessment of verbally expressed evaluations. One type of assessment is based on the presentation to subjects of direct questions regarding behavior (their own or that of others) in particular situations. As examples, subjects might first be asked whether one should cheat on a test (Hartshorne & May, 1928–1930) or to whom they do and should give help (Mussey, 1977, as cited in Blasi, 1980), and then are observed in behavioral situations providing the opportunity for cheating or helping behavior. The other type of verbal assessment is based on the administration of what have been referred to as moral knowledge tests, which are presumed to measure the extent of knowledge and commitment to cultural values. Scores on such moral knowledge tests are compared with performance in natural or experimental situations. More recently a third type of assessment of verbal evaluation has been included, among those studies, that presumably provides evidence for the proposition that judgment and behavior are not closely linked. It is maintained by Aronfreed (1976) and others (e.g., Hogan, 1973; Kurtines & Greif, 1974; Mischel & Mischel, 1976) that studies using measures of developmental level of moral judgment, such as those of Kohlberg (1969) or Piaget (1932), also demonstrate that there are large discrepancies between thought and action. Specifically referring to Kohlberg's measure, Mischel and Mischel (1976, p. 101) stated, "The predictive validity from moral reasoning to moral behavior does not appear to be better than the modest, albeit often statistically significant, personality co-efficients (averaging .30) typically found in correlational personality research linking measures across diverse response modes."

Each of these modes of assessment is actually very different, and they all tap different aspects or levels of thought. Only the last-mentioned of the three measures (those based on the Piaget or Kohlberg formulations) represent methods of assessing how individuals reason about moral issues. Posing subjects with direct questions about their habitual behavior or their future behavior in particular types of situations is, in effect, asking them to make psychological assessments and predictions (about the self or others). The calculation of the correspondence between psychological assessments or predictions and actual behavior does not constitute a study of the relations of thought and action, but is rather the study of the accuracy of psychological knowledge and ability to predict behavior. The individual's predictive abilities in moral or nonmoral events are likely to be inaccurate for at least two reasons. First, the psychological knowledge of most persons is far from perfect (see Nisbett & Ross, 1980; Ross, 1977). There is also a good deal of evidence (Bem, 1972; Nisbett & Wilson, 1977) that indicates that individuals are not able to predict their own behavior (or that of others) with great accuracy. The second reason that predictions are likely to be inaccurate is that subjects would not be cognizant of all the variables of the behavioral situation. Indeed, psychologists have much less than perfect success in predicting behavior even in situations that they have experimentally manipulated.

Studies conducted by Hartshorne and May (1928–1930) on children's honesty are often cited as providing results that demonstrate a tenuous or modest link between thought and action. In the Hartshorne and May research a large sample of elementary-school-age children were administered moral knowledge tests and their cheating behavior was measured. Although moral knowledge tests of the sort used by Hartshorne and May do not assess psychological knowledge nor do they provide measures of abilities to predict behavior, they are also inadequate measures of judgment because they are designed to measure surface attitudes toward moral issues. Typically, the test items present statements depicting a transgression and the test-taker is requested to rate (for example, on a 5-point scale) the wrongness of the act. The extent of moral knowledge is calculated by summing the ratings of the wrongness of the acts. Hence, such tests provide only a quantitative measure of attitudes toward moral acts, but do not assess judgment or reasoning components. On the basis of studies like those of Hartshorne and May, one could, at best, draw the conclusion that surface attitudes toward cultural values are not closely related to moral behavior. Such results, however, would have little bearing on the relations between the structure of moral judgment and behavior.

Moreover, it is not clear to what extent moral knowledge tests are valid measures of attitudes. It had generally been found that by the time children reach the first or second grade they obtain high scores on moral knowledge tests. In a recent study (Turiel, 1976), a moral knowledge test was administered to a group of subjects who were between 10 and 16 years of age. It was found that test scores decreased, rather than increased, with age. On the average, the 10-year-olds obtained higher scores than the 13-year-olds, who in turn obtained higher scores than the 16-year-olds. The observed decline in "moral knowledge" is not difficult to explain. Children do not lose their knowledge as they become older. Rather, it is likely that the test scores decreased because, as children grow older, their ways of thinking about the issues presented undergo change, so that they take new factors into account in rating the wrongness of the transgressions depicted in the test items. For example, older children may give more weight to extenuating circumstances than do younger children in judging a given act and, thereby, rate it less severely.

The large majority of recent studies comparing behavior with an assessment of moral judgments (i.e., how moral issues are conceptualized) have relied on measures of the stages formulated by Kohlberg. Varied interpretations have been made of the data from these studies. Focusing on studies that produced low or moderate levels of correlation, some have concluded, as noted earlier, that close links do not exist between judgment and behavior (Aronfreed, 1976; Mischel & Mischel, 1976). However, on the basis of his very comprehensive review of the research, Blasi (1980, p.10) was led to the conclusion that "the empirical literature supports the hypothesis of a significant relationship between moral thinking and moral behavior. To a large extent, the opposite opinion, that moral reasoning and moral behavior are independent dimensions, is revealed to be a well-advertised myth."

Those drawing the conclusion that moral judgment is not highly related to behavior focused on those studies that showed low correlations between the two measures. By contrast, Blasi reviewed the research in a thorough manner and concluded that consistency was found in a large number of studies. He also found inconsistencies in a number of other studies. The clearest relations were between stages of moral judgment and what is an assessment of general naturalistic behavior: delinquency and nondelinquency. Somewhat weaker relations were found between stages of moral judgment and behavioral measures of honesty (e.g., cheating on tests or games, failing to return someone else's property) and altruism (e.g., sharing, helping others in need). Little relation was found between stages of moral judgment and behaviors in situations that give rise to social pressures to act in ways discrepant with one's moral choice (e.g., adherence to an experimenter's instructions to administer electric shocks to another person).

The facts of the matter are that high levels of consistency and inconsistency have been and could be found in research on moral judgment–action relations. In an important respect, the extant research findings underestimate the degree of consistency in judgment and action that actually exists. In an effort to provide stringent tests of the hypothesis, researchers have frequently concentrated on ambiguous and conflictful situations for the behavioral assessments. For example, many studies have assessed children's cheating in competitive games and in academic test situations; from the viewpoint of the child's moral judgments these are either situations (Turiel, 1978a) not likely to be clearly moral (competitive games) or situations that pose a conflict over achievement standards imposed by adults (academic tests). As another example, studies have been done on issues that reflect strong conflicts between individual judgments and elements of the social system (e.g., situations requiring civil disobedience or contradiction of the demands of a person in authority). One consequence of such a research strategy may be the underestimation of the consistency between people's actions and their judgments.

Indeed, researchers could spend many years conducting studies that would undoubtedly show a high consistency between behavior and verbally expressed evaluations or judgments (using any of the three types of assessment mentioned earlier, including predictions of behavior). Consider a few obvious examples. Suppose a study were designed to deal with the following specific behaviors: robbing money from a bank, stealing money from a friend, killing another person, running over a person with one's car, driving through red lights, setting fire to a house. These are only a few examples to illustrate the point; many more could be listed. Our hypothetical study has a simple design. A large, randomly chosen sample of subjects would be administered a measure of their moral judgment and/or asked direct questions regarding what they do or would do in situations pertaining to the behaviors in question. Subjects could be posed the following types of questions: Would you steal money from a bank? Would you steal money from a close friend? Do you think you will kill anyone in the next five years? Suppose that, while driving your car, a pedestrian is crossing the street; would you make every effort to avoid hitting that person? Similar questions could be posed for any of the other behaviors included in the study. In this hypothetical study subjects would then be systematically observed in order to determine whether or not their behaviors are consistent with their verbally expressed judgments, evaluations, and predictions.

This type of study has not been conducted! If the study were carried out with a randomly chosen sample from the population, it is almost certain that high consistencies would be found between the verbal and behavioral assessments. One can only conjecture why these kinds of studies have not been conducted. In the first place, there are logistical problems in systematically observing such behaviors in naturalistic settings. Perhaps just as important, the anticipated results may seem so obvious that, in this sense, the study is considered a trivial one to conduct. The self-evident nature of the research stems from the assumption that people's judgments do correspond closely with these behaviors. Indeed, many everyday behaviors are consonant with judgments. Were such studies to be conducted, it is likely that even greater consistency would be found than that assumed by Blasi (1980) in his contention that the belief that moral reasoning and moral behavior are independent dimensions "is a well-advertised myth."

It is not being claimed here that judgment and action are always in synchrony with each other. The claim is that synchrony exists for a large number of behaviors and that it cannot be legitimately concluded that moral judgment and action are independent of each other. At the same time, it is apparent that significant inconsistencies between the two do exist.

Consistencies and inconsistencies in judgment and action

Simply on the basis of consistencies documented in research already conducted (and ignoring the anticipated consistencies in many instances of judgment and behavior), it can be concluded (Blasi, 1980) that an empirical relation exists between measures of moral judgment and measures of moral behavior. The research also yields what may seem to be discrepant findings, that inconsistencies exist between moral judgment and behavior. The two sets of findings are not necessarily in contradiction with each other. Whether or not they are viewed as contradictory depends upon one's interpretation of judgment–behavior relations. As was pointed out by Langer (1975), one prevalent assumption has been that, insofar as relations do exist between judgment and behavior, they are of a causal nature. Findings of consistency are interpreted to mean that judgment is the antecedent causal condition for behavior. Findings of inconsistency are interpreted to mean that judgment is not the causal condition for the action and that other factors (e.g., situational pulls, noncognitive personality forces, irrational considerations) provide or contribute to the causal conditions for the behavior.

One derivative of the causal position is that consistencies between judgment and behavior are neither subjected to rigorous explanatory analyses nor given much attention in empirical analyses. Findings of consistencies are taken as explanatory, in themselves, and inconsistencies are regarded as requiring explanation and further empirical exploration. As Langer (1975, p. 1) has put it: "It has often been thought that inconsistent coordinations should be the prime target of developmental research since the explanation of consistent coordinations is self-evident." The explanations for consistencies should not be regarded as self-evident and they do require elaboration and verification. Explanations of the relations between judgment and behavior are required, both where there is empirical consistency and where there is empirical (apparent) inconsistency. Moreover, an alternative explanation to the causal model for either consistent or inconsistent empirical associations stems from the structural-developmental perspective on judgment and action: Consistencies and inconsistencies are forms of coordination of systems of judgment and systems of action (Langer, 1975). From the structural perspective, there are two general and researchable issues in the judgment–action problem. First is the structural-developmental issue: that is, that coordinations of judgments and actions are integral to the process of development. The proposition that development stems from coordinations of judgment and actions is another way of stating that development is a function of individual–environment interactions. The child's actions serve as a source of direct feedback about the social environment. Actions can serve to inform judgments and provide conditions for transformations in judgments. The role of coordinations of judgments, actions, and social interactions in development within domains was discussed in Chapter 3. The present concern is with the second and interrelated structural aspect of the judgment–action problem: how the coordination of social judgments in behavioral situations is related to the individual's behaviorally implemented decisions.

The basic proposition is that explanation of the relations of judgment and behavior requires analyses of the coordination of different domains of social judgments. Many situations that entail moral decisions on the part of an individual also include components entailing nonmoral social judgments. Such situations may vary in the salience of a particular type of judgment they evoke. A given situation may, for instance, include considerations of a moral nature, of a pragmatic nature, of a social-organizational and conventional nature, and so on. In such situations consideration only of the relation of the individual's moral judgment to the behavioral outcome would omit relevant nonmoral social judgments and erroneously lead to the conclusion that the individual's judgment is inconsistent with his or her behavior. Higher levels of consistency between judgment and action may be assessed if the situation were analyzed for its different judgmental components. In other words, assessments of consistency between moral judgment and behavior provide only partial information regarding the relations of different types of judgments and social behavior.

In a philosophical context, this point has been made by Harman with regard to general life action-choices and the moral requirements of the philosophical conception of utilitarianism (Harman, 1977, p. 157):

Utilitarianism says that you always ought to do that act that will maximize utility and it is extremely rare for anyone ever to do that. Consider your own present situation. You are reading a philosophical book about ethics. There are many courses of action open to you that would have much greater social utility. If, for example, you were to immediately stop reading and do whatever you could to send food to places like Africa or India, where it is scarce, you could probably save hundreds, even thousands of lives, and could make life somewhat more tolerable for thousands of others. That is something you could do that has a greater utility than anything you are now doing; it probably has a greater utility than anything you are ever going to do in your whole life. According to utilitarianism, therefore, you are not now doing what you ought morally to be doing and this will continue to be true throughout your life. You will always be doing the wrong thing; you will never be doing what you ought to be doing. That conclusion is very different from any ordinary view of the matter. Utilitarianism implies that it is morally wrong of you to be reading this book. That is not the sort of thing people ordinarily think of as morally wrong.

There are, indeed, many examples of everyday behavior, in addition to reading a philosophical book about ethics, that could be used to illustrate Harman's point with regard to the dictates of the utilitarian position. These would include reading books that have nothing to do with ethics (after all, it may be argued, reading about ethics provides knowledge relevant to your moral decisions), watching television, going to the movies, cultivating your garden, and even educational endeavors and some types of occupational activities. All these examples pertain not only to utilitarian principles, but to most other concepts of morality. People's activities are not solely guided by moral considerations. Moral considerations and one's moral judgments will have implications for action; nonmoral considerations and corresponding judgments will also have implications for action. In this context, it is difficult to know what a search for moral judgment–behavior consistencies or inconsistencies would reveal. Instead, behavioral choices of the general sort mentioned by Harman, if put to empirical analyses (which would be difficult), would entail investigation of multifaceted judgment–action relations and would have to begin with a delineation of the relevant moral and nonmoral components.

The same analytic model applies to research on behavior in specific experimental or naturalistic situations. Moral and nonmoral considerations are applied in such behavioral situations as well, so that definitions and classifications of behavioral situations are essential to investigations of judgment–action relations. It does not suffice to assume that a particular situation (e.g., involving deception or altruism) can be used to assess moral judgment and action consistencies on the basis of an identification of its moral components alone. Indeed, explanations of specific behaviors in delineated situations will also vary in accordance with the moral and nonmoral parameters of the situation.

As an illustrative example, consider a previously researched situation. In 1964, on the Berkeley campus of the University of California, there occurred a student demonstration and sit-in at an administration building that was part of what came to be known as the Free Speech Movement. The sit-in itself was the culmination of a series of activities by students to protest a university ban on political action on the campus. The sit-in ended with the forcible removal and arrest of approximately 800 persons.

The Free Speech Movement has been used to research relations of moral judgment and behavior (Haan, Smith, & Block, 1968). It was assumed that the sit-in entailed morally relevant decisions because it concerned conflicts over freedom of speech and political rights. In the study, university students who had not participated in the sit-in and students who had been arrested were given a test of their moral judgment (based on the Kohlberg methods and stage descriptions discussed in Chapter 7). The general expectation was that participation in the sit-in would be more closely associated with the higher stages of moral judgment than with the lower stages. In a general sense the results confirmed this expectation: almost all students (80%) at the highest stage (stage 6 in Kohlberg's scheme) participated in the sit-in; approximately half of the students at the next lower stage (stage 5) participated; and very few of the students at the middle stages (stages 3 and 4) participated. One finding inconsistent with the general trend was that approximately half of the students at stage 2 participated in the sit-in. There is some question about the validity of that stage assessment (see Haan, 1975; Kohlberg & Candee, 1979) with additional findings indicating that those students were actually in transition from stage 4 to stage 5.

It may perhaps be assumed, therefore, that actual participation in the Free Speech Movement is an example of consistency between moral judgment and moral behavior. It is at the highest stage of moral judgment that the principle of the right to freedom of speech is most clearly understood, and most students tested who were at that stage participated in the protest (Haan, Smith, & Block, 1968; Kohlberg & Candee, 1979). However, the attribution of consistency or inconsistency to the types of empirical associations observed in the study is not as unambiguous as it may appear. That the meaning of consistency between one's moral judgments and actions is not given in empirical associations can be illustrated by considering some possible, hypothetical variations in the parameters of a situation like a sit-in at Berkeley. Suppose, as one example, that it was known by all concerned that individuals who participated in the sit-in would be expelled from the university and never allowed to enroll at any other. What would constitute judgment–action consistency in such circumstances? Is it to be expected that individuals reasoning at the highest stages of moral judgment would participate in the sit-in under those conditions? Not necessarily! And it is not apparent that individuals who do not participate are acting in ways that are inconsistent with their morality. Clearly, it would be more difficult to predict behavior under the proposed circumstances because pragmatic (e.g., one's live-lihood) and societal (e.g., one's place, role, and status in the social system) considerations are highly relevant – in addition to the moral considerations.

The altered Free Speech Movement situation represents the other side of the coin of the example posed by Harman. Harman referred to everyday activities, such as reading a book, that do not serve moral functions. Our example pertains to the choice of a morally relevant activity that would be at the expense of important and legitimate pragmatic and societal ends. There are two points to be stressed about the proposed example. First, expectations regarding the consis-tency or inconsistency of moral judgment and moral behavior become more ambiguous by the addition of the pragmatic considerations. It is not clear what one would refer to as the consistent behavior, if the focus is only on the moral components of the person's judgments. Second, apparent empirical "consistency" in behavior (i.e., participation in the sit-in) would not be any more readily explicable than apparent empirical inconsistency.

The example of behavior involving protest or civil disobedience, in the two forms presented here, is meant to illustrate how the salience of moral and non-moral ends influences actions taken in a given situation. The pattern of findings from research designed with the aim of examining moral judgment and behavior, as summarized by Blasi (1980), indicates that the salience of moral and nonmoral components of behavioral situations is an important variable in explaining behav-ioral outcomes. It will be recalled that, according to Blasi, the clearest associa-tions found are between measures of moral judgment and delinquent behaviors. Delinquent actions of a criminal nature are most likely to be primarily classifi-able within the moral domain and are, indeed, found to be closely associated with levels of moral judgment. Also, according to Blasi, the least clear-cut empirical associations between measures of moral judgment and behavior appear in studies that examined situations in which individuals were faced with social pressures to act in ways discrepant with their moral choices. In several experi-mental studies (e.g., Fodor, 1971; Saltzstein, Diamond, & Belenky, 1972; Turiel & Rothman, 1972), the subject was faced with a moral choice and an opportunity to adhere to the rules and authority expectations of the experimental situation. As discussed in greater detail below with regard to Milgram's (1963) experiment on obedience, such situations include both moral and societal/conventional compo-nents that may account for the findings of moderate or low empirical associations between behavior and the moral judgment measure.

The results of one other study support the proposition that the salience of domain-specific considerations contributes significantly to behavioral outcomes.

Table 9.1. *Frequencies of social-conventional levels for disruptive and nondisruptive subjects at Time 1*

Group	Level 4	Level 4(5)	Level 5(4)	Level 5
Disruptive	7	8	6	1
Nondisruptive	1	2	4	13

Source: Geiger and Turiel (1981).

In a study by Geiger and Turiel (1981) the attempt was made to identify behaviors that pertained specifically to conventional and social organizational issues. In the first part of the study, comparisons were made between the social-conventional concepts of adolescents who displayed school-related disruptive social behaviors and those who did not. The subjects in the study were seventh- and eighth-grade students (male and female) from two junior high schools. Two groups were identified. One group consisted of students who, as identified through the records of school counselors, had persistently engaged in disruptive school behavior. The students included in that group had engaged in transgressions related only to conventional aspects of the social organization of the school, and not in actions of a criminal or delinquent nature. Some examples of disruptive school-related behaviors are talking back to the teacher, talking during class, eating in class, and refusing to wear designated clothing in physical education classes. The second group in the study consisted of randomly chosen students from the same seventh and eighth grades who had had no histories of disruptive behavior.

The two groups of students were administered the social-convention interview described in Chapter 6 in order to determine if disruptive school behavior was associated with specific types of conventional thinking. The expectation was that among junior high school students disruptive behavior would be associated with level 4 thinking. Level 4 is characterized by a negation or rejection of convention in which conventional expectations of authorities and conventional regulations are regarded as arbitrary and unnecessary constraints. The comparison of the levels of social-conventional thinking of the two groups is presented in Table 9.1. The table shows a clear contrast (statistically significant) between the two groups. The thinking of students in the disruptive group (with only one exception) was either at level 4 or included a mixture of levels 4 and 5. Although some of the students in the nondisruptive group showed a mixture of levels 4 and 5, the majority were at level 5. These results show, therefore, that the behaviors were associated with levels of conventional thinking, but were not completely isomorphic with it. Level 5 thinking was not associated with disruptive behavior, but it cannot be said that being at level 4 completely accounts for the behavior. Some students whose thinking was at level 4 did not display school-related disruptive behavior.

Table 9.2. *Social convention scores at Time 1 and Time 2 for longitudinal subjects as grouped by behavior classification at Time 2*

Subject	Time 1	Time 2	Direction of change
Disruptive group			
1	4	4	0
2	4	5(4)	+
3	4(5)	4(5)	0
4	4(5)	5(4)	+
5	4(5)	5(4)	+
6	5(4)	5(4)	0
7	5(4)	5(4)	0
Nondisruptive group			
1	4	4(5)	+
2	4	5(4)	+
3	4	5(4)	+
4	4	5(4)	+
5	4(5)	4(5)	0
6	4(5)	5(4)	+
7	4(5)	5	+
8	4(5)	5	+
9	4(5)	5	+
10	4(5)	5	+
11	5(4)	5	+
12	5(4)	5	+
13	5	5	0

Source: Geiger and Turiel (1981).

The association between conventional thinking and behavior was further demonstrated by longitudinal findings in a second part of the study. One year after
the initial assessments of behavior and judgment the students originally classified
as disruptive were again administered the social-convention interview. In addition, the students' behavior during the intervening year was identified through
the counselors' records as disruptive or nondisruptive. As shown in Table 9.2, 7
students continued to display disruptive behavior during the intervening year,
whereas 13 students shifted in their behavioral patterns. The table also presents
the levels of social-conventional thinking for each of those students at time 1 and
time 2. Again, the results show that there is some relation between the two
measures, although changes in one measure do not entirely account for changes
in the other measure. That is, all the students who in the intervening year shifted
to level 5 thinking also changed from disruptive to nondisruptive behaviors; but
among students whose thinking shifted toward a greater proportion of use of
level 5, some changed in their behavior but others did not.

The Geiger and Turiel findings support the proposition that behaviors pertaining to conventional aspects of social organization are related to the level of social-conventional thinking. Nevertheless, the results suggest that conventional behavior may be influenced by other aspects of judgment. As an obvious example, prudential judgments regarding academic achievements are likely to influence social behaviors in school. Like the other examples mentioned earlier, the Geiger and Turiel study demonstrates that identification of the different domains (more or less salient) of behavioral situations requires the use of specified criteria. Indeed, one can see upon a reexamination of Table 7.1 that a diverse set of situations and behaviors have been used in studies of moral behavior. Not all of those behaviors are clearly in the moral domain – at least not in accordance with the criteria presented here. One example, the experimental prohibition on playing with toys, has already been considered in some detail (Chapter 8). Similar analyses could be made of several of the studies listed in that table, such as adherence to game rules, cheating in games, cheating in classroom tests (which often pose children both moral and pragmatic conflicts), or deviation from a work assignment.

The need for criteria to identify the domains of behavioral decisions means, therefore, that the situational context is important. It is important not in the sense that external conditions determine behavior, but in the sense that behavior is related to interactions among domains of social judgments, interpretations of the situational context, and the parameters of the situation. It should be stressed, as has been noted several times before (Blasi, 1980; Damon, 1977; Kohlberg, 1971; Kohlberg & Candee, 1979) that the meaning attributed by actors to the situation is central to analyses of behavior. Actions recorded only at the behavioral level may appear similar but differ in their intent and meaning. In another context, and for a different purpose (i.e., a discussion of ethnographic description), this point was well-articulated by the anthropologist C. Geertz. Geertz provides a good example for a seemingly insignificant (and usually morally neutral) act, a contraction of the eyelid (Geertz, 1973, pp. 6–7):

Consider. . . two boys rapidly contracting the eyelids of their right eyes. In one, this is an involuntary twitch; in the other, a conspiratorial signal to a friend. The two movements are, as movements, identical; from an I-am-a-camera, "phenomenalistic" observation of them alone, one could not tell which was twitch and which was wink, or indeed whether both or either was twitch or wink. Yet the difference, however unphotographable, between a twitch and a wink is vast; as anyone unfortunate enough to have had the first taken for the second knows. The winker is communicating, and indeed communicating in a quite precise and special way: (1) deliberately, (2) to someone in particular, (3) to impart a particular message, (4) according to a socially established code, and (5) without cognizance of the rest of the company. As Ryle points out, the winker has not done two things, contracted his eyelids and winked, while the twitcher has done only one, contracted his eyelids. Contracting your eyelids on purpose when there exists a public code in which so doing counts as a conspiratorial signal *is* winking. That's all there is to it: a speck of behavior, a fleck of culture, and – voilà! – a gesture.

Analyses of judgment–behavior relations, then would (and must) include the meanings attributed to acts by the actors involved. In addition, the components discussed thus far regarding analyses of the coordination of social judgments and of judgments and actions include the following: (1) assessment of the domains relevant to the behavioral situation; (2) assessment of the subject's conceptual orientation to the domains of the situation; (3) description of the forms of judgment applied to the situation; (4) measures of behavioral outcomes; and (5) the ways in which the different conceptual domains are coordinated.

The coordination of domains of social judgments in nonbehavioral contexts was discussed in Chapter 6. The remainder of this chapter deals with domain coordinations in the context of behavioral analyses. And the one study (Smetana, 1981b, 1982) that has investigated judgment–behavior relations by taking into account the components just mentioned is considered. Then the experiment on obedience by Milgram (1963, 1974) is examined as a case study of how moral and social-conventional considerations are coordinated in behavioral decisions.

Domains of judgment and action

Smetana's study examined women's judgments about abortion and the related decision whether to abort their pregnancies. The study was aimed, first, at determining the domain or domains of judgment used by subjects in their reasoning about abortion and, second, at relating such domain attributions to behavioral decisions. Subjects in the study were first-time pregnant single women between the ages of 13 and 32 years, some of whom (25 of them) decided to have an abortion and some of whom (23 of them) decided to continue their pregnancies. A group of women who had never been pregnant were also included in the study.

The research procedures were guided by the assumptions that perhaps not all subjects would classify abortion as a moral issue and that some subjects may classify it in more than one domain. Subjects were given an interview consisting of a set of standardized questions designed to determine the types of issues taken into account in reasoning about abortion. Details regarding the questions, interview format, coding procedures, and reliability data can be found elsewhere (Smetana, 1982). Of central interest for the present purposes is the finding that different domain identifications were made of the issue of abortion. Indeed, not all subjects placed abortion in the same category. For some, abortion was primarily a moral issue (25% of the sample), but for others (35%) it was a nonmoral issue of a personal nature (i.e., not appropriately governed by moral considerations). Moreover, not all subjects classified abortion solely within one of these domains. There were some subjects (24%) who coordinated moral and personal considerations and others (16%) who used both considerations in an uncoordinated and conflicted fashion. These findings were obtained from both the never-pregnant and pregnant groups.

The following four domain-related types of reasoning were identified (Smetana, 1981b, pp. 217–218):

1. Subjects...for whom moral issues or issues of justice concerning two human lives were salient for the entire course of pregnancy. They considered the genetic or spiritual potential of the embryo at conception sufficient to define it as a human life and thus were concerned with possible justifications, or lack of justifications for taking life.
2. Subjects for whom personal issues were salient for the entire pregnancy and who considered the criterion of physical and/or emotional independence from the mother (occurring at birth) as the relevant feature in considering the child a human life....These subjects considered the unborn an equal human life only after birth and thus made clear distinctions between the act of abortion and killing a (born) human life....Abortion was considered an action outside the realm of societal regulation and moral concern. Either decision...was viewed as a personal issue.
3. Subjects who considered abortion first a personal and then a moral issue....For these subjects, concepts in (successively) the personal and moral domains were coordinated by their definition of life, full fetal development, and/or resemblance to human form, which was seen to occur with varying biological accuracy between three to six months in a pregnancy. After the point at which these subjects believed human life begins, abortion was considered a justice issue similar to other issues of life.
4. Those types of thought lacking in coordination between the domains. Subjects who treated abortion as a personal issue until viability and then experienced conflict between issues in the personal and moral domains were in conflict when considering the entire course of a pregnancy....Subjects whose responses were characterized by equivocation and confusion and who lacked a clear definition of life....

The significance of identifying the subjects' domain orientations to the issue is evident in the analyses of their behavioral decisions. The main finding of the study was that the categorization of subjects in accordance with the domain-related form of reasoning corresponded with their behavioral decisions. All but one of the subjects whose judgments about abortion were based on moral considerations continued their pregnancies to term. In turn, all but one of the subjects who regarded abortion as a nonmoral issue did have abortions. Those coded as showing coordinated and uncoordinated reasoning were about evenly split in their behavioral decisions. Furthermore, the reasoning categories evident in the women who were in the process of deciding whether to continue the pregnancy were the same ones used by a sample of women who were not pregnant (the same categories were also used by a sample of men). It should also be noted that the categories of subjects' reasoning about abortion parallel those found in the analyses of the domain combination issue presented in Chapter 6 (i.e., the question of whether the husband should give up his job so as to allow his wife to accept a position in another state). The analyses presented in Chapter 6 were based on an interview about a hypothetical situation. Yet, the observed categories of reasoning were close to those observed in reasoning about abortion, an issue about which the subjects were making an actual decision.

The correspondence of behavioral choices regarding abortion and conceptual orientations to the issue cannot be accounted for by differences in the subjects' general level or type of moral judgment. That is, the assessed differences in subjects' domain identifications of abortion did not correlate with their moral thinking about other issues. All of the participants in the study were administered separate interviews to assess their moral judgments (based on Kohlberg's methods of assessment). On that measure, no differences were found in type of moral reasoning between the group of subjects who considered abortion a personal issue (and had abortions) and the group of subjects who considered abortion a moral issue (and did not have abortions). Consequently, the results show that the conceptual orientation to abortion was not determined by level of moral judgment, which in turn was not correlated with the behavioral decision. The behavioral decisions were related to the conceptual criteria used to classify the domain of the event. Note that if the level of moral judgment were considered the only relevant measure in this research, the results would have led to the incorrect conclusion that actions do not closely correspond to judgments (because subjects at the same moral judgment levels make different behavioral choices regarding abortion). By attending to the domain issue and to individuals' identification and conceptualizations, Smetana provides a more complete picture of the types of correspondences that exist between judgment and action than is provided by correlational analyses of moral judgment and behavior.

The abortion decision, as analyzed in the Smetana study, represents one type of behavioral decision that includes more than one domain of judgment. The decisions taken by individuals were closely related to the domain identification and interpretation, with different people making different domain interpretations of the event. However, for most subjects the event did not pose a conflict between domains of judgment. Insofar as the abortion decision did pose a conflict, it was about how to define the issue. Some subjects were conflicted over a personal or moral attribution to abortion. Subjects who coordinated the two domains did so successively over time, first treating it as a personal issue (for the first three to six months of pregnancy) and then as a moral issue.

Many behavioral situations, as maintained earlier, do include components from more than one domain that require their simultaneous coordination. A clear example of a situation posing the individual with a conflict between moral and social organizational-conventional considerations is provided by the set of experiments on obedience to authority conducted by Milgram (1963, 1974). Most commonly, the experiments have been regarded as dealing with the subject's obedience or disobedience to an authority's request to commit an act that violates a moral standard – inflicting harm on another person. As mentioned earlier, study of the relation of judgment and behavior in the experimental situation has focused solely on moral judgments (Blasi, 1980; Kohlberg & Candee, 1979). However, in addition to a strong moral component, the experimental situation includes salient social organizational-conventional features, making it likely that the behavior of subjects involves a coordination of moral and conventional judgments. An examination of the parameters of the experimental manipulation, a subject's protocol, and the quantitative findings will illustrate the basis for the proposition that the behaviors involve coordination of the two domains. Such an interpretation should be regarded as a hypothesis because, originally, the experiments were not analyzed from this perspective.

First consider the parameters of the experimental situations reported by Milgram. Several variations were used (some of which are described shortly), but the main features of the standard experimental manipulations were as follows:

A subject is brought into an experimental room and told that he will participate in a study dealing with the effects of punishment on learning. The subject, along with another person posing as a second subject (but who was actually an accomplice of the experimenters), is first given a lengthy explanation about the possible influences of punishment on learning and the purposes of the experiment. They are then told that one of them will have the role of a teacher and the other the role of a learner. A rigged drawing of lots results in the assignment of the subject as teacher and the accomplice as learner. The subject is told that his task as the teacher is to administer increasing volts of electric shock (up to a point of ostensibly inflicting severe pain) to the learner, whose task is to correctly memorize a series of word-associations. The learner is strapped into a chair, with electrodes attached to his wrist. The subject is then seated in a separate room in front of a generator with 30 lever switches labeled in 15-volt increments from 15 to 450 volts. The learner is not visible to the subject, but can be heard. The subject is instructed to administer an increased level of shock each time the learner gives an incorrect answer in the paired-associate learning task. In actuality, the accomplice is not being shocked, though according to a predetermined schedule he makes a very convincing pretense of experiencing great pain when the subject presses the levers (especially beginning with the administration of 150 volts). Also according to a predetermined schedule, at several points the learner demands to be let out. Whenever the subject questions or protests the punishment, the experimenter instructs him to continue the experiment.

The experimental condition has been described in some detail in order to provide enough information to analyze the structure of the situation confronting subjects. But first the results should be mentioned. In the experimental condition described, the majority (65%) of subjects continued to administer shocks to the very end of the scale (the experiment was terminated after the 450-voltage was administered three times). The remainder of the subjects decided to terminate their participation at a point prior to the end of the scale and in contradiction to the experimenter's instructions. It should also be noted that, according to Milgram's report, most subjects who continued the experiment did so with much conflict and reluctance. Many stated that they wanted to stop the experiment, but remained in it in the face of the experimenter's repeated statements that the experiment had to continue. The components of the conflict have been alluded to by Milgram (1974, p.9):

Most subjects in the experiment see their behavior in a larger context that is benevolent and useful in the pursuit of scientific truth. The psychological laboratory has a strong claim to legitimacy and evokes trust and confidence in those who come to perform there. An action such as shocking a victim, which in isolation appears evil, acquires a totally different meaning when placed in this setting.

Only in part did the meaning of the act of shocking a victim take on a different meaning for the subjects. In most cases, the subject's aversion to the harm experienced by the other person was sustained throughout the experiment. For the majority of subjects, that aversion did not lead to discontinuation of their participation. This was because of the conflicts posed, not only by the legitimacy of the pursuit of scientific truth, but also by the social-organizational features of the situation. The perceived legitimacy of the rules and, especially, the authority in the situation was, it will be argued, a central reason for the subjects' continued participation in the experiment. The presence of two compelling features – the judgment that one should not be harmed and the judgment that the experiment is a legitimate institution – made for the conflict experienced by subjects.

That the organizational features of an experiment can be separated from the moral component is best illustrated through an example. Suppose a subject were brought into an experiment on learning that did not involve harming another person. The subject may agree to participate on the assumption that the research is worthwhile, that the researcher knows what he or she is doing, and that the information sought must be useful. The subject accepts the role and status in a situation perceived as legitimate and normally would continue this participation, avoiding disruption of the activity or interference with the scientific process (this does not necessarily imply extensive knowledge on the part of the subject of the scientific enterprise).

All these usual features of experiments and subject attitudes were present in the Milgram situation. The moral consideration did not eliminate the organizational features; the moral consideration is an additional and important factor that makes for serious conflicts. Correspondingly, the organizational features usually did not eliminate the moral consideration. In other words, subjects generally did not lose sight of the moral issue; it is evident from the reports of the research that almost all subjects were acutely aware of the moral component.

An illustrative example comes from the following protocol of the performance of a 50-year-old subject who continued administering shocks to the very end of the generator scale. The protocol is taken from Milgram's volume on *Obedience to Authority* (1974, pp. 73–76). A more vivid account is presented in a filmed account of the experiment (Milgram, 1965).

Immediately after the 150-volt shock was administered the learner began to protest and loudly request that he be released from the chair. At that point the subject began to express some reluctance. By the time the 180-volt shock was administered, the learner's complaints were even more forceful and the subject's concern for that person's welfare had increased. The protocol presents all the interactions that followed after the 180-volt shock was administered:

Subject: I can't stand it. I'm not going to kill that man in there. You hear him hollering?
Experimenter: As I told you before, the shocks may be painful, but –
Subject: But he's hollering. He can't stand it. What's going to happen to him?
Experimenter (his voice is patient, matter-of-fact): The experiment requires that you continue, Teacher.
Subject: Aaah, but, unh, I'm not going to get that man sick in there . . . know what I mean?
Experimenter: Whether the learner likes it or not, we must go on, through all the word pairs.
Subject: I refuse to take the responsibility. He's in there hollering!
Experimenter: It's absolutely essential that you continue, Teacher.
Subject (indicating the unused questions): There's too many left here; I mean, Geez, if he gets them wrong, there's too many of them left. I mean who's going to take the responsibility if anything happens to that gentleman?
Experimenter: I'm responsible for anything that happens to him. Continue, please.
Subject: All right. [Consults list of words.] The next one's "Slow – walk, truck, dance, music." Answer please. [A buzzing sound indicates the learner has signaled his answer.] Wrong. A hundred and ninety-five volts. "Dance."
Learner (yelling): Let me out of here. My heart's bothering me! [Teacher looks at experimenter.]
Experimenter: Continue, please.
Learner (screaming): Let me out of here, you have no right to keep me here. Let me out of here, let me out, my heart's bothering me, let me out! [Subject shakes head, pats the table nervously.]
Subject: You see, he's hollering. Hear that? Gee, I don't know.
Experimenter: The experiment requires . . .
Subject (interrupting): I know it does, sir, but I mean – hunh! He doesn't know what he's getting in for. He's up to 195 volts! [*Experiment continues, through 210 volts, 225 volts, 240 volts, 255 volts, 270 volts, at which point the teacher, with evident relief, runs out of word-pair questions.*]
Experimenter: You'll have to go back to the beginning of that page and go through them again until he's learned them all correctly.
Subject: Aw, no. I'm not going to kill that man. You mean I've got to keep going up with the scale? No sir. He's hollering in there. I'm not going to give him 450 volts.
Experimenter: The experiment requires that you go on.
Subject: I know it does, but that man is hollering in there, sir.
Experimenter: (same matter-of-fact tone): As I said before, although the shocks may be painful . . .
Subject (interrupting): Awwww. He – he – he's yelling in there.
Experimenter: Start with "Blue," please, at the top of the page. Continue, please, Teacher. Just go ahead.
Subject (concentrating intently on list of words in front of him, as if to shut everything else out): "Blue – boy, girl, grass, hat." [Buzz indicates answer.] Correct. "Night – day, sky, job, chair." [Buzz.] Wrong. The answer is "day." Two hundred and eighty-five volts.
Learner: Ohhuhhoohhh!

Subject: "Fat – man, lady, tub, neck." Answer, please. [Buzz.] Wrong. The answer is "neck." Three hundred volts.

Learner: Ohhh. I absolutely refuse to answer any more. [Shouting urgently, now.] Let me out of here. You can't hold me here. Get me out. Get – me – out – of – . . .here.

Experimenter: Continue. The next word is "Green," please.

Subject: "Green – grass, hat, ink, apple." [Nothing happens. No answering buzz. Just gloomy silence.]

Subject: I don't think he's going to answer.

Experimenter: If the learner doesn't answer in a reasonable time, about four or five seconds, consider the answer wrong. And follow the same procedures you have been doing for wrong answers. Say, "Wrong," tell him the number of volts, give him the punishment, read him the correct answer. Continue, please.

Subject: "Green – grass, hat, ink, apple." Answer, please. [More silence. Subject just sits there.]

Experimenter: Go on with the procedure, please, Teacher.

Subject: Three hundred and fifteen volts. The answer is "ink."

Learner: Ohh. Ooohh.

Subject (relieved to hear response): Next one. . .

Learner: I absolutely refuse to answer.

Subject: You got to. You get a shock if you don't answer. [Experiment continues with learner refusing to answer, and, finally, failing even to grunt or groan. At 375 volts, the subject stands up.]

Subject: I think something's happened to that fellow in there. I don't get no answer. He was hollering at less voltage. Can't you check in and see if he's all right, please?

Experimenter (with same detached calm): Not once we've started. Please continue, Teacher.

Subject (sits down, sighs deeply): "Cool – day, shade, water, paint." Answer, please. Are you all right in there? Are you all right?

Experimenter: Please continue, Teacher. Continue, please [Subject pushes lever.]

Subject (swiveling around in his chair): Something's happened to that man in there. [Swiveling back.] Next one. "Low – dollar, necklace, moon, paint." [Turning around again.] Something's happened to that man in there. You better check on him, sir. He won't answer or nothing.

Experimenter: Continue. Go on, please.

Subject: You accept all responsibility?

Experimenter: The responsibility is mine. Correct. Please go on. [Subject returns to his list, starts running through words as rapidly as he can read them, works through to 450 volts.]

Subject: That's that.

Experimenter: Continue using the 450-volt switch for each wrong answer. Continue, please.

Subject: But I don't get no anything!

Experimenter: Please continue. The next word is "white."

Subject: Don't you think you should look in on him, please?

Experimenter: Not once we've started the experiment.

Subject: But what if something happened to the man?

Experimenter: The experiment requires that you continue. Go on, please.

Subject: Don't the man's health mean anything?

Experimenter: Whether the learner likes it or not. . .

Subject: What if he's dead in there? [Gestures toward the room with the electric chair.] I mean, he told me he can't stand the shock, sir. I don't mean to be rude, but I think you should look in on him. All you have to do is look in on him. All you have to do is look in the door. I don't get no answer, no noise. Something might have happened to the gentleman in there, sir.

Experimenter: We must continue. Go on, please.

Subject: You mean keep giving him what? Four-hundred-fifty volts, what he's got now?

Experimenter: That's correct. Continue. The next word is "white."

Subject (now at a furious pace): "White – cloud, horse, rock, house." Answer, please. The answer is "horse." Four hundred and fifty volts. [*Administers shock.*] Next word, "Bag – paint, music, clown, girl." The answer is "paint." Four hundred and fifty volts. [*Administers shock.*] Next word is "Short – sentence, movie..."

Experimenter: Excuse me, Teacher. We'll have to discontinue the experiment.

A striking feature in this protocol is that a genuine concern on the part of the subject for the welfare of the learner remains throughout the experiment and is manifested in several actions. It cannot be said that the subject failed utterly to act upon his concern for the learner. The subject protested, argued, asked that the experimenter look in on the learner, and was agitated. The subject requested that the experimenter accept responsibility for the welfare of the victim and even castigated him for failing to meet up to that responsibility (e.g., "What if something happened to the man?"; "Don't the man's health mean anything?"). At the same time, there is a concern on the part of the subject with the viability of the experiment and the corresponding legitimacy of the experimenter's authority. That concern is manifested in his responses to the experimenter and in his participation to the end in spite of a strong desire to discontinue. The two forms of judgment were coordinated by him in a way that gave sufficient weight to the social-organizational features, resulting in his continuation of the shocks to the end of the scale. In the experimental condition described above (referred to here as the standard condition), the majority of subjects, though not all, coordinated the two forms of judgment in that way.

This interpretation of the experiment as involving domain coordinations is supported by the results from several other experimental conditions (as reported by Milgram, 1974). The prediction would be that, relative to the standard condition, experimental conditions in which either the salience of the moral component is increased or the salience of the conventional component is decreased would result in a greater number of subjects discontinuing their participation. The expectation fits the results of the experiments.

First consider three of the experimental conditions, including the standard one, which can be ordered along the dimension of the saliency of the moral component. (1) In the standard condition the subject is placed in a different room from the learner and can only hear him (referred to by Milgram as the "voice-feedback" condition). (2) In what was referred to as the "proximity" condition the learner was placed a few feet from the subject and could be seen and heard. (3) And in the "touch-proximity" condition the learner and subject were in the same room and the learner received a shock only when his hand was on a shock plate. After the 150-volt level the learner refused to place his hand on the plate and the experimenter instructed the subject to force the learner's hand onto the plate. The social-organizational features of these three conditions are the same, whereas the salience of the harm inflicted on the other person varies. The findings are consistent with what we would expect: In the voice-feedback condition 65% of the subjects continued to the end of the scale; in the proximity condition 40% of the subjects continued; and in the touch-proximity condition 30% continued.

A similar analysis can be made of conditions that varied in the salience of the conventional component. Four experimental conditions can be ordered on this dimension, relative to the standard condition, on the basis of the role and place of the experimenter as the authority. Briefly stated, the four conditions were (details are given in Milgram, 1974):

(1) "Experimenter absent": after providing the initial introduction the experimenter left the room and gave the instructions by telephone.

(2) "Ordinary man gives orders": this condition was designed so that the subject would have the impression that another subject (actually an accomplice of the experimenter), in the absence of the experimenter, decided the procedure and gave instructions to administer shocks.

(3) "Authority as victim; an ordinary man gives orders": in this condition the experimenter received the shocks and at some point demanded to be let out, while a person posing as a second subject insisted that the experiment continue.

(4) "Two authorities; contradictory commands": two experimenters gave instructions, but after the 150-volt level one experimenter instructed the subject to continue while the second experimenter instructed the subject to stop.

In each of these conditions the structure of the situation is different from the standard condition. In the first the experimenter is absent physically, giving instruction through remote means. In the second the experimenter is totally absent and a person of the same status as the subject takes charge. In the third condition the hierarchy is reversed, so that a subject is instructing while the experimenter is protesting. In the fourth condition, by taking opposing positions, the two authorities cancel each other out. The results in these conditions are as striking as the results of the standard condition: in each of the first two conditions only 20% of the subjects continued administering the shocks; in the last two conditions none of the subjects continued. As expected, a decrease in the saliency of the social-organizational component in the situation results in behavior consistent with the subject's moral decision.

These results bear directly upon the issues raised earlier regarding empirical consistencies and inconsistencies between moral judgment and action. The findings from the standard condition in the Milgram experiment show inconsistency between moral judgment and behavior. However, it is not necessarily the case that there is inconsistency between *judgment* and behavior. The findings from the standard condition can also be interpreted as showing consistency between behavior and concepts of social organization. The behaviors in that condition can be best explained as a function of the coordination of two different domains of judgment.

In actuality, the results of the various experimental conditions show that, with regard to the same behavior (i.e., shocking another person), there is both consistency and inconsistency between moral judgment and behavior. The degree of consistency is related to the salience of each domain being coordinated by the subject in the situation. Judgment–behavior consistencies, as well as inconsistencies, require explanations that take domain coordinations into account. Rather than restricting the problem to relations between moral judgments and behavior, the question can be posed as: What are the relations between social judgments and behavior? In empirical investigations this question would then be translated into analyses of the parameters of behavioral situations, identification of the domains, assessments of behavioral outcomes, assessments of within-domain judgments, and explanation of the coordination of judgments manifested in behavioral outcomes.

10   Conclusions: Interaction, development, and rationality

In 1926 the anthropologist Bronislaw Malinowski wrote about *Crime and Custom in Savage Society*. He presented an ethnographic account of the legal conditions in the Melanesian community, located in the Trobriand Archipelago to the northeast of New Guinea, and concluded that "The savage is neither an extreme 'collectivist' nor an intransigent 'individualist' – he is, like man in general, a mixture of both." (p. 56). Malinowski's conclusion was not in accord with characterizations of whole cultural groups as predominantly either individualistic or collectivistic. His conclusion was also not in accord with a prevailing assumption among anthropologists that in so-called primitive societies the individual (the savage) is dominated by the commands of the community, has deep reverence for tradition and custom, and is bound by a pervasive group sentiment (an assumption of "the French school of Durkheim, in most American and German works and in some English writings"). The legal system in Melanesian savage society, like that of civilized societies, was based on considerations of both group solidarity and personal interest. Malinowski observed that although the legal system is generally maintained, as in most places, conflicts, contradictions, and violations exist.

On the basis of his ethnographic studies Malinowski characterized the Melanesian native as having a differentiated understanding of a multifaceted social system. The native does not fail to distinguish the personal from the social. The native applies rationality to an understanding of different cultural practices. Thus, the native distinguishes law from custom, practical utility from taboo, moral obligation from convention, religious practice from the rules of personal relations, and manners from rules of games ("rules which are the soul and substance of the amusement or pursuit and are kept because it is felt and recognized that any failure to 'play the game' spoils it").

Malinowski's studies demonstrated that there are complex legal, moral, conventional, and political systems in Melanesia, as well as differentiated understandings of those systems by members of the society. The culture is not an integrated system to which the individual accommodates:

211

The most important fact from our point of view in this struggle of social principles is that it forces us to re-cast completely the traditional conception of law and order in savage communities. We have to abandon now definitely the idea of an inert, solid 'crust' or 'cake' of custom rigidly pressing from outside upon the whole surface of tribal life. Law and order arise out of the very processes which they govern. But they are not rigid, nor due to any inertia or permanent mould. They obtain on the contrary as the result of a constant struggle not merely of human passions against the law, but of legal principles with one another. . . .

We have reached a number of conclusions about the existence of positive and elastic and yet binding obligations, which correspond to the civil law in more developed cultures; about the influence of reciprocity, public enactment and the systematic incidence of such obligations, which supply their main binding forces; about the negative rulings of law, the tribal prohibitions and taboos, which we have found as elastic and adaptable as the positive rules although fulfilling a different function. [Malinowski, 1926, pp. 122–124]

If Malinowski thought that he had put to rest the issue of stereotyped characterizations of individualistic and collectivistic societies, he was mistaken. In the past few years – about 50 years after Malinowski's studies – we have seen once again characterizations of social systems and their members as either individualistic or collectivistic (Hogan, 1975; Hogan, Johnson, & Emler, 1978; Sampson, 1977; Simpson, 1974). It has been maintained that North American and Western European societies are mainly individualistic, in contrast with collectivistic societies, and that, therefore, the findings obtained by psychological researchers working within these contexts reflect the cultural orientation. An individualistic culture produces an individualistic psychology; a solid "crust" of individualistic custom and ideology rigidly presses from outside upon Western life. Moreover, the pervasive individualistic culture produces individualistic psychologists, so that their theories actually reflect and reify the values and biases of the society.

An example relevant to the concerns of this volume pertains to the explanations of moral development provided by Piaget and Kohlberg (which were described in Chapter 7). It has been stated (e.g., Hogan, 1975; Sampson, 1977) that those explanations are essentially reproductions of the morality of one type of culture. More specifically, it is claimed that propositions of a developmental shift toward autonomy or self-constructed principles idealize independence from the collectivity and are, therefore, reflective of individualistic values. Presumably, this is the case for the sequence proposed by Piaget, with its shift from heteronomy to autonomy, as well as for Kohlberg's formulation, with its shifts from preconventional to conventional to principled (postconventional) morality.

The notion that the Piaget or Kohlberg formulations idealize individualism is, in one sense, puzzling because they both described the most advanced levels of moral judgment in terms discrepant with individualism. The essence of morality at the most advanced level, as described by Piaget, is cooperation and interdependence. The mutuality and reciprocity of cooperative social relations characterize the autonomous orientation and contrast it with the unilateral (nonmutual, noncooperative) orientation to authority of the heteronomous level. Similarly, Kohlberg's most advanced level is characterized by reciprocity, mutuality, and general welfare. In fact, the clearest form of individualism in Kohlberg's formulation appears at an early level of development (the egoism of stage 2).

The perception of an individualistic bias in these theories comes from two sources. First is the proposition that moral judgments are not defined by constituted social systems but by principles that can be evaluated independently of what exists in given social systems (as was discussed in Chapter 3). In that case, there is the possibility that the individual may apply moral criteria (pertaining to cooperative relations) that are discrepant with and independent of the existing practices of the collectivity. The second source of the perception of an individualistic bias apparently comes from a confusion of the descriptions of moral judgments with the explanations of the psychological principles of cognition and development. Structural theorists have proposed that the development of thinking is a constructive process stemming from individual–environment interactions (see Chapter 2). This self-constructive aspect of the explanation of the process of development is taken as individualistic. However, the aim of theory and research on processes of development is to formulate explanations of the mechanisms of ontogenetic changes. A variety of such explanations has been offered, including those viewing development as an accommodation to the social environment or as the emergence of biologically determined behaviors. In all these cases, cultural labels like individualistic or collectivistic, or any others, are beside the point. Propositions regarding mechanisms of development may be evaluated as correct or incorrect, as more adequate or less adequate; cultural labeling does not constitute evaluation.[1]

Of greatest importance is that the research findings discussed throughout this volume have shown that individuals cannot be stereotyped in the cultural categories. As in Malinowski's research on the Melanesians, we have seen that social

---

[1] The cultural labels have also been used to criticize explanations of moral development through the contention that the cultural (or individual) biases of the researcher account for the formulations – that is, that the researcher is being ethnocentric. The purported cultural biases of the researcher are also beside the point and do not constitute evaluations. These kinds of criticisms merely substitute a characterization of the researcher for analyses of the scientific merits of theory and data. A theory can be evaluated by criticism of supporting or disconfirming data, or by logical analysis of its premises, but not through speculations or accusations regarding the motives, biases, or cultural commitments of its proponents.

Accusations of ethnocentrism in the guise of criticism of a theory is analogous to claims of bias recently made by proponents of creationism against proponents of evolutionary theory. Creationists have asserted that evolutionary theory is consistent with the religious beliefs (i.e., secular humanism) of its proponents, which differ from the religious beliefs of those upholding a creationist explanation of the origins of life. It is thus asserted that evolutionary theory stems from a set of religious biases and is no more legitimate an explanation than creationism. However, the fact that proponents of evolution might hold certain religious beliefs has no bearing on the scientific validity of evolutionary theory. Correspondingly, that proponents of a particular theory of moral development might hold certain moral or cultural beliefs has no bearing on the scientific validity of the theory.

judgments in the United States samples do not fall into categories reflecting holistically integrated cultural schemes. Instead, it has been found that the social cognition of individuals reflects differing orientations, whose manifestation depends, at least, on the issue and domain in question. With regard to conventions, the orientation is primarily collectivistic because they are regarded as coordinating social interactions. With regard to morality, the orientation is toward interdependence, though the requirements of justice sometimes demand individualism insofar as they conflict with institutional practices. The same individuals are relativists and universalists. They are concerned with group solidarity *and* individual rights. They can be absolutistic and flexible. In some instances individuals account for rules and in others they do not. Some judgments are based on authority and social hierarchies, whereas other judgments are based on equality. In some conditions behavior is in conformity to the dictates of authority, but in other conditions it is in contradiction with dictates of authority (as seen in the experiments by Milgram discussed in the previous chapter). Some issues are evaluated by the criterion of impersonality; in other cases the validity of personal choice or inclination is affirmed.

The coexistence of the impersonal and personal is of particular relevance to the individualism–collectivism dichotomy. In the study by Nucci (1981) that was considered in Chapter 4, subjects classified a series of social actions as "the person's own business." In that some acts were regarded as legitimately determined by personal choice, the subjects may appear to have an individualistic orientation. And indeed they do! Moreover, the acts regarded as personal were highly influenced by societal practice. Another set of acts were judged to be out of the realm of personal choice insofar as social rules and expectations were associated with them. Therefore, the subjects may appear to have a collectivistic orientation. And indeed they do! The individualism–collectivism dichotomy is insufficient, however, to account for the orientation of individuals. Yet another set of actions were considered apart from both the personal and conventional realms and judged to be wrong regardless of social expectations or personal inclination. These subjects also have an orientation to the categories of justice and welfare.

A dichotomy between social regulation or restriction and personal choice or freedom from regulation is also inadequate in accounting for the orientations of individuals. Contrasting types of judgments in the same individuals are typical. The research suggests that a coherent cultural scheme is not the direct source of the social judgments and behaviors of individuals. The coexistence of categories like individualism and collectivism or relativism and universality is tied to the types of judgments involved.

Rationality and nonrationality in social domains

The coexistence of social concepts cutting across typically stated cultural categories can be interpreted to support the general hypothesis that social domains do involve rational processes. The issue of rationality in relation to cultural analyses was raised in the introductory chapter. Although the research discussed in the intervening chapters only begins to address the relations between individual development and culture, we are now in a better position to evaluate alternative hypotheses. As stated in Chapter 1, the assumption of cultural determination has been coupled with the assumptions of morality as nonrational, symbolic, and conventional. A view of morality as entailing nonrational processes proposes that social content is ultimately arbitrary; that development is the enculturation of children; that culture is primary in social judgments and actions; and that, given the arbitrariness of social content and the primacy of culture, there are no systematic relations between forms of social judgment and the content of the domain. These propositions rest on the idea that all social domains are constitutive; that is, social practices are largely symbolic and expressive, and based on arbitrary cultural constructions.

The French school of Durkheim (1924/1974, 1925/1961), as it was referred to by Malinowski, is the classic example of a nonrational interpretation of morality as consisting of symbolic expressions of cultural constructions. An aspect of Durkheim's viewpoint was mentioned earlier (Chapter 3) with regard to connections between social acts and their moral status. It will be recalled that Durkheim disassociated social acts from intrinsic consequences. Whereas the violation of a prudential rule (e.g., rules of hygiene or safety) brings with it direct, observable, and analyzable consequences, the violation of a moral rule (e.g., the rule that prohibits killing) does not. Analyses of an act like killing do not lead to its blameworthiness or moral proscription. The link is "synthetic" in that it is the existence of a social rule that connects the act to blame or sanctions.

The implication, then, is that social actions (including killing), in themselves, must be morally neutral. It is something other than analysis of social acts that transforms them into moral acts: it is their place in the group, in the collectivity. According to Durkheim, society as an entity distinct from the different individuals it comprises is both the source and authority for moral duties and obligations ("Society... for me is the source and end of morality"). Transcending individual interest or welfare, society is the only legitimate source of moral authority. The social order is a moral order and the basis for moral obligation.

Some of Durkheim's formal criteria for morality resemble the ones we have used (as derived from Gewirth and others). Included among Durkheim's criteria are obligatoriness and impersonality (see Durkheim, 1924/1974, pp. 35–38). However, for Durkheim, obligation and impersonality do not stem from concepts or inferences – they are not the products of reason – but stem from sentiments of attachment and respect for the collectivity. Impersonality is what transcends individuals, namely, the group. Obligation and duty are directed toward the group and stem from a shared sentiment of respect for society and an attribution of sacredness for its moral authority.

Morality is, therefore, highly symbolic. It is manifested in the expressions of respect for society; it is symbolized through the authority, rules, and conventional signs of the social order. Morality is symbolic because the source of praise or blame is not in analytic judgments of intrinsic features of acts, or their consequences, but in a synthetic link to something else. The obligatory, the valued, or the sacred obtain value and meaning from what is symbolized. Therefore, the relation between rules or actions and the social system they represent is arbitrary and conventional. That is, social conventions are often symbolic of the moral order.

From the Durkheimian perspective, institutional practices, traditions, and customs take the form of categorical moral obligations. For Durkheim, it could not be said that "judgments of moral obligation are categorical" and set requirements "that they cannot rightly evade by consulting...institutional practices" (as in Gewirth). Institutional practices are, as Shweder (1981) has explicitly asserted (following Durkheim), part of the nonrational realm of moral obligation. As a nonrational realm, the social order must be viewed as a global and undifferentiated system that is not subject to comparative evaluation.

Moreover, the relation between the content or substance of moral codes and the formal criteria defining morality is conventionally variable. For example, the criteria of obligatoriness and impersonality are applied by Durkheim to content in a very different way from that of Gewirth. The source of obligation and impersonality for Durkheim is affect, not reason; obligation and impersonality stem from symbolic cultural expressions and not analytic discoveries through deductive or inductive inference. Any content or set of acts can be, by cultural determination, symbolic and morally obligatory.

The symbolic and expressive view of morality-convention is the view that the individual is dominated by the community, by tradition and custom, and by a pervasive group sentiment (insofar as it exists). It is a view that contains the two interrelated assumptions of nonrationality and of development as the child's acquisition of cultural codes transmitted by others (see especially Durkheim, 1925/1961, and Shweder, 1981). These assumptions, which are discrepant with Malinowski's observations on Melanesia, were not supported by the body of findings presented in this volume. To account for these findings from the nonrational perspective it would be necessary to postulate (a) that those subjects (as well as those in Malinowski's observations) were from a diversified culture which, unlike some others, includes category distinctions (e.g., individualism/ collectivism; relativism/universality; hierarchy/equality) and (b) that they adopted the categories in a nonrational fashion.

Such an interpretation would again invoke cultural categories, but with the additional feature, to account for the findings, that cultures can be contrasted on a dimension of relative diversity or uniformity. Indeed, by continually stretching one's cultural categories most research findings can be explained with the enculturation proposition. The implausibility of this interpretation was mentioned earlier with regard to the findings of the observational studies of children's social interactions considered in Chapter 3. The results of the research considered in subsequent chapters are also not supportive of such an interpretation in that it has been found that children construct systematic, nonarbitrary social concepts. It has been seen that analyses of social development require the formulation of categories of social knowledge and elements of social interactions, along with the categories of cultural systems. Rationality and the construction of categories of social knowledge go together.

In what ways do the research findings demonstrate rational processes in social domains? A major conclusion that can be derived from the research is that individuals form coherent systems of thinking, including discriminations, in their understandings of the diverse elements of their social world. Social judgments are neither random nor simply reflective of external content. Constitutive aspects of social systems are not equated with principles pertaining to how people ought to relate to each other. Individuals are not by any means unaware of arbitrariness in social coordination or of the role of constitutive rules in systems of social organization. There is rationality in the recognition of the arbitrary and its relation to cultural and social organizational systems. Rational processes are reflected in discriminations between what coordinates and what prescribes, as well as between the contextual and the noncontextual. As an example, children's concepts of games as constitutive systems and of game rules as definitional of the context reflect the application of analysis and reason to a social realm. It has also been documented that there is recognition of acts that are not arbitrary in their consequences to others or for systems of social relations. Sanctions and rules are not required for the individual to form a link between concepts of obligation or rights and actions. Analyses of certain acts (such as one person harming another) do lead to inferences about rules that ought to guide conduct.

Several of the studies, through different types of data, have shown that moral functions are conceptualized differently from social-organizational functions. If obligation were based primarily on sentiments of attachment and respect, it would follow that the moral and conventional stem from the same source and serve similar functions. However, the individual's relation to the social system is not solely one of attachment to an entity held to be sacred nor sentiment of moral respect for the collectivity. As intuitive sociologists, individuals attempt to understand the principles that govern systems of social organization. There is an analytic orientation to social organization, so that conventions, rules, and authority are understood as alterable and relative elements serving to coordinate social interactions. In addition, it is an analytic orientation that can include criticalness of adult conceptions and social system practices. There are efforts at self-correction and at corrections of what are perceived to be errors of institutional practices. The analytic orientation toward social organization is part of one of the central social conceptual systems that has its origins at an early age. It is a conceptual system with major significance for children's interactions in social units, as was documented by observational studies in schools. It is also a conceptual system that is nontrivially related to behavior, as was shown by the analyses of the conflicts and behavioral outcomes in Milgram's experiments.

Conflicts between moral judgments and concepts pertaining to functions served by adherence to the social system require more attention than thus far accorded. Insofar as observations are made of behaviors that contrast with moral prescriptions regarding harm, for instance, they are attributed to a cultural source and regarded as evidence for the cross-cultural variability of morality. Benedict (1934, p. 45), for example, used instances of homicide as evidence for the strong claim that cultures are integrated wholes, and that they determine the acceptability or unacceptability of social actions:

Standards no matter in what aspect of behavior range in different cultures from the positive to the negative pole. We might suppose that in the matter of taking life all peoples would agree in condemnation. On the contrary, in a matter of homicide, it may be held that one is blameless if diplomatic relations have been severed between neighboring countries, or that one kills by custom his first two children, or that a husband has right of life and death over his wife, or that it is the duty of the child to kill his parents before they are old.

Benedict's solution to the complex problem of explaining instances of harm, including homicide, is to reduce it to a matter of cultural determinism. There is more than meets the eye in the types of examples cited by Benedict, as shown by Asch (1952) and Wertheimer (1935). The findings of the Milgram experiment also illustrate that these examples require more complex explanation than the force of custom. Given the likelihood that avoidance of harm is a moral consideration in most societies, examples of the infliction of harm would require further explication of conflicts and inconsistencies in judgments as well as between judgments and actions. In this regard, the analyses of the Milgram experiments indicated that instances of harm are not linked to one cultural orientation. Under certain conditions subjects from this culture inflicted harm, but in other conditions the same subjects refused to do so. Furthermore, the Milgram experiments demonstrated that situations in which harm is inflicted can involve conflicts between moral and societal considerations.

It also needs to be recognized that the definition of persons has a bearing on differential treatment of classes of persons (of those within and external to the group). The coordination of moral judgments with the much less than perfect psychological concepts (concepts of persons) that individuals hold is another route to explaining behaviors of the sort listed by Benedict. Rather than the reductionism of invoking custom and culture to account for those actions, our explanations should be broadened to include the conflicts and coordinations that are inherent to multidimensional social actions.

In constructing concepts of social organization, individuals may respect or form an attachment to a constitutive system, but they do not generally view adherence to that system's rules, authority, or conventions to be a universal necessity. The proposition that individuals form concepts of social organization has far-reaching implications for anthropological and sociological perspectives on the study of culture. For the most part, individuals' concepts of culture and social organization have been ignored. Social scientists often attribute nonrationality to the layperson in those very realms that they (the social scientists) are attempting to explicate in a rational fashion. No credence is given to the cultural and social-organizational theories of the members of cultures under investigation. Insofar as a constitutive realm is concerned, the presumption is made that those who are part of the system do not make judgments about it. The assumption of the primacy of culture and society has resulted in a failure to explicate the richness of individuals' understandings of constituted systems by those who are most concerned with those systems.

As an example, students of culture have neglected concepts of social organization in their interpretation of social convention. For instance, Shweder (in press) accepts that moral judgments regarding harm or welfare may be related to nonculturally specific social experiences with intrinsic consequences. At the same time, however, he maintains that conventions are part of the individual's morality. The reasoning is as follows. Conventions, which are arbitrary in themselves, represent constitutive elements of given social systems and vary from one system to the next. Yet the conventions of a social system are treated as important and meaningful (nonarbitrary) by its members. Hence, conventions actually represent a nonrational (symbolic) morality that obtains its force from attachments to culture.

These formulations lack an appreciation for conceptualizations of culture and social organization. The research has documented that subjects can understand the arbitrary quality of conventions, as well as their constitutive role in social systems. Nevertheless, conventions are treated as important and meaningful. This is because of an understanding of their importance and function (nonarbitrariness) in the makeup of the social system or the group. If we attribute to the individual concepts of social organization, without assuming an affectively based dominance of culture over his or her attitudes and behavior, it becomes necessary to consider the varying conceptual sources for attributions of meaning and importance. Children will attribute much importance to conventional transgressions (such as the outlandish ones of a boy wearing a dress or pajamas to school), but still conceptualize them in nonmoral terms; they view the convention as different even from moral transgressions with minor consequences (e.g., stealing an eraser). An even more informative set of findings in this regard comes from research by Nucci (1982), who examined discriminations made by high school and college-age devout Catholics regarding strongly held religious beliefs. In brief, Nucci found that religious beliefs in the moral domain were generalized by the subjects to other religious groups, whereas nonmoral religious beliefs were not regarded as applicable to other religious groups.

Evidence sometimes provided for the proposition that conventions are nonrational and moral is from examples of subjects who consider the harmful consequences to persons of conventional transgressions (Shweder, in press). This is what was referred to earlier as a second-order phenomenon – which actually provides a very good example of conceptual-transformational activity in the social realms. As was discussed in Chapter 6, subjects' perceptions of the moral implications of a conventional transgression (e.g., public nudity in the face of objections from others) were not based on the violation of symbolic expressions of group solidarity or loyalty. There is a two-step process of reasoning by which two conceptual systems are coordinated. The conventional issue of public nudity took on moral considerations for many subjects only insofar as its violation would cause harm or offense to others. The issue was then transformed into an issue of harm. Nevertheless, the primary conventional understanding of the issue was maintained and coordinated with the moral concern for avoidance of harm to others (hence it is a second-order phenomenon). The perceived arbitrariness of the convention had sufficient force for a number of other subjects that they gave it priority over avoidance of harm; they stated that others ought not to take offense.

The complex and systematic nature of the theories children construct about the social world is perhaps best illustrated by the distinction and complementarity of criterion judgments and justification categories. Systematic and non–age-related criteria are used in defining domains of social knowledge and in identifying social events in accordance with domain. Through assessments of criterion judgments, evidence was obtained that a given subject uses the opposing orientations, referred to earlier, that are often construed as cultural orientations. Subjects also apply the justification categories, which represent reasons within domains. The justification categories are complementary with criterion judgments in that reasons vary in accordance with domain (e.g., the categories of welfare, fairness, and obligation are associated with the moral domain, whereas authority, custom, and social coordination are associated with the conventional domain).

Although the criterion judgments were not age-related, sequential shifts were found in concepts reflective of justification categories. Qualitative changes in social reasoning are apparent in the developmental sequences of concepts of social convention and concepts of distributive justice. The observed developmental patterns regarding sequentiality and transformation do not support the second assumption of the symbolic-expressive cultural position, that children acquire cultural codes through transmission from others. Assumptions made about the acquisition of cultural codes are just assumptions in the absence of an empirically based explanation of processes of development. Such assumptions are more often informed by concerns with culture and presumptions of the overriding impact of culture on the individual (Durkheim, 1925/1961; Geertz, 1973; Shweder, 1981) than by an explanation of developmental processes. These assumptions, however, need to be informed by investigations of individual development. A clear example of an analysis of patterns of individual development that is in conflict with the cultural transmission assumption can be seen in the systematic shifts between affirmation and negation throughout childhood and adolescence in the development of concepts of social convention. An explanation of the child's development as the direct acquisition of cultural codes implies consistency between adult and child attitudes, once they are acquired by the child. Once acquired, conventions would be maintained as the child grew older (perhaps with changes in their strength and scope). However, the observed patterns of consistency or inconsistency are not straightforward. Individuals shift back and forth, in one phase accepting convention and in the next rejecting convention. Development involves a process of reorganization of one conceptual system into another.

This is not to say that communications from others and cultural content are unimportant in the development of social concepts. Communications are, indeed, significant components of children's interactions with the social environment. If, however, we are to take seriously the individual's inferential activities, then it is necessary to consider how explicit or implicit communications are interpreted by children. Similar considerations apply for communications of "cultural messages" (D'Andrade, 1981). An interactional interpretation of the relevance of communications would account for the contextual domain of the communications, the developmental level of the receiver of the communications, and how change might be stimulated by the interchanges.

An interactional interpretation of development also has to account for the role of experiences that are not solely prepackaged units in the form of communications or cultural codes. Participation in (and observation of) social interactions constitutes direct action from which information is extracted and knowledge is derived. All too often this significant element of social experience is omitted from proposed factors influencing social development. It is worth reiterating that meaning derived from events with intrinsic consequences is one of the central sources of the development of moral reasoning. A class of social actions having intrinsic consequences and revolving around interpersonal relations is likely to be perceived as nonarbitrary. Thus, the relation between the content of social actions and moral judgments is not determined solely by the institutional context.

The institutional context is a primary source of the content of (arbitrary) social actions that are part of conventional systems. The relation of the content of conventional acts would, in large measure, be determined by the cultural context. The specific conventions considered significant in one context may very well differ from those in another context. Behaviors considered in the purview of personal choice in one context may be judged as conventionally binding in another context.

Categories of social knowledge

The proposed cultural dichotomies discussed earlier are paralleled in the research strategies used in comparative investigations (including cross-cultural investigations) of social behavior, attitudes, or judgments. A common research strategy is to establish, as a standard of comparison, one group (e.g., a national or cultural group) that is characterized as uniform in sociocultural orientation. Observations of other orientations in other cultures are taken as evidence for cultural determinism. A potential fallacy in this research strategy comes from the likelihood that the group used as the standard of comparison has been inappropriately characterized (stereotyped?) as primarily one-dimensional. The search, then, for other dimensions in another group as evidence for the hypothesis of cultural determinism would be misplaced. Alternative research strategies would be required if the coexistence of diverse social dimensions were to be explored within all the groups.

A related strategy in comparative investigations of morality is to search for norms, customs, or conventions that are intensely held in one group but not in another. Most frequently, the intensity is located in "primitive" or isolated groups, as compared with more "complex" societies. Differences in the intensity of adherence to customs or conventions are interpreted as evidence for culturally determined differences in the content of morality and for its acquisition from the external environment. However, there are other possible explanations of the observed differences. The differences can be on account of other factors, such as misattributions, conflicts, or coordinations between moral and conventional domains of reasoning. In the previous chapter it was maintained that both consistencies and inconsistencies in judgment and behavior require explanation. Observation of consistency does not constitute explanation. Analogously, observations of both group similarities and differences require explanation. From the structural and developmental perspectives, explanations of observed similarities or differences require analyses of the individual's interactions with the social environment, of domains of social knowledge and their reorganizations in development, and a multidimensional perspective on the social system.

Social knowledge is, of course, not restricted to morality and convention. They are two aspects of social knowledge that form part of a broader set of domains and categories that will be considered in the subsequent volume. The present volume does provide guidelines for the parameters to be encompassed in the study of the development of moral judgments and concepts of social convention in any setting. The factors to be included are schematized in Table 10.1. As illustrated in the table, the starting point is the definitional basis for each domain of knowledge, which guides the research methodology. The findings have shown that definitional criteria, which were substantially derived from considerations suggested by philosophers, are not discontinuous with the reasoning of subjects. Essential aspects of the definitional characteristics were reflected in the social epistemology of the subjects represented in the research. Assessment of subjects' knowledge includes criterion judgments and justification categories, with analyses of the levels of organization and reorganization of the justification categories. In analyses of the social environment, a distinction is drawn between the nature of events (intrinsic or arbitrary) and sociocultural facts. Note that aspects of social-environmental events and facts are interactive with each domain. As examples, communications can revolve around moral or conventional issues and rules may pertain to each domain. Also note that a definitional characteristic in one domain may be a sociocultural fact in the other (e.g., social consensus as definitional for convention and as a fact for morality) or that a type of social event in one domain is a fact in the other (e.g., uniformities).

The specification of distinctions in subjects' reasoning and in the social environment has implications for the units of analysis, as listed in Table 10.1. The first task is to ascertain within-domain criterion judgments and justification categories. This requires identification of prototypical domain-specific events for use as the stimuli in assessments of concepts of justice, harm, and rights, as well as assessments of concepts of social organization.

The determination of systems of reasoning in each domain is a prerequisite for study of the subjects' relation to sociocultural facts and domain combinations. An advantage of this procedure is that it controls for the subject's conceptual activities – a control lacking in attempts simply to map cultural content onto behavior or attitudes. That is, it provides the necessary subject assessments in an interactional analysis of the relations between social judgments and aspects of the social environment. As an example, the severity of consequences for the violation of convention is a sociocultural fact established by the social system. The existence of severe consequences for conventional violations (or even intensely held conventions) should not necessarily be interpreted as part of moral reasoning or moral fact. Assessments of criterion judgments and justification categories may show that conventions can be regarded as important for the members of the group, though still recognizing that they are not necessarily applicable to other groups.

One means for understanding variations in sociocultural facts is through investigation of the interface of the two domains of reasoning. We have already

Table 10.1. *Elements of interactional analyses*

Domain	Definitional basis for system of knowledge	Subject assessments	Social environment I) Social events	II) Sociocultural facts

Morality	Justice
	Welfare
	Rights
		a) Criterion judgments
		  Obligatoriness
		  Impersonality
		  Generalizability
		b) Level of organization of thought (e.g., levels of concepts of distributive justice); justification categories
		  Welfare
		  Fairness
		  Obligation
		  Equality of Distribution
			Intrinsic
			Communications
				Norms
				Rules
				Authority dictates
				Sanctions
				Attribution of seriousness of violation
				Social consensus
				Uniformities

Convention	Coordination of social interactions
	Constitutive aspects of social units
	Social consensus
		a) Criterion judgments
		  Rule contingency
		  Authority jurisdiction
		  Punishment
		  Contextualism
		  Relativism
			Arbitrary
			Communications
			Uniformities
				Norms
				Rules
				Authority dictates
				Sanctions
				Attribution of seriousness of violation

b)Level of organization of
  thought (levels of concepts
  of social convention); justification
  categories
      Custom
      Authority
      Punishment
      Prudence
      Personal Choice
      Social Coordination

Units of Analysis
Domain-specific criterion judgments and justification categories
Correspondences of domain of reasoning and actions in social events: feedback of actions to
    judgment and judgment to action; interpretations of communications
Relations among domain of reasoning, social events, and the content of sociocultural facts
Domain combinations:
    Coordination of domain mixture
    Conflicts and misattributions of domain mixtures
    Second-order phenomena
    Ambiguously multidimensional

considered an example, the experiments by Milgram, of a situation in which the individual's moral judgments come into conflict with social-organizational concepts. It was also evident in those experiments that variations in the environment served, for subjects, to alter the salience of the moral or social-organizational considerations and to shift the parameters of the conflict.

Variations in social-environmental events and facts (within and between groups) can be approached in a similar fashion. Only after having obtained assessments of domains of reasoning can the problem of their coordination be addressed. Coordinations may involve integration or conflict. At some times and in some situations it may indeed occur that social system or institutional practices are in contradiction with moral considerations. Assuming that individuals do form a core set of concepts of justice, welfare, and rights, such institutional practices may produce conditions for potential conflict. It should be kept in mind that the data have shown the coexistence of strong social organizational concerns and moral concerns. As demonstrated by the Milgram experiments, moral judgments do not always prevail over social-organizational considerations when they are in conflict. As was also demonstrated by those experiments, social-organizational considerations do not always prevail over moral ones. One task is to closely examine coordinations and conflicts between distinct conceptual systems and the role of variations in sociocultural facts. Another task is to consider possible sources of contradictions and misattributions in subjects' efforts at coordinating domains.

The proposition of the coexistence of diverse social orientations reflective of categories of social knowledge is consistent with the hypothesis of development stemming from individual–environment interactions. To say, with Malinowski, that a mixture of orientations characterizes social behavior and judgments is to assert the importance of categories of social knowledge that are not restricted to specific group affiliations. It is also to agree, with Piaget, that psychological explanation of the individual is an attempt at understanding "humans in general and notably of 'the subject' in a universal sense" (1978, p. 648). Working with epistemological categories from the logical, mathematical, and physical realms, Piaget and others have documented the subject's construction of cognitive structures. The research described here has provided documentation for the proposition that the subject constructs categories of social knowledge. The research has shown that the study of social development is, in important respects, the study of distinctions in social domains. Investigations of behavior and processes of acquisition are well-served when they are coordinated with analyses of the types of knowledge acquired, which, in part, constitute cultural orientations.

References

Allinsmith, W. The learning of moral standards. In D. R. Miller & G. E. Swanson (Eds.), *Inner conflict and defense*. New York: Holt, 1960.

Aronfreed, J. Moral standards. III. Moral behavior and sex identity. In D. R. Miller & G. E. Swanson (Eds.), *Inner conflict and defense*. New York: Holt, 1960.

Aronfreed, J. The effects of experimental socialization paradigms upon two moral responses to transgression. *Journal of Abnormal and Social Psychology*, 1963, *66*, 437–448.

Aronfreed, J. *Conduct and conscience: The socialization of internalized control over behavior*. New York: Academic Press, 1968.

Aronfreed, J. The concept of internalization. In D. A. Goslin (Ed.), *Handbook of socialization theory and research*. Chicago: Rand McNally, 1969.

Aronfreed, J. Moral development from the standpoint of a general psychological theory. In T. Lickona (Ed.), *Moral development and behavior: Theory, research and social issues*. New York: Holt, Rinehart & Winston, 1976.

Aronfreed, J., Cutick, R., & Fagen, S. Cognitive structure, punishment, and nurturance in the experimental induction of self-criticism. *Child Development*, 1963, *34*, 281–294.

Aronfreed, J., & Reber, A. Internalized behavioral suppression and the timing of social punishment. *Journal of Personality and Social Psychology*, 1965, *1*, 3–16.

Asch, S. *Social psychology*. Englewood Cliffs, N.J.: Prentice-Hall, 1952.

Austin, J. *The province of jurisprudence determined*. New York: The Noonday Press, 1954. (Originally published, 1832).

Baldwin, J. M. *Social and ethical interpretations in mental development: A study in social psychology*. New York: Macmillan, 1897.

Baldwin, J. M. *Thought and things*. London: Swan Sonnenschein, 1906.

Baldwin, J. M. *Genetic theory of reality*. New York: Putnam, 1915.

Bandura, A. Social learning through imitation. In M. R. Jones (Ed.), *Nebraska Symposium on Motivation*. Lincoln: University of Nebraska Press, 1962.

Bandura, A. Social learning theory of identificatory processes. In D. A. Goslin (Ed.), *Handbook of socialization theory and research*. Chicago: Rand McNally, 1969.

Bandura, A. *Social learning theory*. Englewood Cliffs, N.J.: Prentice-Hall, 1977.

Bandura, A., & Huston, A. C. Identification as a process of incidental learning. *Journal of Abnormal and Social Psychology*, 1961, *63*, 311–318.

Bandura, A., & McDonald, F. J. The influence of social reinforcement and the behavior of models in shaping children's moral judgments. *Journal of Abnormal and Social Psychology*, 1963, *67*, 274–281.

Bandura, A., Ross, D., & Ross, S. A. Imitation of film-mediated aggressive models. *Journal of Abnormal and Social Psychology*, 1963, *66*, 3–11. (a)

227

Bandura A., Ross, D., & Ross, S. A. A comparative test of the status of envy, social power, and secondary reinforcement theories of identificatory learning. *Journal of Abnormal and Social Psychology*, 1963, *67*, 527–534. (b)

Bandura, A., & Walters, R. *Social learning and personality development*. New York: Holt, Rinehart & Winston, 1963.

Bechtoldt, H. P. Construct validity: A critique. *American Psychologist*, 1959, *14*, 619–629.

Bem, D. J. Self perception theory. In L. Berkowitz (Ed.), *Advances in experimental social psychology*, Vol. 6. New York: Academic Press, 1972.

Benedict, R. *Patterns of culture*. Boston: Houghton Mifflin, 1934.

Benedict, R. *The chrysanthemum and the sword: Patterns of Japanese culture*. Boston: Houghton Mifflin, 1946.

Berg-Cross, L. Intentionality, degree of damage, and moral judgments. *Child Development*, 1975, *46*, 970–974.

Binet, A., Simon, T. (1916) The measurement of intelligence. In W. Kessen (Ed.), *The child*. New York: Wiley, 1965.

Blasi, A. Bridging moral cognition and moral action: A critical review of the literature. *Psychological Bulletin*, 1980, *88*, 1–45.

Bower, T. G. R. *A primer of infant development*. San Francisco: W. H. Freeman, 1977.

Brainerd, C. J. The stage question in cognitive-developmental theory. *The Behavioral and Brain Sciences*, 1978, *1*, 173–213.

Bregman, E. O. An attempt to modify the emotional attitudes of infants by the conditional response technique. *Journal of Genetic Psychology*, 1934, XLV(1), 169–198.

Broughton, J. M. The cognitive-developmental approach to morality: A reply to Kurtines and Greif. Unpublished manuscript, Wayne State University, 1975.

Broughton, J. M. Development of concepts of self, mind, reality and knowledge. In W. Damon (Ed.), *New directions for child development. Vol. 1: Social cognition*. San Francisco: Jossey-Bass, 1978. (a)

Broughton, J. M. The cognitive-developmental approach to morality: A reply to Kurtines and Greif. *Journal of Moral Education*, 1978, 7(2), 81–96. (b)

Burton, R., Allinsmith, W., & Maccoby, E. Resistance to temptation in relation to sex of child, sex of experimenter and withdrawal of attention. *Journal of Personality and Social Psychology*, 1966, *3*, 253–258.

Burton, R., Maccoby, E., & Allinsmith, W. Antecedents of resistance to temptation in four-year-old children. *Child Development*, 1961, *32*, 689–710.

Campbell, D. T. Recommendations for APA test standards regarding construct, trait, or discriminant validity. *American Psychologist*, 1960, *15*, 546–553.

Cheyne, J. A. Some parameters of punishment affecting resistance to deviation and generalization of a prohibition. *Child Development*, 1971, *42*, 1249–1261.

Cheyne, J. A., Goyeche, J. R. M., & Walters, R. H. Attention, anxiety, and rules in resistance to deviation in children. *Journal of Experimental Child Psychology*, 1969, *8*, 127–139.

Cheyne, J. A. & Walters, R. H. Intensity of punishment, timing of punishment and cognitive structure as determinants of response inhibition. *Journal of Experimental Child Psychology*, 1969, *7*, 231–244.

Chomsky, N. On cognitive structures and their development: A reply to Piaget. In M. Piatelli-Palmarini, *Language and learning: The debate between Jean Piaget and Noam Chomsky*. Cambridge, Mass.: Harvard University Press, 1980.

Colby, A., Kohlberg, L., Gibbs, J., & Lieberman, M. A longitudinal study of moral judgment. *Monographs of the Society for Research in Child Development*, in press.

Cowan, P. *Piaget with feeling*. New York: Holt, Rinehart & Winston, 1978.

Cronbach, L. J., & Meehl, P. E. Construct validity in psychological tests. *Psychological Bulletin*, 1955, *52*(4), 281–302.

Damon, W. Early conceptions of justice as related to the development of operational reasoning. Unpublished doctoral dissertation, University of California, Berkeley, 1973.

Damon, W. *The social world of the child*. San Francisco: Jossey-Bass, 1977.

Damon, W. Patterns of change in children's social reasoning: A two-year longitudinal study. *Child Development*, 1980, *51*, 1010–1017.

Damon, W. Exploring children's social cognition on two fronts. In J. H. Flavell & L. Ross (Eds.), *Social cognitive development: Frontiers and possible futures*. New York: Cambridge University Press, 1981.

D'Andrade, R. G. *Cultural meaning systems*. Paper presented at the Social Science Research Council Conference on Conceptions of Culture and Its Acquisition. New York, 1981.

Davidson, P., Turiel, E., & Black, A. The effect of stimulus familiarity on the use of criteria and justifications in children's social reasoning. *British Journal of Developmental Psychology*, in press.

Dawkins, R. *The selfish gene*. New York: Oxford University Press, 1976.

DeMersseman, S. A developmental investigation of children's moral reasoning and behavior in hypothetical and practical situations. Unpublished doctoral dissertation, University of California, Berkeley, 1976.

Dodsworth-Rugani, K. J. The development of concepts of social structure and their relationship to school rules and authority. Unpublished doctoral dissertation, University of California, Berkeley, 1982.

Durkheim, E. *Sociology and philosophy*. New York: Free Press, 1974. (Originally published, 1924.)

Durkheim, E. *Moral education*. Glencoe, Ill.: Free Press, 1961. (Originally published, 1925.)

Dworkin, R. *Taking rights seriously*. Cambridge, Mass.: Harvard University Press, 1978.

Elkind, D., & Dabeck, R. F. Personal injury and property damage in moral judgments of children. *Child Development*, 1977, *48*, 518–522.

Enright, R. D., Franklin, C. C., & Manheim, L. A. Children's distributive justice reasoning: A standardized and objective scale. *Developmental Psychology*, 1980, *16*, 193–202.

Flavell, J. H. Structures, stages and sequences in cognitive development. In A. Collins (Ed.), *Minnesota Symposia on Child Psychology*, Vol. 15. Hillsdale, N.J.: Erlbaum, 1982.

Fodor, E. M. Resistance to social influence among adolescents as a function of level of moral development. *Journal of Social Psychology*, 1971, *85*, 121–126.

Freud, S. *Three essays on the theory of sexuality*. New York: Avon, 1962. (Originally published, 1905.)

Freud, S. Instincts and their vicissitudes. In *Collected papers*, Vol. 4. New York: Basic Books, 1959. (Originally published, 1915.)

Freud, S. *Beyond the pleasure principle*. New York: Liveright, 1970. (Originally published, 1920.)

Freud, S. *The ego and the id*. New York: Norton, 1960. (Originally published, 1923.)

Freud, S. The passing of the oedipus-complex. In *Collected papers*, Vol. 2. New York: Basic Books, 1959. (Originally published, 1924.)

Freud, S. *The future of an illusion*. New York: Liveright, 1953. (Originally published, 1927.)

Freud, S. *Civilization and its discontents*. New York: Norton, 1961. (Originally published, 1930.)

Furth, H. Children's societal understanding and the process of equilibration. In W. Damon (Ed.), *New directions for child development. Vol. 1: Social cognition*. San Francisco: Jossey-Bass, 1978.

Geertz, C. *The interpretation of culture*. New York: Basic Books, 1973.

Geiger, K., & Turiel, E. Disruptive school behavior and social convention in early adolescence. Unpublished manuscript, University of California, Berkeley, 1981.

Gewirth, A. *Reason and morality*. Chicago: University of Chicago Press, 1978.

Gilligan, C., Kohlberg, L., Lerner, J., & Belenky, M. Moral reasoning about sexual dilemmas: The development of an interview and scoring system. Unpublished paper, Harvard University, 1971.

Gould, S. J. On human nature. *Human Nature*, 1978, *1*(10), 20–28.

Grinder, R. New techniques for research in children's temptation behavior. *Child Development*, 1961, *32*, 679–688.

Grinder, R. Parental child-rearing practices, conscience, and resistance to temptation of sixth-grade children. *Child Development*, 1962, *33*, 803–820.

Grinder, R. E. Relations between behavioral and cognitive dimensions of conscience in middle childhood. *Child Development*, 1964, *35*, 881–891.

Haan, N. Hypothetical and actual moral reasoning in a situation of civil disobedience. *Journal of Personality and Social Psychology*, 1975, *32*, 255–270.

Haan, N., Smith, M., & Block, J. Moral reasoning of young adults: Political-social behavior, family background, and personality correlates. *Journal of Personality and Social Psychology*, 1968, *10*, 183–201.

Harman, G. *The nature of morality: An introduction to ethics*. New York: Oxford University Press, 1977.

Harris, B. Whatever happened to Little Albert? *American Psychologist*, 1979, *34*, 151–160.

Hart, H. L. A. *The concept of law*. London: Oxford University Press, 1961.

Hart, H. L. A. Positivism and the separation of law and morals. In R. M. Dworkin (Ed.), *The philosophy of law*. New York: Oxford University Press, 1977.

Hartshorne, H., & May, M. S. *Studies in the nature of character*: Vol. I, *Studies in deceit*; Vol. II, *Studies in self-control*; Vol. III, *Studies in the organization of character*. New York: Macmillan, 1928–1930.

Heider, F. *The psychology of interpersonal relations*. New York: Wiley, 1958.

Hoffman, M. L. Moral development. In P. H. Mussen (Ed.), *Carmichael's manual of child psychology*, Vol. 2. New York: Wiley, 1970.

Hoffman, M. L. Moral internalization. In L. Berkowitz (Ed.), *Advances in experimental social psychology*, Vol. 10. New York: Academic Press, 1977.

Hoffman, M. L., & Saltzstein, H. D. Parent discipline and the child's moral development. *Journal of Personality and Social Psychology*, 1967, *5*, 45–47.

Hogan, R. Moral conduct and moral character: A psychological perspective. *Psychology Bulletin*, 1973, *79*, 217–232.

Hogan, R. Theoretical egocentrism and the problem of compliance. *American Psychologist*, 1975, *30*, 533–540.

Hogan, R., Johnson, J., & Emler, N. P. A socioanalytic theory of moral development. In W. Damon (Ed.), *New directions for child development. Vol. 2: Moral development*. San Francisco: Jossey-Bass, 1978.

Hogan, R., & Mills, C. Legal socialization. *Human Development*, 1976, *19*, 261–276.

Hubbard, R. From termite to human behavior. *Psychology Today*, October 1978, 124–134.

Hull, C. L. The concept of habit-family hierarchy and maze learning. *Psychological Review*, 1934, *41*, Part I, 33–52; Part II, 134–152.

Imamoglu, E. O. Children's awareness and usage of intention cues. *Child Development*, 1975, *46*, 39–45.

Inhelder, B., & Piaget, J. *The growth of logical thinking from childhood to adolescence*. New York: Basic Books, 1958.

Inhelder, B., & Piaget, J. *The early growth of logic in the child (classification and seriation)*. New York: Harper, 1964.

Inhelder, B., & Sinclair, H. Learning cognitive structures. In P. H. Mussen, J. Langer, & M. Covington (Eds.), *Trends and issues in developmental psychology*. New York: Holt, Rinehart & Winston, 1969.

Inhelder, B., Sinclair, H., & Bovet, M. *Learning and the development of cognition*. Cambridge, Mass.: Harvard University Press, 1974.

Irwin, D. M., & Moore, S. G. The young child's understanding of social justice. *Developmental Psychology*, 1971, *5*, 406–410.

Isaacs, S. *Intellectual growth in young children.* New York: Schocken Books, 1930.

Jones, E. E., & Davis, K. E. From acts to dispositions. In L. Berkowitz (Ed.), *Advances in experimental social psychology*, Vol. 2. New York: Academic Press, 1965.

Kahneman, D., & Tversky, A. Subjective probability: A judgment of representativeness. *Cognitive Psychology*, 1972, *3*, 430–454.

Kahneman, D., & Tversky, A. On the psychology of prediction. *Psychological Review*, 1973, *80*, 237–251.

Karmiloff-Smith, A., & Inhelder, B. If you want to get ahead, get a theory. *Cognition*, 1975, *3*, 195–212.

Keasey, C. B. Children's developing awareness and usage of intentionality and motive. In C. B. Keasey (Ed.), *Nebraska Symposium on Motivation*, 1977, (Vol. 25). Lincoln: University of Nebraska Press, 1979.

Kelley, H. H. Attribution theory in social psychology. In D. Levine (Ed.), *Nebraska Symposium on Motivation* (Vol. 15). Lincoln: University of Nebraska Press, 1967.

Kelley, H. H. The processes of causal attribution. *American Psychologist*, 1973, *28*, 107–128.

Kohlberg, L. The development of modes of moral thinking and choice in the years 10 to 16. Unpublished doctoral dissertation, University of Chicago, 1958.

Kohlberg, L. Moral development and identification. In H. Stevenson (Ed.), *Child Psychology. 62nd Yearbook of the National Society for the Study of Education.* Chicago: University of Chicago Press, 1963. (a)

Kohlberg, L. The development of children's orientations toward a moral order: 1. Sequence in the development of moral thought. *Vita Humana*, 1963, *6*, 11–33. (b)

Kohlberg, L. Stage and sequence: The cognitive-developmental approach to socialization. In D. A. Goslin (Ed.), *Handbook of socialization theory and research.* Chicago: Rand McNally, 1969.

Kohlberg, L. From is to ought: How to commit the naturalistic fallacy and get away with it in the study of moral development. In T. Mischel (Ed.), *Psychology and genetic epistemology.* New York: Academic Press, 1971.

Kohlberg, L. Moral stages and moralization: The cognitive-developmental approach. In T. Lickona (Ed.), *Moral development and behavior: Theory, research and social issues.* New York: Holt, Rinehart & Winston, 1976.

Kohlberg, L., & Candee, D. Relationships between moral judgment and moral action. Unpublished manuscript, Harvard University, 1979.

Köhler, W. *The place of value in a world of facts.* New York: Liveright, 1938.

Kuhn, D. Mechanisms of change in the development of cognitive structures. *Child Development*, 1972, *43*, 833–844.

Kuhn, D., & Langer, J. Cognitive developmental determinants of imitation. Unpublished paper, University of California, Berkeley, 1968.

Kurtines, W., & Greif, E. The development of moral thought: Review and evaluation of Kohlberg's approach. *Psychological Bulletin*, 1974, *81*, 453–470.

Langer, J. Disequilibrium as a source of development. In P. H. Mussen, J. Langer, & M. Covington (Eds.), *Trends and issues in developmental psychology.* New York: Holt, Rinehart & Winston, 1969.

Langer, J. Interactional aspects of cognitive organization. *Cognition*, 1974, *3*, 9–28.

Langer, J. The coordination of moral conduct. Unpublished manuscript, University of California, Berkeley, 1975.

Langer, J. *The origins of logic: Six to twelve months.* New York: Academic Press, 1980.

Langer, J. From sensorimotor to representational cognition. Paper presented at Biennial Meeting of the Society for Research in Child Development, Boston, 1981. (a)

Langer, J. Concept and symbol formation by infants. Paper presented at the H. Werner Institute Conference, Clark University, 1981. (b)

Langer, J. Dialectics of development. In T. G. R. Bever (Ed.), *Regressions in mental development: Basic phenomena and theories.* Hillsdale, N.J.: Erlbaum, in press.

La Voie, J. Type of punishment as a determinant of resistance to deviation. *Developmental Psychology*, 1974, *10*, 181–189.

Lewin, K. *A dynamic theory of personality*. New York: McGraw-Hill, 1935.

Lickona, T. The acceleration of children's judgments about responsibility: An experimental test of Piaget's hypotheses about the causes of moral judgmental change. Unpublished doctoral dissertation, State University of New York at Albany, 1971.

Lockhart, K. L., Abrahams, B., & Osherson, D. N. Children's understanding of uniformity in the environment. *Child Development*, 1977, *48*, 1521–1531.

Lord, C., Ross, L., & Lepper, M. R. Biased assimilation and attitude polarization: The effects of prior theories on subsequently considered evidence. *Journal of Personality and Social Psychology*, 1979, *37*, 2098–2109.

Luria, A. R. *Cognitive development: Its cultural and social foundations*. Cambridge, Mass.: Harvard University Press, 1976.

Maccoby, E. E. *Social development*. New York: Harcourt, Brace, Jovanovich, 1980.

Malinowski, B. *Crime and custom in savage society*. London: Routledge & Kegan Paul, 1926.

Mead, G. H. *Mind, self, and society*. Chicago: The University of Chicago Press, 1934.

Milgram, S. Behavioral study of obedience. *Journal of Abnormal and Social Psychology*, 1963, *67*, 371–378.

Milgram, S. *Obedience* (a filmed experiment). Distributed by the New York University Film Library, 1965.

Milgram, S. *Obedience to authority*. New York: Harper & Row, 1974.

Mill, J. S. *Utilitarianism*. New York: Washington Square Press, 1963. (Originally published, 1863.)

Miller, N. E., & Dollard, J. *Social learning and imitation*. New Haven: Yale University Press, 1941.

Mischel, W., & Mischel, H. N. A cognitive social-learning approach to morality and self-regulation. In T. Lickona (Ed.), *Moral development: Theory, research and social issues*. New York: Holt, Rinehart & Winston, 1976.

Much, N., & Shweder, R. A. Speaking of rules: The analysis of culture in breach. In W. Damon (Ed.), *New directions for child development. Vol. 2: Moral Development*. San Francisco: Jossey-Bass, 1978.

Nisbett, R., & Ross, L. *Human inference: Strategies and shortcomings of social judgment*. Englewood Cliffs, N. J.: Prentice-Hall, 1980.

Nisbett, R. E., & Wilson, T. D. Telling more than we can know: Verbal reports on mental processes. *Psychological Review*, 1977, *84*, 231–259.

Nucci, L. The development of personal concepts: A domain distinct from moral or societal concepts. *Child Development*, 1981, *52*, 114–121.

Nucci, L. Can morality be separated from religion in the teaching of values? Paper presented at the Annual Meeting of the American Educational Research Association, New York, 1982.

Nucci, L., & Nucci, M. Children's social interactions in the context of moral and conventional transgressions. *Child Development*, 1982, *53*, 403–412.

Nucci, L., & Nucci, M. Children's responses to moral and social conventional transgressions in free-play settings. *Child Development*, in press.

Nucci, L., & Turiel, E. Social interactions and the development of social concepts in preschool children. *Child Development*, 1978, *49*, 400–407.

Nucci, L., Turiel, E., & Gawrych, G. E. Preschool children's social interactions and social concepts in the Virgin Islands. Unpublished manuscript, University of Illinois at Chicago Circle, 1981.

Parke, R. Nurturance, nurturance withdrawal and resistance to deviation. *Child Development*, 1967, *38*, 1101–1110.

Parke, R. D. (Ed.), *Readings in social development*. New York: Holt, Rinehart & Winston, 1969.

Parke, R., & Walters, R. Some factors influencing the efficacy of punishment training for inducing response inhibition. *Monographs of the Society for Research in Child Development*, 1967, *32*(1).

Piaget, J. *The language and thought of the child.* New York: Harcourt, Brace, & Co., 1923.

Piaget, J. *The child's conception of physical causality.* Totowa, N. J.: Littlefield Adams, 1960. (Originally published, 1927.)

Piaget, J. *Judgment and reasoning in the child.* New York: Littlefield Adams, 1928.

Piaget, J. *The child's conception of the world.* London: Routledge & Kegan Paul, 1929.

Piaget, J. *The moral judgment of the child.* London: Routledge & Kegan Paul, 1932.

Piaget, J. *The origins of intelligence in children.* New York: Norton, 1963. (Originally published, 1936.)

Piaget, J. *The psychology of intelligence.* London: Lowe and Brydore, 1950. (Originally published, 1947.)

Piaget, J. *Play, dreams and imitation in childhood.* New York: Norton, 1962. (Originally published, 1951.)

Piaget, J. *The child's conception of number.* London: Humanities Press, 1952.

Piaget, J. *The construction of reality in the child.* New York: Basic Books, 1954.

Piaget, J. *The mechanisms of perception.* London: Routledge & Kegan Paul, 1969.

Piaget J. Piaget's theory. In P. Mussen (Ed.), *Carmichael's manual of child psychology.* New York: Wiley, 1970. (a)

Piaget, J. *Psychology and epistemology.* New York: Viking Press, 1970. (b)

Piaget, J. *Structuralism.* New York: Basic Books, 1970. (c)

Piaget, J. *The grasp of consciousness: Action and concept in the young child.* Cambridge, Mass.: Harvard University Press, 1976.

Piaget, J. *The development of thought: Equilibration of cognitive structures.* New York: Viking Press, 1977.

Piaget, J. What is psychology? *American Psychologist,* 1978, *33,* 648–652.

Piaget, J. The psychogenesis of knowledge and its epistemological significance. In M. Piattelli-Palmarini (Ed.), *Language and learning: The debate between Jean Piaget and Noam Chomsky.* Cambridge, Mass.: Harvard University Press, 1980. (a)

Piaget, J. *Experiments in contradiction.* Chicago: University of Chicago Press, 1980. (b)

Piaget, J., & Inhelder, B. *The psychology of the child.* New York: Basic Books, 1969.

Piaget, J., & Inhelder, B. *Mental imagery in the child: A study of the development of imaginal representation.* New York: Basic Books, 1971.

Piaget, J., & Inhelder, B. *Memory and intelligence.* New York: Basic Books, 1972.

Pool, D., Shweder, R. A., & Much, N. Culture as a cognitive system: Differentiated rule understandings in children and other savages. In E. T. Higgins, D. N. Ruble, &. W. W. Hartup (Eds.), *Social cognition and social development: A sociocultural perspective.* Cambridge: Cambridge University Press, in press.

Rawls, J. *A theory of justice.* Cambridge, Mass.: Harvard University Press, 1971.

Rest, J. Patterns of preference and comprehension in moral judgment. *Journal of Personality,* 1973, *41,* 86–108.

Rest, J. Morality. In J. Flavell & E. Markman (Eds.), *Carmichael's manual of child psychology: Cognitive development.* New York: Wiley, in press.

Rest, J., Turiel, E., & Kohlberg, L. Level of moral development as a determinant of preference and comprehension of moral judgments made by others. *Journal of Personality,* 1969, *37,* 225–252.

Ross, L. The intuitive psychologist and his shortcomings: Distortions in the attribution process. In L. Berkowitz (Ed.), *Advances in experimental psychology* (Vol. 10). New York: Academic Press, 1977.

Ross, L. The "Intuitive Scientist" formulation and its developmental implications. In J. Flavell & L. Ross (Eds.), *Social cognitive development: Frontiers and possible futures.* Cambridge: Cambridge University Press, 1981.

Saltzstein, H. D., Diamond, R. M., & Belenky, M. Moral judgment level and conformity behavior. *Developmental Psychology,* 1972, *7,* 327–336.

Sampson, E. E. Psychology and the American ideal. *Personality and Social Psychology*, 1977, *35*, 767–782.

Schwartz, T. Where is the culture? Personality as the distributive locus of culture. In G. D. Spindler (Ed.), *The making of psychological anthropology*. Berkeley: University of California Press, 1978.

Searle, J. R. *Speech acts*. London: Cambridge University Press, 1969.

Sears, R. R., Maccoby, E. E., & Levin, H. *Patterns of child rearing*. Evanston, Ill.: Row, Peterson, 1957.

Sears, R. R., Rau, L., & Alpert R. *Identification and child rearing*. Stanford, Calif.: Stanford University Press, 1965.

Selman, R. L. Social cognitive understanding: A guide to educational and clinical practice. In T. Lickona (Ed.), *Moral development and behavior: Theory, research and social issues*. New York: Holt, Rinehart & Winston, 1976.

Selman, R. L. *The growth of interpersonal understanding: Developmental and clinical analysis*. New York: Academic Press, 1980.

Shweder, R. A. Rethinking culture and personality theory. Part I: A critical examination of two classical postulates. *Ethos*, 1979, *7*, 255–278. (a)

Shweder, R. A. Rethinking culture and personality theory. Part II: A critical examination of two more classical postulates. *Ethos*, 1979, *7*, 279–311. (b)

Shweder, R. A. Rethinking culture and personality theory. Part III: From genesis and typology to hermeneutics and dynamics. *Ethos*, 1980, *8*, 60–94.

Shweder, R. A. Anthropology's romantic rebellion against the Enlightenment; or, there's more to thinking than reason and evidence. Paper presented at the Conference on "Conceptions of Culture and Its Acquisition," Committee on Affective and Social Development in Childhood, Social Science Research Council, New York, 1981.

Shweder, R. A. Beyond self-constructed knowledge: The study of culture and morality. *Merrill-Palmer Quarterly*, in press.

Simpson, E. L. Moral development research: A case of scientific cultural bias. *Human Development*, 1974, *17*, 81–106.

Skinner, B. F. *Beyond freedom and dignity*. New York: Knopf, 1971.

Slaby, R. E., & Parke, R. D. Effect on resistance to deviation of observing a model's affective reactions to response consequences. *Developmental Psychology*, 1971, *5*, 40–47.

Smetana, J. Prosocial events and transgressions in the moral and societal domains. Paper presented at the annual meeting of the American Educational Research Association, Boston, 1980.

Smetana, J. Preschool children's conceptions of moral and social rules. *Child Development*, 1981, *52*, 1333–1336. (a)

Smetana, J. Reasoning in the personal and moral domains: Adolescent and young adult women's decision-making regarding abortion. *Journal of Applied Developmental Psychology*, 1981, *3*, 211–226. (b)

Smetana, J. *Concepts of self and morality: Women's reasoning about abortion*. New York: Praeger, 1982.

Stein, A. Imitation of resistance to temptation. *Child Development*, 1967, *38*, 157–169.

Stein, J. L. Adolescents' reasoning about moral and sexual dilemmas: A longitudinal study. Unpublished doctoral dissertation, Harvard University, 1973.

Stent, G. S. Introduction: The limits of the naturalistic approach to morality. In G. S. Stent (Ed.), *Morality as a biological phenomenon*. Berlin: Dahlem Konferenzen, 1978.

Stouwie, R. J. Inconsistent verbal instructions and children's resistance to temptation. *Child Development*, 1971, *42*, 1517–1531.

Strauss, S. Inducing cognitive development and learning: A review of short-term training experiments. I. The organismic-developmental approach. *Cognition*, 1972, *1*, 329-357.

Strauss, S. (Ed.). *U-shaped behavioral growth*. New York: Academic Press, 1981.

Strauss, S. Appearances, disappearances, nonappearances, and reappearances of various behaviors: Methodological strategies of experimentation and their implications for models of development. In T. G. R. Bever (Ed.), *Regressions in mental development: Basic phenomena and theories.* Hillsdale, N.J.: Erlbaum, in press.

Sugarman, S. The development of classification and correspondence from 12 to 36 months: From action to representation. Paper presented at the biennial meeting of the Society for Research in Child Development, San Francisco, 1979.

Tapp, J., & Kohlberg, L. Developing senses of law and legal justice. *Journal of Social Issues,* 1971, *27,* 65–92.

Terman, L. M., & Merrill, M. A. *Measuring intelligence.* Boston: Houghton Mifflin, 1937.

Tisak, M., & Turiel, E. Children's conceptions of moral and prudential rules. Paper presented at the annual meeting of the American Psychological Association, Washington, D.C., 1982.

Trivers, R. L. The evolution of reciprocal altruism. *Quarterly Review of Biology,* 1971, *46,* 35–57.

Turiel, E. An experimental test of the sequentiality of developmental stages in the child's moral judgment. *Journal of Personality and Social Psychology,* 1966, *3,* 611–618.

Turiel, E. Developmental processes in the child's moral thinking. In P. H. Mussen, J. Langer, & M. Covington (Eds.), *Trends and issues in developmental psychology.* New York: Holt, 1969.

Turiel, E. Conflict and transition in adolescent moral development. *Child Development,* 1974, *45,* 14–29.

Turiel, E. The development of social concepts: Mores, customs and conventions. In D. J. De Palma & J. M. Foley (Eds.), *Moral development: Current theory and research.* Hillsdale, N. J.: Erlbaum, 1975.

Turiel, E. A comparative analysis of moral knowledge and moral judgment in males and females. *Journal of Personality,* 1976, *44,* 195–209.

Turiel, E. Conflict and transition in adolescent moral development. II. The resolution of disequilibrium through structural reorganization. *Child Development,* 1977, *48,* 634–637.

Turiel, E. The development of concepts of social structure: Social convention. In J. Glick & A. Clarke-Stewart (Eds.), *The development of social understanding.* New York: Gardner Press, 1978. (a)

Turiel, E. Social regulations and domains of social concepts. In W. Damon (Ed.), *New directions for child development. Vol. 1: Social cognition.* San Francisco: Jossey-Bass, 1978. (b)

Turiel, E. Distinct conceptual and developmental domains: Social convention and morality. In H. E. Howe & C. B. Keasey (Eds.), *Nebraska Symposium on Motivation, 1977: Social Cognitive Development* (Vol. 25). Lincoln: University of Nebraska Press, 1979.

Turiel E. Domains and categories in social cognitive development. In W. Overton (Ed.), *The relationship between social and cognitive development.* Hillsdale, N. J.: Erlbaum, in press.

Turiel, E., & Guinsburg, H. Cognitive factors in children's imitative activities. Unpublished paper, Columbia University, 1968.

Turiel, E., & Rothman, G. R. The influences of reasoning on behavioral choices at different stages of moral development. *Child Development,* 1972, *43,* 741–756.

Tversky, A. Features of similarity. *Psychological Review,* 1977, *84,* 327–352.

Tversky, A., & Kahneman, D. Judgment under uncertainty: Heuristics and biases. *Science,* 1974, *185,* 1124–1131.

Vygotsky, L. S. *Thought and language.* Cambridge, Mass.: M.I.T. Press, 1962. (Originally published, 1934.)

Walters, R., Parke, R., & Cane, V. Timing of punishment and the observation of consequences to others as determinants of response inhibition. *Journal of Experimental Child Psychology,* 1965, *2,* 10–30.

Watson, J. B. *Behaviorism.* Chicago: University of Chicago Press, 1924.

Watson, J. B., & Rayner, R. Conditional emotional reactions. *Journal of Experimental Psychology,* 1920, *3,* 1–14.

Werner, H. Process and achievement. A basic problem of education and developmental psychology. *Harvard Educational Review*, 1937, *7*, 353–368.

Werner, H. *Comparative psychology of mental development*. New York: International Universities Press, Inc., 1957.

Werner, H., & Kaplan, B. *Symbol formation*. New York: Wiley, 1963.

Wertheimer, M. Some problems in the theory of ethics. *Social Research*, 1935, *2*, 353–367.

Weston, D., & Turiel, E. Act-rule relations: Children's concepts of social rules. *Developmental Psychology*, 1980, *16*, 417–424.

Whiting, J. M. W., & Child, I. L. *Child training and personality: A cross-cultural study*. New Haven: Yale University Press, 1953.

Wilson, E. O. *Sociobiology: The new synthesis*. Cambridge, Mass.: Harvard University Press, 1975.

Wilson, E. O. *On human nature*. Cambridge, Mass.: Harvard University Press, 1978.

Winch, P. *Ethics and action*. London: Routledge & Kegan Paul, 1972.

Wolf, T. Effects of televised modeled verbalizations and behavior in resistance to deviation. *Developmental Psychology*, 1973, *8*, 51–56.

Youniss, J., & Volpe, J. A relational analysis of children's friendship. In W. Damon (Ed.), *New directions for child development. Vol. 1: Social cognition*. San Francisco: Jossey-Bass, 1978.

Index